ALASKA
BOUND

by TAMMY JONES

Pennock
Island
Productions

www.PennockIslandProductions.com

LCCN 2011901211
ISBN 978-0-615-44237-2

Author photo by Nathan Miller
All other photos courtesy of Tom and Tammy Jones

This book is dedicated to my dad, Ray Porter, who for many years longed to experience the "Alaska Dream." 1932-2004

Acknowledgements

A large thank you should be handed out to my husband, Tom, for encouraging me to share many of our most personal experiences even though they don't shed him in the best light; to my editors Nancy Morris and my sister, Donna Harwell, for their awesome attention to detail; to Kari Lundy-Ping, Julie Deaton and my sister, Kimber, all of whom offered helpful suggestions and tremendous encouragement.

Much appreciation also goes to Tom's parents, Vern and Nancy, for their continual patience, love and support.

A heartfelt thank you to my wonderful kids, Tiffany, Nathan, and Nicole, all of whom answered my urgent calls about technical issues and who continue to make me proud. I love you guys!

Thanks to Prairie Rose Tucker for her compassionate instruction in regards to my computer. I love you!

CONTENTS

SECTION III: A SUMMER WONDERLAND

THE ALASKA COMPROMISE

1

On the Move

Outside Ketchikan, Alaska
March 22, 2009

The fully encompassing darkness is absolute. Suspiciously, I stare out over the small sputtering fire I am struggling to keep lit, and as my Border collie, Pup, begins to fiercely growl at something beyond our meager firelight, the hairs bristle on the back of my neck. Is something out there? The pounding of my heart inside my chest is rapidly increasing as I strain to open my eyes as wide as possible, but all is simply pitch black. What could be lurking? Bear? Wolf? Badger? In a forced whisper I call over to Tom, who is resting on the beach a short distance away. "Sweetie!" No response. I swallow hard, wondering if he's still there or not. A little louder this time I call out again, "Can you hear me?" Don't make me face this alone, I plead silently.

What a devastating feeling it is to be officially marooned in the Alaskan wilderness. It is just the three of us—my husband Tom, Pup, and me—who made the grueling weeklong journey, leaving behind our comfy new home in eastern Oregon. The long list of reluctant decisions that had led up to my participation in my husband's idea of this adventure of a lifetime hadn't happened overnight, either! There had been years of short-lived debates before I'd finally agreed to make this trip north to Ketchikan, the closest town to our new remote property. Just this morning, the last leg of our nearly sixteen hundred-mile journey had been before us. It had seemed simple on paper;

we'd launched our boat at the south end of town, and from there it had been just ten short miles to our destination.

Now, huddled close to my fire, I wonder for the hundredth time, how did our circumstances deteriorate to this level? How did the three of us become stranded overnight, forcing us to endure the icy-cold March climate on a secluded Alaskan beach with almost no provisions? Was it bad luck or bad planning? What had possessed us to think we could do this and survive? We had spent the last six months meticulously discussing, planning, checking and rechecking our plans; we thought we were prepared. But there was no denying that within the first two hours of setting foot on our new Alaska real estate, things had gone definitely wrong. How the heck did I end up here, I wondered to myself again. Deep in thought, I pondered how we would solve our current dilemma. But this wasn't the first time I'd been in a mess of this magnitude; Tom was always pushing me beyond what I thought I could ever handle, or so it felt like to me anyway. Looking back on it all, I realized that it was actually five years earlier when unbeknownst to me, our initial transition to Alaska really began.

Long ago, Tom had fallen in love with Alaska. He was fresh out of high school when he'd begun his twenty-seven year long career as a commercial fisherman. Most of his fishing endeavors had been spent in Alaska's well-known Bristol Bay, but he'd also crabbed for months at a time in the intimidating Bering Sea. In recent years I'd heard bits and pieces of his visits to St. Paul Island, King Cove, Dillingham, and Dutch Harbor, Alaska. I also recall him telling tales of places like Cold Bay, Petersburg, Homer and Sitka, among other frigid-sounding coastal towns along the way. But until recently, all the time he'd spent in Alaska had been entirely work-related, and as a result, it hadn't satisfied his curiosity of a remote existence in a land of such golden opportunity. Instead, the infrequent exposure had only enhanced his lifelong dream of living there someday.

My talented husband, Tom, is an extremely resilient individual full of unbelievable determination, coupled with a boat load of ingenuity and a splash of controlled recklessness, perhaps. In other words, for him, living as one with Mother Nature was no doubt an adventure he was capable of enduring. The majority of his life, it seemed, has been a preparation period for just such a transition, with most of his spare time spent on both hunting and fishing excursions of one kind or another. Add to that his extensive work in the fishing industry, which has allowed him plenty of experiences in The Last Frontier. Lucky for him, the outdoorsy lifestyle we were about to embark on fit him to a "T." Myself….not so much! Going to Alaska didn't appear intriguing whatsoever! It sounded extremely uninviting, horribly cold and even more intimidating.

Tom and I were such opposites. It was fate, as they say, when he and I crossed paths in 1998. His commercial fishing season had just ended; consequently, he'd resumed his regular off-season work in construction. It was then that we'd met; I was the Administrator of the local Public Market with a full-time construction business of my own. We hit it off immediately, and our relationship bloomed. We found that we not only had plenty in common, but our individual strengths seemed to offset each other perfectly.

Within two years we were married; by then, he and I were a self-employed construction team. In our partnership, Tom might have been considered the "engine," where I felt more like the "grease." On our many projects together, Tom's talent shone brightly during the land development phase and "rough framing" process. At work, his well-thought out actions commanded impressive results, but his intense focus also rendered his personality rather abrasive, especially to me. Complimenting his naturally stern countenance, his salt and pepper-colored hair was typically hidden beneath the rain-soaked hood of a gray or sometimes navy blue sweatshirt; either color combined with any dark shade of sweat pants was for sure his outfit of choice. Even at work, he didn't sport the distinctive garb of a contractor. In fact, the typical carpenter's belt was never seen cinched around his waist. He claimed that the bulky pouch was forever in his way, never worth the trouble to wear. Since he rarely allows anything to slow his progress, in the wet coastal climate he also avoided wearing raingear at all costs. I didn't care for the cumbersome attire either, but even more so, I disliked being cold and wet.

Although I also loved pounding nails, my end of the construction business focused more on people skills, finish work, and the monotonous details of continual clean-up. For sure, it was our contrasting talents that made us a good team, but it was the differences of opinion that came along with that asset which over time had become the source of many an argument! In spite of our frequent opposing viewpoints, though, I had been extremely content with my life; I enjoyed an endless list of tasks and a very flexible schedule.

Since Tom and I spent nearly twenty-four hours a day together, I'd frequently hear him suggest to me, "Sweetie, let's just move to Alaska!" Over time, my response had been whittled down to brief, yet habitual, "No way!" I routinely shot down one gentle suggestion after another without even a second thought. I loved him, but I was keenly aware that in his vocabulary, "Alaska" didn't mean pavement, stores, or schedules; it translated into remote wilderness. I certainly didn't feel I owed him a compromise of such epic proportions!

As the years went by, the subject of me going to Alaska with my husband became an ongoing tug of war. For lack of a suitable compromise, we continued to keep ourselves engaged in our full-time business: building homes, constructing metal buildings, and taking on endless remodels. Yet, it was clearly understood that even in the midst of our busy existence, it was always very important to Tom that our schedule still allowed him time to continue his summer fishing endeavors as a commercial fisherman in Alaska's Bristol Bay. Each June he would leave for six weeks no matter what.

By 2004, even though I still wouldn't consider Alaska, I eventually felt myself beginning to soften. He was forty-two; I was thirty-seven. Finally, in an effort to "meet in the middle" somehow, I agreed to consider buying a piece of hunting property in eastern Oregon, which was four hundred miles from the Washington coast where we'd both lived our whole lives. It was all his idea. As far as he was concerned, eastern Oregon wasn't Alaska, but it did have two of the three vital elements for which he was looking: excellent hunting and secluded property. And since his occupation as a fisherman still allowed him ample time up north, he'd convinced himself that as long as he could hunt the big bucks on his own private land, he could most likely manage without the third ingredient for his definition of true happiness: a large body of water straight out the back door.

Originally, when he brought up the Oregon property concept, he felt certain that this end-all, grandiose acquisition would satisfy his longings to live up north. I wasn't sure what to think of his change of heart, but at that stage of the game, I was grateful for the compromise and felt that his most recent suggestion might be a fair trade. On my mental chalk-board I quickly erased "Alaska" as his supreme destination and replaced it with "Oregon," before cheerfully moving along with my already satisfying daily routine.

As far as I was concerned, with the Alaska monster finally under wraps, I was able to experience some much appreciated relief. As a result, we were more on the same page again when Tom's earnest search for Oregon property began. While thumbing through the agricultural newspaper, he came across an interesting piece of real estate which was well within our price range.

"This could be the perfect huntin' property," he told me.

After spreading out the map, he pointed out the acreage, which was situated in the foothills of the Blue Mountains of eastern Oregon. The decisive factor was that the proposed property had over twenty thousand acres of timberland adjacent to it—all of which was open to the public. The vast expanse of neighboring land had only one restriction; it was four-wheeler access only—apparently a dream come true for a devoted hunter.

Tom was intrigued. This proposal offered more real estate than he thought he'd ever be privileged to own. I checked my pulse, but the news of his magnificent find hadn't caused my heart to skip a single beat. All I knew was that the 624 acres was a massive upgrade from the sixteen acres on which we were currently living.

It was March, when after contacting a realtor, Tom drove to look at a couple of parcels. To be honest, I was hopeful that once he'd finished the long, thirteen-hour round trip to eastern Oregon, he would've grown tired of the whole idea. Instead, he fell in love with the openness of the land and the potential freedom it could offer. For him, the hunting privileges alone would be heaven-sent. On that particular day in Oregon, he and his agent hiked across miles of various snow-covered parcels. While Tom calculated the value of the timber, the agent located corner markers. Even with the long drive each way and twelve hours of investigation in between, he was back in just twenty-four hours. His unstoppable determination had prevented him from sleeping a wink! Upon his return home, his feet were still drenched from slogging through the wet snow during spring melt. Although he wasn't jumping up and down, he was ecstatic by his standards. His stunning blue eyes sparkled during his quiet conversation about the cool piece of property he'd found. That spring, the glowing reports of his discovery had me signing documents for a "vacation" property I never really wanted.

By then, I had come to the conclusion that buying a piece of property in Oregon would barely stir the nest we already had going; it really wouldn't change my life, whatsoever. I envisioned that during the summer he could fish in Alaska like he wanted, and in the fall, he would always have the option to go hunting; neither of which would upset my world. I wasn't thrilled in the least with the thought of having access to a recreational property so far away from home, but after thinking it through, I decided that I could adjust to owning land in two states. The place in Washington would continue to be our home; in Oregon, Tom could enjoy his hunting getaway.

Following our purchase, our lives were once again, back to a normal routine. But little did I know, this simple compromise would not be my last! Just ahead in my future I'd be in stranded in the Alaskan wilderness, struggling to get a fire going in the midst of a terrifying night on a remote beach.

2

Leap of Faith

The ambitious Tom that I knew was famous for churning out ideas for seemingly unachievable projects. He was forever on the hunt for something that presented more of a challenge. Although I also thrived in a challenging environment, I disliked traveling, and as a result, I made a point to focus my energy on tackling projects in my own back yard. But now that we owned property in Oregon, instinctively I knew that Tom would be figuring out a way to get me to trek back and forth to eastern Oregon with him from time to time. Either way, from the outside looking in, our lives were in order.

But to my surprise, even after the recent property purchase, Tom's scheming continued! He quickly gave birth to another brainstorm, plotting that if we bought a second piece of land in the same area, and "if" it was heavily timbered, then we could quit our jobs, move to Oregon and log the second piece to pay for both. Where did this idea come from? At first, I was not even close to being on board because we'd most likely be forced to sell our new home.

"We could build a house on the first parcel we bought, which is mostly steep hillside," he energetically explained. "It has two canyons full of gushing creek waters that could have gold somewhere."

The more he spoke, I have to admit, the unlikely concept he proposed of being out of debt in five years began to sound pretty amazing! Of course, I didn't experience the same glorious vision, but we were in agreement that the monumental idea of a second parcel would be a life-changing event if we actually followed through with another purchase. So on the next trip to Oregon I half-heartedly made the long drive with Tom to visit our next prospective investment. Before we even left the driveway, I felt that my mind was already made up. I knew that once we'd returned home again, I'd be able to honestly comment, "Sorry Sweetie, I tried."

We headed out early one morning. After many hours on the road, at last we'd arrived in eastern Oregon where I was introduced to our realtor, a friendly, ambitious gentleman whom Tom had met on the previous trip. In recent months, I'd been privy to only Tom's half of their many lengthy phone conversations, which consisted of dialogue revolving solely around property. Now, after seeing the two of them together, I could tell that they definitely had an unspoken connection—both of them, in my opinion, were in serious fantasy land. Their non-stop chatter skipped from an enormous 8,000 acre ranch in Pilot Rock to a $2 million dollar "steal" in last week's real estate flier. Was I even on the same planet, I wondered? Get real!

Nevertheless, during a brief yet enthusiastic summary, I listened carefully as our agent described our future property, "This particular piece is situated in the middle of wilderness at the top of Stubblefield Mountain," he explained. Our agent, Ben, spoke dreamily of the many attributes, and he couldn't wait to show it to us.

So off we went. We followed Ben in his pickup as we headed for the property, which I'd overheard was located several miles out of town. Perhaps if I had been paying closer attention, I would've picked up on the word "wilderness" and put the skids on the whole idea, once and for all! Although Tom wasn't saying much, I could tell that he was extremely excited. Inquisitively, his body leaned away from the driver's seat and his eyes were completely fascinated by the new scenery. In a matter of minutes we'd turned off the highway onto a gravel road, leaving the driving comforts of smooth pavement behind. Surprisingly, without reducing our rate of travel, we continued to speed toward the distant mountain range. Curling dust billowed from either side of his back bumper, and probably ours, too, as we zoomed past one weather-worn homestead after another. I watched intently as the rolling hills, grazing cattle and miles of barbed wire fencing streaked past my window. After twisting and turning past acres of farmland, it appeared we'd driven beyond civilization.

"How much further?" I asked impatiently on a couple of occasions.

"We should be getting close," Tom would cheerfully reply more than once. I could see he was absorbing every detail of our journey deep into the woods. Finally, we slowed down just a bit, taking a left turn off of the main gravel road. Within moments we had come to a dip in the terrain where a babbling mountain stream crossed in front of us, and without a bridge present we were invited to ease through the shallow water and then up a smaller and obviously less-traveled road leading to the top of Stubblefield Mountain.

As our vehicle climbed the narrow path, I must admit, the ride seemed like it might go on forever. And the longer we drove, for sure the less enthused I was becoming. Huge ruts of dried mud made for bumpy travel on the primitive trail, our vehicle nearly stopping at times so we could avoid whiplash. Bouncing, jarring movements turned me into a rag doll as my body eventually gave in to the relentless pounding. I questioned Tom's proposal that if we bought this piece of land that we'd actually be logging up there every day.

"It wouldn't be that big of a deal," he replied.

Quite frankly, I could never imagine getting used to this experience! As we pushed onward up the winding mountain road, I wondered how long the journey might continue before we actually reached our destination at the top, while at the same time, I was highly skeptical that any piece of land would be worth making this miserable commute both in and out each day.

Forty-five minutes had passed since leaving town, when at last, I felt great relief as our Durango slowly came to a halt. Up in front of us, Ben had jumped out, unhooked a ram shackled gate and tossed it aside. I watched the barbed wire and wooden posts coil into a tangled mess as they hit the ground. We inched forward a few more feet where we found ourselves officially on the property. The dusty trail we were following continued, but we stopped right away in an open field where the landscape leveled out on top of the mountain. The tall, lanky Ben bounded out of his pickup again and when he approached our car, his face was beaming.

"This is it," he proudly announced now that we'd arrived just inside the 664 acre parcel we would be considering for purchase.

Right off, I didn't find it overly enthralling; however, it did feel good to finally be out of the car, and once we were, the serene setting invited us to deeply inhale the pure mountain air. We stood waist-high in a sea of flaxen grass that was leaning in the gentle winds blowing on Stubblefield Mountain that day. The property's designated name was less than endearing, but in every direction the sights were absolutely gorgeous, just as the realtor had described earlier that day. We walked to the east where an awe-inspiring rock canyon came into view where the mostly flat terrain instantly dropped off hundreds of feet. As we gazed in the other directions, the majority of the panorama was beautifully timbered with unending stands of ponderosa pine. We strolled through fields dotted with wild flowers while Ben enthusiastically narrated in great detail the facts about the promising real estate. Judging by the animal sign present on the ground, the area appeared the perfect habitat for grazing deer and elk as well, no doubt a great selling point for Tom. After our brief investigation on foot, both men each unloaded his four-wheeler, which we immediately climbed aboard to explore the remainder of the trails that snaked throughout the property. No matter where we looked, endless acres of mature trees covered what could potentially be ours someday.

After several miles of investigations, we had a good feel for what the acreage had to offer. We'd already poked around on the old homestead where only remnants of a log cabin remained. Decrepit apple trees still stood on either side of the once well-used entrance to the now overgrown driveway. From there, off we went again, into another fifty acre patch of timber. Looking over at Tom, I could tell that he was in heaven.

"What d'ya think, Sweetie?" he asked. The unusual upbeat tone in Tom's voice was evident as he asked the real estate agent one question after another; this was completely uncharacteristic of the quiet, soft spoken Tom that I knew. His eyes danced as they scanned in all directions while he spoke to me about his plan to cut thousands of board feet of timber. As studiously as I tried to follow along with his conversation, I couldn't quickly compute the jargon of board feet, necessarily, or how that equated to log truck loads and eventually money, but it seemed like a project that would last a long time. I soon discovered that even though a couple hours earlier I'd been completely opposed to owning land so far out of town, now once I was there, somehow the idea of this long-term project had become more appealing.

As we walked through the large stands of timber, Tom began counting trees.

"There are 179 trees just in this small area and you gotta figure on average six trees this size would fill a truck," he said, pointing into the patch of timber. As I attentively absorbed the information, I wondered how he could even keep track of where he'd started or ended his random count; there weren't rows, just a sprawling forest.

According to Tom's calculations, this huge piece of land could be very profitable if all went well. Part of me wanted him to be wrong. But over the years I'd learned that I could trust his recommendations. I still had to wonder, though, if he could really accurately calculate what the timber was worth, or was he just guessing? After all, I could tell he was smitten. Was there a chance he might be exaggerating, even a little, I questioned?

The majority of the forest consisted of Ponderosa Pine, a completely different species than the coastal timber back home. As we gazed about, the fresh and somewhat overwhelming fragrance of pine emanated from the towering trees. I reached out to touch one of the many huge trunks that I couldn't even begin to wrap my arms around. The pinkish-tinted bark consisted of overlapping, scaly layers which reminded me of the finest pastry, the top layers flaking off without much effort. I tried to visualize a single pine tree as if it were lying on the ground with all the limbs removed and then I even took the whole concept a step further where it might be cut into lengths that would fit on a log truck. But standing there in the forest, I couldn't comprehend the actual sizes of anything, except for my serious doubts about the entire far-fetched plan. I mean, I knew Tom was very adept at running a chainsaw, but I had no idea how much wood he could process in a day. What if he couldn't get it all done? Would we lose it all? Realistically, I couldn't imagine this enormous project ever panning out.

I was certain that I personally wouldn't be a major factor in the logging equation, since for sure I wasn't planning on cutting any trees down myself. And at the moment, my mind couldn't begin to compute all of the details.

I was overwhelmed not only with the monstrosity of the proposed project, but also the size of our potential financial investment. We'd be jumping in at $400,000 with the owner carrying half. Then added to it was the cost of our other new land purchase as well; how could that even work? We didn't have that kind of cash, or even credit for that matter!

Surprisingly, as our explorations continued, I have to admit, I began to catch the fever! After listening to Tom's convincing interpretation of the proposed project, I began to feel like we couldn't go wrong; we were invincible almost. About halfway into the long drive back home I found myself brimming with nervous hope, thinking about what might be possible with such a risky venture. However, since we'd have to take out a substantial loan to explore this dream, we'd have everything to lose if it didn't pan out. It was no doubt a "go big or go home" scenario.

There were so many "ifs" on the subject of whether to buy the property or not. The project would be successful "if" the log market held steady, "if" we didn't get injured, "if" the owners accepted our offer, and so on. First and foremost, I was uneasy about the possibility of losing everything we'd worked so hard to achieve up to this point in our lives. In all reality, if we invested and failed, it could be a mistake from which we might not ever recover.

Back at home on the coast, we ran the calculator and weighed our many options. Over the next week, our kitchen's countertops were buried beneath maps and multiple pages of property information. More than once we looked over the professional estimate of the timber still standing on the property. Of the types of trees listed, fir was the only species with which we were familiar; besides Pine, the others were Western Larch and Alpine Fir.

Several weeks had passed since we'd been to Oregon together, and our deep discussions continued. It didn't matter if it was while we were eating dinner, driving to work, or lying in bed at night, we made conservative guesses on how many log trucks we could fill with logs, and then how much that truck's load would be worth at the mill. Eventually, I began to agree more with Tom's line of thinking, while at the same time, I searched for the courage to look beyond my personal fears and insecurities. Maybe we could handle a project of this magnitude. I certainly wouldn't mind being out of debt before our retirement years, I pondered. But, I'd been used to living in the small town of Raymond nearly my whole life. What would this new lifestyle entail? Where would I fit into the equation?

One evening, after processing all the facts and figures at our dining room table, I leaned back into a slouch as I looked out the window in deep thought. While Tom remained "Mr. Full Speed Ahead," my cheerful-talkative side became a bit subdued, most likely a subconscious effort to offset his abnormally over-zealous behavior. I knew that up to this point in our lives together, every waking minute had been about trying to get out of debt. The more time I had to think about the concept of moving, the less realistic it was becoming. After all, we'd just finished our new home, and I really had no desire to abandon ship. On the other hand, if we didn't try, I wondered if it might be something we'd regret in twenty years. We'd be too old; it would be too late. Back and forth I went from being excited to feeling overwhelmed.

"I don't know, Sweetie," I said, apprehensively, on more than one occasion, contemplating whether I really wanted to disrupt my somewhat predictable lifestyle.

Tom kept referring to all the positive aspects of the logging project in eastern Oregon. It obviously fit in with his adventurous personality far more than it did mine, that was for sure. If we were to move, then he would not only have two pieces to hunt on, but he'd also have truckloads of timber to cut down for years to come. As I searched for positive attributes—besides a chance at financial freedom down the road—I wasn't sure if there was really anything in it for me. Was that enough to go "all in," I thoughtfully considered?

It was actually a relief when the month of June arrived and Tom left for work in Bristol Bay, Alaska. As usual, whenever he's gone for the fishing season, we are typically out of touch, communicating on more of an emergency basis. During that period, I gladly put the entire overwhelming idea out of my mind. I had six peaceful weeks to clear my head. I was busy working various on jobs anyway, so very little of my time was spent thinking about a possible move. However, when Tom called from the cannery's payphone at the end of the fishing season, I sensed our situation beginning to ramp up. I could tell by his line of questioning that, unlike me, he must have remained on fire about the bigger-than-life Oregon land acquisition. And to his delight, a few days later when he returned home from Alaska, it began to appear as if the stars were aligning themselves. I was shocked when the enormous loan to buy the property had been approved, and our offer on the second piece of property had been accepted. Other than my fear of the unknown, there was no good reason not to go ahead. "You only live once!" became our motto, which eventually pushed me over the conservative edge. As it turned out, in late July we took the plunge, signing documents for the second much more expensive Oregon parcel we planned to log.

Now we'd officially planted ourselves in the middle of a massive project! The second property purchase was the most daring decision I'd ever been part of in my sheltered small-town life. On this wild adventure in which I'd agreed to take part, I fully understood that plenty of hard work and personal sacrifice lay ahead. As a practical person, I've always prided myself in making sensible choices, but it wasn't long before I was wondering if our current state of affairs might be a case of "mid-life crisis;" whether it was mine or Tom's, I couldn't say.

The transition to Oregon was fairly simple for us to execute. Our construction business had been at a standstill while he'd been in Alaska, making it an easy shift for us to break away without much notice. Without delay, we put our Washington dream home up for sale and left town. It felt surreal to be distancing ourselves from all I'd ever known. I wondered if I'd be able to meet Tom's high expectations in this colossal expedition. For the last thirty-odd years I'd been like a rat, taking the same path to the same store to buy the same groceries. Although I'd moved four times since high school graduation, in my small world, my places of residence were always less than ten miles away from my childhood home.

Before I knew it, the time had come for us to leave on our adventure. It had been only one week since Tom had returned from fishing when I found myself following along with his well-thought out instructions on how to most efficiently load our flatbed pickup with the bare necessities we'd most likely need for our move to Oregon.

Full of both determination and anxiety, we'd locked up the newly completed home and said our good-byes! We headed south to Portland, Oregon, then east along the magnificent Columbia River gorge. The farther east we drove, the more never-ending sunshine, beautiful scenery, and bright blue skies we could see. It was such a stark contrast from the dreary gray coastal weather that I'd always known, possibly giving me just enough encouragement to stay tuned in to Tom's wild plan for our future.

Once the six hours of highway driving were behind us, we made our way through the main drag of one modest town and then another. At last Tom announced that we were less than two miles away from our first piece of property which he'd picked out on his own several months earlier. A few minutes later we rolled into a small community whose sign announced that it was our intended destination: it read Elgin—population 1710. I was filled with nervous excitement as I tried to remember what Tom had told me during our previous conversations; gushing creeks, gold, deer, elk and trees. All that in addition to sunshine sounded great! I was smack in the middle of my new daydream when I was abruptly brought back to reality. The blaring noise of a train whistle caused my eyes to come back into focus as we slowed to a stop just outside the run-down post office building.

3

Awakening

We were held up for a few minutes while we waited for a train to inconveniently cross the main two-lane highway that passed through the middle of town. As we paused for the string of box-cars to clatter by, I began to absorb the details of my new home town. Taking a long hard look out my window, I noted that the road was paved, but the cement sidewalks were few and far between. All of the buildings in view could've been considered quaint, I suppose, but in poor condition. Judging by the facial expressions of local motorists, it appeared that this time-consuming delay we were experiencing was a regular occurrence. Soon enough, the train had passed, the warning lights had stopped flashing, and once again, we were on our way.

My first impression of the new community was that we had taken a step back in time. Even though I'd come from a small town, my current surroundings seemed more like a country western settlement from the distant past.

It was the first of August during the parched summer, which I soon found out was not considered parched by eastern Oregon standards. And the only grocery store in this sleepy little town to which we were moving exhibited a winter motif that didn't fit the current weather conditions, whatsoever—it consisted of a Christmas snowman display that was either eight months late or three months early. As we motored along, I observed various people in jeans and long-sleeved plaid shirts, many sporting cowboy hats, each of whom appeared to be chatting comfortably under the direct rays of the baking sun. "Welcome to cattle country," I said to myself.

It was only minutes before we approached the entrance to our first purchase, the hunting property where we planned to live. It was exactly a mile from the last house located at the edge of city limits. Just like Tom had explained to me several months earlier, the property was situated in a canyon and just off the public road. As our vehicle slowed, my eyes focused in on a row of tall cotton-wood trees. I leaned toward the window to observe what I could. They might be over a hundred feet tall, I calculated. Their leafy presence certainly provided a green wall of privacy between the road and our new property. When we turned off the pavement, the truck rocked from side to side for a couple hundred yards as we journeyed up the hill on a crudely graveled path paralleling the highway. Quietly, I surveyed the steep landscape. It was then I began to ask myself, "What have I done and where am I?" Our brief ascent dead-ended on a small flat spot just big enough to turn the vehicle around. Sadly, it was the only level area in sight. On my side of the truck, the angle of the steep incline was similar to the windshield I'd been staring through since we'd long ago left home this morning. There were dips and occasional benches in the terrain, but for the most part, the property continued upward as far as I could see. Besides hiking straight uphill for an entire mile, I wondered how we'd ever reach the top. How awful, I thought!

My stomach filled with dread. For the life of me, I couldn't imagine how this lackluster piece of ground could have grabbed Tom's attention. Unlike the natural beauty of Stubblefield Mountain property, this backdrop appeared di-sheveled. I could see jagged boulders randomly poking up from widespread ar-eas of scruffy grass. Scraggily pine trees which looked dwarfed and deformed, somehow had a solid hold on the sun-baked hillside. Small clusters of crisp leafy bushes chose to congregate in several small "draws," or gentle folds of the land where water would naturally drain. Clumps of sage brush were gener-ously scattered here and there, and as my eyes inspected their way up the hill toward the skyline, leaning dead trees repeatedly interrupted my line of sight. The wet climate I'd grown up in had always offered plenty of rain, which guar-anteed either mud, or shamrock-green colored grass teaming with a healthy crop of dandelions. As I sat there observing the sights, I knew that from then on, in my vocabulary, the adjectives "lush and green" would be tucked away like a swimming suit at summer's end.

"*This* is the property?" I asked, as I turned to look at Tom.

I was trying to remain strong. Past the curtain of trees lining the road, from what I could tell, we'd bought ourselves one square mile of blistering desert. As I sat inside the truck with the air conditioner running, I could barely get a grip on my frustration. Every last inch of the merciless terrain seemed insurmountable and nearly unusable. Slowly, I opened the passenger door, instantly feeling the hot oven-like air engulf me. Depression began to set in only seconds after I slid off the comfortable cloth seat. When my feet hit the dusty gravel, I felt intense disappointment wash over me as I stood speechless in the blinding sun. My eyes began to tear up as a natural reaction to my overwhelming discontent. This wasn't the picture that Tom had painted for me during the countless hours of conversations we'd had about the property. There were trees alright, but as far as the rest of his sales pitch, I was anxiously awaiting its revelation. How could I have so drastically misconstrued all that he'd told me?

One glance in my direction allowed Tom to assess my devastation. I could tell he knew that he'd misled me in some way, but didn't know exactly how. My high hopes were dashed, my body felt limp, and my spirit was overcome with sorrow. We both felt terrible for different reasons, but there was no turning back.

"Sorry, Sweetie," he whispered, hugging me tightly as the tears streamed down my face. I was aware that there would be no quick fix. We were a mile outside the city limits of a strange town, with no running water, no porcelain toilet, and no electrical outlet to ease the pain. Even though I had known of the primitive circumstances going in, I hadn't pictured the intense heat surrounding me while I attempted to transition from the easy-going lifestyle I knew to the pioneering mentality of the unforgiving Wild West.

The glaring truth was that we had nowhere to live at the moment, but we were in possession of a few of the basic necessities which were still strapped down on the back of our new flatbed pickup. Besides some miscellaneous lumber and a few building materials, we'd also brought along our generator, bedding and a few tools. We unloaded right away, piling all the supplies under a group of young trees beside the dusty gravel driveway. Stashed under the seat of the truck was $10,000 in cash which would keep this unpromising project moving forward. Those funds would have to cover our upcoming living expenses such as a place to stay, food, permits and the initial building materials.

What to do? Back in Washington State the construction business was no more! Returning home at this point would have been more than a humbling experience. There was no turning back; we hadn't lined up any work. I knew that the situation I would be forced to cope with was no one's fault but my own. I was fully aware of how different he and I were, and I should have never committed to this without seeing the property for myself! As the shock began to wear off, I took a deep breath or two before Tom and I left the property in search of a camp trailer we could purchase to live in for the time being.

At the grocery store we scanned the local paper where an ad for a twenty-foot travel trailer caught our attention. With some good directions from the owner, we drove through the peaceful countryside, eventually coming to farmhouse with a 1970's model camp trailer out front.

"There it is!" I said optimistically. As we followed the narrow driveway up toward the house, off to our left, we could see our potential refuge from the overwhelming heat. The unappealing accent colors on the exterior consisted of the less-than-stylish shades of gold and orange. It did, however, appear sparkling clean in the midday sun. After talking to the owner, Tom and I stepped inside to have a look around. Our "tour" consisted of standing in one spot and turning our heads. Just like the outside, the interior of the trailer was spotless as well. The fold-out table provided ample seating complete with the rust-colored cushions which easily transformed from an eating area into a large bed. The propane stove was crammed conveniently between the miniature stainless steel sink and the pint-sized fridge which I knew we'd so desperately need during the hot weather. The floor space in the bathroom was no bigger than a rug sample offered at any carpet store, but the small room housed a toilet, sink and a tub/shower unit. After our quick internal inspection, we agreed to buy it. Perhaps I could stomach this adventure if I had a place to call home. After all, the trailer would allow for a few modern conveniences while we built a permanent place to live. It would also provide an enclosure in which to keep our small assortment of belongings in order.

On the way back to the property I remained optimistic that we'd made the right decision to buy such a small trailer, but after all, it did seem to provide everything we'd need. We wouldn't be hanging out there all day anyway, we'd be busy working. Most importantly, it would afford us a place to cook, sleep and organize our thoughts.

By the time we got back "home," I was anxious to settle into our new acquisition. Call me spoiled, but it wasn't long before my mood plummeted again. Our brows were dripping with sweat as we uncovered the unfortunate facts, immediately learning that our new living arrangement was nothing more than a glorified cot stuffed inside a tin-can shelter. We discovered that the fridge was not in working order like we'd been told. Next we tried the sink and found it to be in similar condition—broken. A quick turn of the faucet revealed a plumbing disaster which instantly sprayed like a fountain from under the cupboards, with barely a drizzle coming from the faucet itself. The small amount of water that ended up making it to the bathroom facilities was dribbling down the wall and onto the floor. This enormous undertaking was feeling more hopeless as the minutes passed. We'd just spent a quarter of our money on this heap and the only redeeming quality that existed in this prize on wheels was the door I could slam at the end of the day! Within ten minutes, my mood had shifted from devastated to furious. Clearly, the previous owners had not been honest with us.

My pace visibly slowed once reality had set in, yet Tom remained unaffected as we continued to get organized in spite of our current shortfall. About then, I found myself wishing that some of his unbelievable optimism would rub off on me. Or was it denial on his part?

"We won't be here forever, Sweetie," Tom said encouragingly. "We'll get something figured out in the next day or two." I wasn't clear on how this might happen in such a dry, dusty, lonely neck of the woods but it instantly offered me a little hope. We carried the bedding and clothes inside and unpacked the small assortment of dishes we'd brought from home. The saving grace was the six-foot awning that the trailer sported, so we stretched that out and enjoyed some much deserved shade while we ate our lunch.

On this hot day we soon realized that we weren't alone! As with any campsite, the presence of humans, food and water was a magnet for bugs of all kinds. Mosquitoes are one thing, but I've never been around such large battalions of yellow jackets, which proved to be meat-eating insects like I'd never seen before. They appeared out of nowhere and were intent on watching our every move. Was this trailer a rolling bee hive, too, I pondered? Over the next couple of days, I noticed that it was during mealtime when they became most aggressive, landing and then offloading parts of my sandwich still in-hand; the greediest ones almost crashed mid-flight after biting off more than they could safely carry. And, thankfully, they did have a nest elsewhere, I later determined after watching them all fly away.

In spite of our hardships, by day two we'd settled into a routine. Eventually, I phoned my family, who couldn't comprehend the situation in which I'd put myself. It was out of character, and therefore, hard for them to believe that I'd willingly agreed to the current arrangement because in the past, their invites to go camping were always quickly denied. For one thing, I couldn't tolerate the lack of progress. And besides the smell of must that has always engulfed every camping device I've ever encountered, in my opinion, the preparations required to be there in the first place and the clean up that followed were the kind of busy work meant for hamsters.

Of course, as expected, the subject of Alaska entered the conversation. We reminisced about what it might have been like in comparison to where we were at the moment. For sure it wouldn't have been blazing hot, but in my mind the state of Alaska still seemed like part of another galaxy. And even though it felt like Oregon was a world away from what I considered home, at least an emergency trip back to Washington was possible if I really couldn't hack it anymore. I felt I had the option to step out of Tom's fantasy at any time.

Nevertheless, we decided to get our heads in the game and do the best we could. In order to refrigerate our groceries, we drove a mile back into town to get some ice. While we were there, we also picked up some two-gallon containers of water to have on hand for the bare necessities. On this miserably hot afternoon, I was forced to come to terms with the fact that the second-rate shelter which we'd set up on our private desert would be referred to as my home for at least the next two months.

4

A Pioneering Spirit

Even in the midst of everything that appeared to be going wrong at the moment, I did at least have confidence in our construction abilities, and I knew that once we made a plan, it wouldn't take long to get something whipped up. The first obstacle we had to deal with was the less-than-suitable area we had available on which to build. It was quite undersized, so we discussed a few building options. First, if we built a simple metal building with an apartment on one side, it would provide a little storage as well as a cozy place to live. Although it would be very quick to assemble it would not be as aesthetically pleasing as perhaps a wood-sided structure. Second, we could build a small house, but there wouldn't be room for a storage building of any kind. Third, our excavator would soon be delivered from the coast, so Tom suggested that he could loosen and resituate what would be the equivalent of twenty dump-truck loads of material from the hillside made up of solid rock that was adjacent to the only level ground we could see. Chipping and then shifting that amount of rock would be time consuming, but it would ultimately develop a larger flat area on which we could build. With that extra space we could erect two separate structures: first the barn and then the house. That made the most sense. Best of all, the barn didn't require a permit, so we could start on that immediately while we waited two weeks for the building permit to be issued for the house.

Working with what was available, we quickly put together a mental picture of what size the metal building should be and how it should be positioned on the soon-to-be available space that Tom would be creating with the excavator. Even without actual drawings, Tom and I were on the same page in regards to the size and shape of our project, deciding on a structure similar to others we'd built for clients in the past. We agreed that the canyon property would not be the site of our permanent retirement home, which enabled me to cope from one minute to the next and kept me breathing between my crying spells for the next three days. I would have to get over this major bump in the road, somehow someway finding the determination to make it work.

For the house, we decided on a simple two story box-style structure with a covered deck spanning across the entire upper level, and for our short term investment we would need only modest accommodations. We visualized a rustic cabin, complete with log siding and a forest-green metal roof. We planned for real log pillars supporting the decks on both levels, and within the first couple of days, Tom sought out and then cut down four perfectly straight, equally-sized trees to use for the poles. In the meantime we'd ordered materials for the barn which would be delivered the next day, allowing us to start construction right away. Perhaps focusing on this project would help take my mind off the overwhelming negatives that seemed to be filling every spare moment of my thoughts.

The excavator arrived. With machinery at our fingertips, the preparations to build a barn began immediately. To combat the rising temperatures for which we were not yet conditioned, we worked in the early morning and late evening hours. During the heat of the day when it was unbearable for us to function, Tom taught me to play cribbage and other card games. We spent the rest of our spare time ironing out the various details of our new house and also running plenty of errands.

* * *

The intense Oregon heat radiated from every surface within the sun's reach. As nice as it was to be out of the coastal rain, surviving the extreme temperatures presented a huge challenge for both of us. To avoid heat stroke, I routinely made multiple visits to the stream located across the highway where the ice-cold snow melt was still trickling from the nearby mountains. The scorching trek across the pavement was always rewarded as I crested over the bank and down toward the water where I could immediately feel the cool air surround me. Once in the creek, I cupped my hands to scoop up the freezing water which I gratefully poured over my head. The refreshing blast instantly provoked goose bumps as it cascaded down my backside and soaked into my clothes. Standing ankle high in the shallow water, my feet were instantly numb. It was so invigorating, though. Then with slippery rubber clogs I struggled to get enough momentum to climb back up the steep, crumbling embankment along the highway. Looking to avoid motorists who might think I was crazy, I dashed across the blistering asphalt in my gritty shoes, feeling somewhat rejuvenated as I returned to our camp on the other side of the road.

Our primitive accommodations were gradually improving. One afternoon, Tom and I began poking around in the clusters of marsh grass in an area near the towering cottonwood trees along the road. He was pretty sure that if the wetland grass and cottonwood trees were there, then water wouldn't be too far below the surface. He pressed the shovel into the caked soil. Like magic, after three scoops of dirt, an artesian well sprang up. That asset became the jewel in our property's crusty crown. Water—fresh and cold—breathed life back into me, giving me renewed hope. What a treasure! To increase the water supply, using the excavator, Tom dug a trench and then created a small pond. An hour later, after the freshly dug dirt and river rock settled to the bottom, we were pleased to find crystal clear running…..yes, running water. The wet gold bubbled out of the earth, pushing its way through the channel, and then mysteriously disappearing back into the baked soil just feet away. I didn't understand how that could be possible—but I didn't question it either. That was a bright day!

We were slowly making things happen, but in the midst of it all; I desperately missed our old life and the people I was certain I could trust. I longed for the ease that accompanied me while doing my errands back home, merely because I knew the streets in my old town like the back of my hand. The modern conveniences of a furnished home and our nearby friends and family were only part of what used to be taken for granted. Many times over, I wondered how I could have ever done such a thing as to leave it all behind. However, in contrast, Tom remained very upbeat about our circumstances. He always had his eye on the bigger picture at least two years down the road.

As soon as our building materials were delivered, we began work on the 36' by 40' metal building we called "the barn." Within a week of arriving in Oregon, we had developed a good routine: up at daylight, work 'til noon, play cards for a couple hours and then by mid-afternoon get back to the grind until dark. In just a few days, the lofty new building was constructed, and we were able to park our travel trailer under our partially completed shelter, out of the incessant rays of blazing sun. From then on, our camp was headquartered inside where I felt less vulnerable, and oh so grateful to be under cover. What a milestone!

With our enlarged living quarters, I moved most of our daily functions to the spacious area just outside the trailer; as a result, our bed didn't have to be reassembled each night after the kitchen table was put away, ultimately saving me a lot of time and energy.

During our first night inside the barn we gratefully dozed off to sleep while a choir of crickets unknowingly serenaded us from afar. With our trailer stationed inside, we could barely hear the passing cars that occasionally interrupted the pure silence that surrounded our lonely existence. And being under cover was pure bliss in comparison to the first week at camp, when our shelter hadn't cooled down to a reasonable temperature until midnight. It felt so good to climb into bed each night after all the heavy lifting, shoveling, and pounding that was required of us each day there.

Going into the camping experience, I was prepared for the crickets, and of course, the typical mosquito humming in my ear, so as we drifted off to sleep, those pesky noise-makers were bothersome, but not surprising. It was just two days after we'd moved into the barn when we discovered that one screaming cricket that, like us, had also set up camp inside the barn and just outside our trailer. Tom was annoyed, but not to the point of being driven to do something about the problem. I, on the other hand, was becoming infuriated! One night as we endured a good two hours of the agonizing whistle,

I made plans to suffocate the relentless siren. The next day I organized my plan. On the second night, I tiptoed outside of the trailer armed with aerosol cans of various products which included everything from air-freshener to hair spray to engine degreaser. Paying careful attention, I eventually zeroed in on a hiding spot where I squirted the variety of poisons into the crack from which I thought the high-pitched note originated. The racket did subside during the initial spray treatment, giving me instant hope that I'd taken care of the problem. But apparently I'd missed the intended target because the unbearable vocals resumed shortly after I was settled back into bed. After many failed attempts, Mrs. Cricket carried on with her whistling like she was a tea-kettle boiling out of control.

It didn't seem to bother me that off in the distance I could hear the harmless croaking frogs as they joined in song with the large population of resident crickets. I could easily fall asleep listening to their steady hum. But within the week, there were two lead croakers that had moved just inside the barn who also regularly treated us to a front row performance well into the night. Who else might move in, I wondered?

Night after night, the ensemble grew. Soon I could pick out the hooting owls which provided a muffled, yet gentle intermittent beat that echoed throughout. Lying in bed, listening hour after hour to the unwanted entertainment, oddly enough, I eventually began to appreciate the rhythm. It was like a junkyard band missing only the clashing of the garbage can lids from time to time. Little did I know….that void would soon be filled!

5

Three's A Crowd

Unfortunately, the crickets, frogs, owls and mosquitoes weren't the worst of our guests whose hectic schedules also began just after dark. It got much worse! We soon learned that there was another unidentified party-goer on the loose. The chain of events always started with an unwelcome thump to the top of the trailer. I must admit, it was the initial pounce that sent my imagination running wild. Judging by how this creature's acrobatic dismount from the barn's rafters rocked our tiny home, I knew the intruder must be well-fed. As it trotted heavily across the roof above our bed, I pictured an animal much larger than a mouse, yet I was hopeful it was smaller than a poodle. Right away, the sounds of scratching, scraping, and gnawing joined the ongoing rustic musical that dared us to fall sleep each night. Snapping rubber band noises resonated in the night air as the caulking was energetically removed from the seams canvassing our trailer's roof. An occasional pound of Tom's fist on the flimsy ceiling would quiet the movement for a while, but whatever it was, until the creature had eaten his fill of dried caulking for dinner, he wasn't about to quit.

To ease my frustration and calm my swelling rage, I tried to imagine his perhaps bubbly personality as we listened to the activities which seemed to be on the increase night after night. If nothing else, the critter sounded very ambitious. When the scraping episode was finished, the intruder routinely made his way through the barn, which always entailed clamoring over many of our belongings that must have appeared useful for his personal freeway.

What a nuisance! When we were fortunate enough to have fallen asleep, a clank, bang and a wobble of the aluminum extension ladder would often jar us awake. There went the cymbals! Whatever this creature was, it was big, and definitely not a mouse! We kept our large spotlight handy, hopeful that we could catch a glimpse of the perpetrator, but when we actually got the chance, a quick flash of light spotted absolutely nothing but our own bright reflection in the trailer's dusty, screen-covered window.

Then there was one night when it was dark but not bedtime yet. With the generator blaring as it did each evening, we were playing cards at the kitchen table when we felt a rocking motion brought about by a boarding passenger.

"What's that noise?" I asked Tom. He didn't answer, but kept listening.

For some reason, the bothersome activity had resumed earlier than usual. Unfortunately for us, this time, instead of being outside on the roof, somehow the camp invader had apparently weaseled a way inside. As we sat holding our breath in a state of shock, our eyes followed the movement as it traveled through the block of cabinets just two feet away. It began in the cupboard under the fridge, and then moved to beneath the stove, the sink, finally ending up in the drawers at the end of line. We could hear jostling in our candy stash. With complete disgust, we witnessed the drawer wiggle under the weight of the unsolicited visitor. Tom and I looked at each other in silent disbelief. I sat frozen with fear as I saw Tom pitch his handful of cards onto the table before reaching past me toward the noise. Without notice he yanked the drawer open, hopeful I guess, of decapitating the intruder.

"What are you doing?" I wailed! In our cramped space I jerked away but had nowhere to go. Thank goodness nothing jumped out. Like Houdini, somehow the varmint had vanished from the compartment, most likely trailing back the same route through which he'd entered moments ago. We waited in quiet disappointment as we felt his heavy carcass leave our home, fully aware that our food had been officially ransacked.

Our patience was wearing thin! As it was, we were exhausted from being baked in the sun all day after yet another restless night. Without a doubt I knew we had to put a stop to whatever had just happened. But how? What was it? I was almost afraid to find out!

It was a known fact that for the time being, a sound night's sleep would be hard to come by. But the next day, we were pleased to find that the artesian spring Tom had tapped into a few days earlier appeared unstoppable. To capture the benefits, he created a large hole that was twelve feet deep and twelve feet across. To our delight, the cavity, once again, instantly filled with water as quickly as he excavated the area. The pit would eventually serve as our water source with clean river rocks ultimately providing a natural filter. To develop the system further, we stood an eighteen-inch culvert upright in the center of the hole and secured it in place. One by one, we surrounded the culvert with river rocks. With all of the trees around, we could work in the shade during the heat of the day and I was grateful for the comfortable working conditions, at last. Besides the shade, each time we heaved a mammoth stone back into the hole we got "ker-plunked" with a splash of chilly water. For me, the cold burst was tremendously invigorating. It wasn't for Tom. I was surprised. For a fisherman, he sure didn't like getting wet. As a result, he stood quite a distance away from the rock's point of entry, instinctively stepping away from the impending shower each time. In the event he did get sprinkled, he'd immediately arch his back, with irritation clearly written all over his face.

Once the rocks were piled up to the natural ground level, Tom ran some plumbing into the culvert and then hooked up a pump he'd bought in town. Somehow, one by one, he managed to make our major obstacles disappear! Now, we had access to fresh running water whenever we started the generator. Before long we had a system set up so that the ice-cold water could be pumped through a hose that was hanging over a portable clothes rack. We were thankful for the cold running water, but we made sure that our breath-taking showers always took place in the mid-day heat, ensuring we didn't freeze to death during the session.

After each long day, we were understandably tired. And without fail, every night after climbing into bed, the animal kingdom proceeded to come to life one species at a time. Like clock-work, the persistent gymnastic rodent returned to our private residence on a regular basis. One night, Tom stepped out of the trailer with a flashlight in hand, this time determined to put a face to whatever was causing the nightly commotion. A few minutes later he re-entered the doorway, his enlarged round eyes and raised brows told me more than I wanted to know.

"It's a *rat*! That sucker's *huge!*" he said, with his hands held up like I've seen when he tells a fishing tale. Tom slid back into his cramped, cushioned bench seat where we were playing cards again for the evening.

"I watched it jump on the trailer's axle and disappear through a hole in the trailer floor," he said as he shook his head in disgust while he explained what he saw.

"Ratty," as we began to call him, seemed quite self-assured, almost like this was his home, not ours. And the thought crossed my mind that he might not be traveling alone. Nevertheless, under the cover of darkness, the invisible circus continued as the camp dweller made his rounds. Once again, after snacking and further contaminating our groceries, the varmint made his way back out of the trailer. I knew just outside the trailer door sat our overflowing dressers of clean clothes. Three plastic drawer units sat side by side against the wall, just below the window. As I rested in the dark, I also recalled the heaps of clean clothing that were folded on top: piles of socks, our underwear, and my favorite white tank top, for starters. Staring at the ceiling, I listened carefully, as I pictured a greasy-haired, buck-toothed, gooey-eyed varmint with wax-filled ears doing gymnastics on our most personal belongings. That revolting image made me want to heave up my dinner. I instantly knew I would be making some changes come first light!

Now knowing what we were up against, all night I resisted the urge to sleep with one eye open. The next day, while Tom remained focused on finishing the barn, I made a quick trip to town in search of a suitable trap. Upon entering the local hardware store, I stopped at the register to explain our dilemma.

"Norway rats," the guy said without hesitation. "A furry tail about yea long?" he asked, holding up his hands up to indicate its approximate length.

"Yep," I sighed, shivering at the thought. Knowing their species didn't make me feel any better. He led me over to the appropriate aisle and my stomach instantly sickened as I focused in on the size of the contraption. Even though its design was much like a standard mouse trap, the size of this device gave me the impression it could very possibly dismember a small child.

Back at camp, with the enormous trap in hand, I was determined to put an end to our nightly disruptions. I optimistically unpackaged the apparatus…. cheese, or peanut butter, I wondered as I removed the cellophane while quickly humming through the verses of *The Farmer in the Dell*.

"The rat takes the cheese?" I questioned out loud to myself. At that very moment, I had a new perception of the chant. I wanted to barf at the mere thought, but I chose cheese, based on the nursery rhyme I'd all but forgotten. I set the trap, and we went to bed with much anticipation of what it might capture once the lights went out!

We waited! From our cozy beds we could hear the familiar romping commence. Like always, it began on the roof. Once the scraping routine was finished, we expected him to make his way inside the trailer and into our food compartment without delay. He did! And to my delight, the movement paused momentarily as if the rat was curiously check out the new grub I'd set in his well-worn path. As I pondered what to do next, I knew that once we put a stop to these home invasions, the groceries which he'd carelessly trampled through each time were going to have to be disposed of like items contaminated by nuclear waste. I tried to imagine his reaction to the latest addition. Was he intrigued? Hungry? Gauging by the size of Tom's hand signals the night he first spotted him, I'd pictured an animal so large that it might just have one foot holding down the spring-loaded arm of the device while he devoured the cheese.

Thankfully, the wait was brief. It was only moments before the trap snapped!

"Got him!" I exclaimed excitedly as I jumped out of bed.

"Good," Tom interjected with his eyes still closed in his groggy pre-sleep voice. At that point he may have been more irritated with me than he was the rat, I couldn't tell.

I flicked on the lights. In unison, off went the noise of the crickets and frogs. After waiting a moment, I carefully opened the cabinet door to view the deceased. Nothing! And the cheese was gone. Was it a malfunction, or was he really that big?

"Grr….ossss!" I announced. I could feel my scalp itching and my skin crawling. My countenance displayed rancid disgust as I slammed the cupboard door and then shimmied back into my warm spot in the bed. Perplexed, I flashed back for a moment. The rhyme did mention that the rat "takes" the cheese. Interesting, I thought!

The next morning, Tom crawled under the trailer to find the possible point of entry. Once there, he plugged one obvious hole with a block of wood.

"Thank goodness!" I said, immediately daydreaming of a good night's sleep.

Somehow I had a hunch that our wide array of treats would entice the mangy rodent to revisit. On this particular day we had treated ourselves to Chinese food. And unfortunately for Ratty, his bait was a hunk of my savory leftover sweet-and-sour chicken which I secured to the trap's activation point using a portion of sturdy dental floss. He wouldn't be getting away this time, I schemed!

We waited for nightfall. It had been only twenty-four hours before the resident rat managed to find a new porthole for what would be his last supper. We heard him on the roof, as usual. Come on, Ratty, I silently cheered.

When the trap snapped I was elated. I heard a valiant struggle. Once the movement stopped, I bolted out of bed. Stooping over at the kitchen cupboard, I gradually opened the door to peer into the cabinet at the lifeless body. To my surprise, the rat wasn't greasy at all…. and no buck teeth. Although I didn't touch him, I could tell that his fur was soft like a mink coat, mocha brown in color, with a white belly and paws. The thought crossed my mind that it was almost cute enough to have been a pet, except for the deeds he had done, and the stench he continually left behind. My emotions flip-flopped from victory to remorse, and within seconds I heard myself expressing my nervous apologies to the deceased. "I'm sorry, Ratty." Wait….what the heck was I saying? In recent weeks I knew that I'd felt deprived of regular human interaction, but was I really that lonely, I wondered?

My sadness was brief. With a great sigh of relief I stood up. There were no antlers present, but he was a trophy catch measuring seven inches, not including his thin furry tail which was almost as long.

Soon enough the external noises resumed, at which point we were disgusted to know that our furry intruder was not acting alone. Although we never had another rat inside our trailer, it was no secret that they still roamed freely throughout the barn. I regularly monitored the enormous traps for the next few weeks while we feverishly built our home. As summer gave way to fall, we couldn't wait to get the house done. Besides escaping the cold temperatures, we were, of course, anxious to elude our persistent visitors, which included not just the rats but all of the irritating pests that came to life once the sun went down. As for the army of starving yellow jackets, we were grateful that like us, at least they retired for the evening.

October was just around the corner, and the night-time temperatures began to plummet. The elevation at the lowest part of our property was just over three thousand feet. Just a quick twelve miles up the road, the recreational ski area was awaiting its first snow of the season. Due to the brisk temperatures, turning on the trailer's furnace was our next project. But guess what? We were about to discover that just like the fridge, toilet, and plumbing, our heating system in the trailer was also a farce. An inspection of the vents revealed only wire coils where insulated ducting once existed. We surmised that every tuft of insulation had probably been removed by the rats. As it turned out, the absence of ducting didn't matter anyway, because the heater itself was also in a state of disrepair.

Despite our poor luck, we continued to work hard and eat well. At least the trailer's propane stove worked adequately, so I fixed plenty of skillet suppers, which on a typical day consisted of hamburger, onions, and fried potatoes. We'd spent six weeks of intense focus on the new house; it was finally completed to the point of sheet rock. At that juncture, we moved our mattress and bedding inside onto the plywood floor and promptly closed the door. What a relief! The peace and quiet was deafening. My ears felt plugged as they do when I slip under water during a hot soak in the bath. I couldn't hear a thing except for the faint sound of occasional cars passing on the highway down below. I quickly got used to the golden silence, but most of all I was appreciative that we had escaped the varmint zone. Just outside of our inaccessible shelter, I imagined rats marching single file, pacing the perimeter while looking for the smallest possible "in." After a diligent effort to invade our space, I'm sure they were tapping their temples in thoughtful determination. We'd won the battle, but instinctively, I knew we hadn't won the war! I was certain that somehow, someway….they had plans to get even!

6

Another Hat for My Wardrobe

In the six weeks immediately following our abrupt move to Oregon, we had been diligently working on the house, not only to escape the growing pest sanctuary, but also so we could nestle into a warm shelter before the cold winter weather set in—the locals had warned us to expect up to five feet of snow during the dead of winter. We couldn't comprehend how we could possibly prepare for that! Even though we were finally headquartered inside a solid structure, our humble provisions were still much like camping, but we'd progressed enough to have a shower, lights and heat, which were adequate living conditions of which I never complained.

With the new house somewhat functional, for income purposes we needed to get to work doing some logging at our Stubblefield Mountain property before the snow season started. I wasn't sure what to expect with that enormous undertaking, but I knew I needed to do all I could. The reality of the situation was that we had bi-annual payments approaching for both pieces of our Oregon property and in addition we'd also purchased a piece of logging equipment: a bulldozer. Now that we were fully committed to the Oregon excursion, I often wondered how I managed to let myself get into such a mess. What a huge risk! There was no doubt that without highly concentrated efforts and hard work, our Oregon project would have been an easy failure to explain, especially to our sensible group of friends and family that shook their heads in dismay as we left town a couple months earlier.

As I began to mentally prepare myself for working in the woods, I knew it wouldn't be a new concept to keep an eye out for danger. I imagined it would be somewhat like our work in the construction business when we had frequently used equipment such as excavators, bulldozers, and large spiraling post-hole diggers as we'd developed various jobs sites. Thankfully, I wasn't going into the logging experience totally unaware. It was to my benefit that thanks to Tom I had sampled just a small taste of logging at our previous property where I'd learned to run our heavy equipment, set chokers and keep out of harm's way.

As for operating a chainsaw, personally, I had run one only once before, and it had taken a lengthy bout of determination for me just to get the saw started. I'd cut down only a nuisance holly tree, hardly a comparison to the hundreds of acres of towering timber we now owned. Tom, however, had been logging off and on for years, so our master plan was while he ran the saw; I would work on the other details of the logging operation, which would entail using the machinery to get the wood skidded out of the woods to a roadside location where a log truck could eventually pick it up. I felt I could handle that.

In preparation for the massive logging project, I gathered all of my courage and collected my memories of any personal experiences associated with the subject. I knew a little about what it took to be a successful logger: early to bed—early to rise, for starters. My dad had worked in the woods years ago and while he told few stories of danger, his body sported numerous scars that marked some of the close calls he'd had over the years. As a little girl I had watched as he re-coiled many a sprung tape measure and repaired damaged saws long after a hard day's work. Most of all, I remember the comforting odor of the fresh wood shavings that were forever being caught in every last one of his pockets.

The daunting task of logging 664 acres seemed overwhelming at first, but Tom and I whole-heartedly dug in. At that point, we really had no choice! As our endeavor began, Tom cut down and then de-limbed tree after tree until he had a large area of logs ready to be collected. Each time he moved to another work zone, repeatedly, I backed the equipment into position before climbing off the machine and down into the brush in order to hook up each choker. To assist me, the winch on the back of the dozer housed a hundred foot long cable—when the equipment couldn't get in close to a log, an outstretched cable could. Once each section was hooked up to the cable, a simple pull of a lever would engage the winch that would reel the heavy log in close to the machinery. Back in the driver's seat, I'd drag the log to its destination.

With the logs gathered, I jumped on our excavator, which had a long arm with a big bucket and a thumb. Those features allowed the machinery to grab the logs, so I could sort them by species—the different types of logs had to be sent to separate mills. I stacked the logs in large piles so that the self-loading log truck could park in one place and easily retrieve the entire load with his "claw" called a grapple. After a brief introduction period, my tasks seemed simple enough. Maybe this project of ours would pan out after all, I thought.

During our commute to and from work on the mountain, the forty-five minute drive gave us time to scheme about our upcoming balloon payments on our loans. We calculated how many log truck loads we'd have to process each week just to make ends meet. With such large numbers, there were many days when our goal felt unreachable; we needed to process at least one log truck load a day. Could we do it? It was such a learning curve, even for Tom. In Oregon, the trees were an unfamiliar species, the mill had different requirements than he was used to, and we had no connections for who would best haul our logs out of the woods.

We were surrounded by magnificent scenery in all directions; plunging rock canyons and plush meadows nestled here and there throughout the property. The healthy stands of flourishing timber made me feel miniscule in comparison. Upon our arrival to work each day, the crisp morning air was exhilarating and unbelievably peaceful! Even as the seasons changed from fall to winter, the sun continued to shine. As we got into a rhythm on the mountain, Tom made quick work of getting the huge trees down, but it soon became obvious that removing the limbs from the felled trees was going to be the most time consuming part. It was even more so in eastern Oregon, because a pine tree's branches were enormous in comparison to the limbs on the coastal timber. Even after piling leftover brush I found myself waiting for Tom to finish his duties. He had the more time-consuming job by far, so seeing the need, I agreed to cut limbs using the smallest of the three saws, but only if he would start it for me. I knew from experience that the jarring, jerking motion it took to get the saw running required almost more strength than I could muster. Once the saw was started, though, I worked enthusiastically and to my delight, my skills steadily improved. Tom continued to cut trees and I focused on cutting limbs. When I was finished with limb removal, then Tom followed up by bucking the freshly de-limbed trees into varying lengths of logs specifically requested by the mill.

Soon, Tom could work outside my immediate area and I rarely needed his help. I could start my own saw, and I had learned how to replace a chain. Maybe we'd finally found a job where we could get along, I thought. Before I'd agreed to move to Oregon, I'd been hopeful that logging would be the answer to our non-stop disagreements at work. In the woods I'd imagined that we would be separated by enough space and somewhat isolated by the blaring noise of the saws and machinery. That didn't last long, though, and as the honeymoon stage wore off, Tom's typically soft-spoken demeanor turned aggressive. It all came about because nothing was ever happening as quickly as he thought it should. Although his work ethic was never intentionally violent 'toward' me, I didn't care for his abrasive conduct, especially in the woods. I was working to my full capacity and his impatient and uncaring manner was causing me a great deal of anger and resentment. I not only had to avoid being hit by falling timber, but I also had to steer clear of getting trampled by him or whacked by his flying elbow.

In the midst of the ongoing turmoil, I kept trying to learn the whole logging routine while also trying to keep up with Tom. After putting in a full day, my arms were tired, but I thoroughly enjoyed it! The fresh air and exercise made me fell alive and productive. Within two weeks of my new career, our schedule found a productive pattern where we'd work separately until midday and then we'd team up to skid the logs from the woods to the landing. This arrangement was more efficient, saving me a lot of time getting on and off the equipment to hook up logs. With that set-up, we were working closely together again and unfortunately, our all-out disagreements were on the increase. I was on the dozer—Tom was setting the chokers when the serious problems began to blossom.

"Back it clear in here," he'd impatiently order after I'd throttled the down the engine while I waited for him to ready the chokers.

Although I wasn't yet an experienced logger, Tom's bossy demands rubbed me the wrong way! After all, I'd already been setting chokers and skidding logs on my own up until then. I just wasn't confident like he was about driving the dozer up over mounds of unstable limbs just to gain a few extra feet—that was what the cable was for! In my opinion, working in the woods was dangerous enough without creating additional chances for injuries.

Since I couldn't run the equipment to his satisfaction, before long we'd switched places. I was setting chokers while Tom was at the helm. That was fine with me. Not only did I love the physical exercise but I was also optimistic that our new arrangement would run more efficiently. But even though I was working as fast as I could go, I couldn't ignore the barely audible ongoing commentary of my partner. "No, pull off more cable," "move it down farther," or "reach under the other log," he'd harshly instruct. My patience was reaching an all-time low!

"Just a second!" I'd reply. I knew I could get the job done.

"What's the hold up now?!" he'd frequently utter from his perch on the equipment.

"Will you give me a freakin' break?" I'd snap back at him time and time again.

Tom was always in such a hurry and he often pulled away before I could get away from the cable. Each time I heard him rev up the engine to take off, I'd yell, "Would you stop!"

I was constantly afraid that I wouldn't be able to get out of the way in time. Sometimes it was my teeth I was worried about saving as the cable pulled tight in a split second, nearly catching me under the chin. Sometimes it was my glove that was still hooked on the spurs of the cable which was being reeled in toward the winch at high speed. I had many nightmares about being wound around the steel drum of that monster, not because Tom meant to hurt me, but it was a well-known fact that the dozer's faulty hydraulics wouldn't always properly shut off. I sounded like a screeching recorded message: "Stop!" "Be Careful!" "Wait!" "Hold it!" His answer to all of the above was a clipped, "I am…hurry up, will ya!"

"And you want me to go to Alaska with you?" I'd frequently ask. But before he could reply I'd interject a resentful, "Well you can forget that!" I didn't want to be trapped somewhere in the wilderness, perhaps a thousand miles away in a strange land. He wasn't proving anything to me, except for the fact that if logging with him was a nightmare, then his dream of disappearing into the Alaskan wilderness sounded like the perfect recipe for disaster!

Life just kept getting worse and the ongoing turmoil at work had turned me into a monster. I knew I didn't want to be blamed for wiping Tom off the face of the earth with an excavator bucket, but let me tell you, at times it felt like a simple solution. This was not who I wanted to be. Once again, I found myself admitting that this was no one's fault but my own. I had chosen to ignore the warning signs which consisted of red flags like overwhelming debt, my uneasy stomach and the fact that I despised traveling, whether it be driving deep into the woods or making the long drive back to the coast to visit my family. Logically thinking, my situation was bound to end badly, no matter how I looked at it.

As I struggled to find to a happy existence, overall, I considered myself a pretty flexible person. Twenty years earlier I'd been a bank teller marching around in high heels all day. Shortly thereafter, I'd given birth to three wonderful kids and in order to stay home with them full-time, I'd transitioned from banking to neighborhood daycare services. During those years I'd raised cows, pigs, and chickens and even taught myself to milk goats, for crying out loud! Once my kids were in school I'd figured out how to build pine furniture and soon had started a home-based business. Those skills eventually extended into managing the local farmers' market in town, an unpaid position that had required many hats. To be successful in that arena, I'd stepped completely out my comfort zone to fulfill promotional speaking engagements. I'd also tracked down vendors, had run monthly meetings….and come to think of it, not only did I build and paint the huge signs for the market, but I'd also installed them along the highway and around town. As my furniture business had evolved into remodels and more, I'd eventually acquired my contractor's license and had begun working full-time in construction. With all of that behind me, this career change which Tom had invited me to experience was quite a transition from where I'd been. However, as I stood there in my cork boots wielding a chainsaw in the wilderness, I knew I was completely capable of learning another new skill and I certainly didn't appreciate his lack of patience during the difficult transition. I truly felt that he owed me a grace period in which I could learn to adjust.

In spite of giving my new lifestyle an honest go-around, after six weeks I was miserable with my decision to "conquer the forest," but somehow I had to make this work. Everything we owned was tied up in this mess. No matter how badly I wanted out, we had to remain partners on the job in order to see it through. This intense project had instigated an ongoing internal war with my emotions; I loved Tom to pieces, but quite frankly, I despised working alongside of him no less than twelve hours of every day. How could I ever find my way out of this hole, I wondered?

I sensed that I was reaching a breaking point. Deep down I knew that I could persevere for a year, perhaps, if I kept the emotional distance, treating our situation as a working relationship, not a marriage. I figured that I would still do the laundry, pack our hefty lunches, and take care of the office duties; similarly, he would still be in charge of loading the truck before work each day, driving us in and out of the woods and making the decisions at the jobsite. Our contrasting strengths could still work for us, just not long-term. Adopting that mentality, perhaps I could cope.

Soon the snow was piling up. The temperatures were extremely cold and the daylight was becoming scarce. Up until the severe winter weather set in, we'd been making the commute in our flatbed pickup, often precariously fishtailing our way up the muddy mountain road to get to work each day. Even though the truck wasn't a practical vehicle for winter use, it allowed us to always have our four-wheeler with us which made it more convenient to run around up in the woods. Eventually, due to the increasing amounts of snow, the road became impassable in the flatbed, at which point we swapped over to our Durango. Although the car didn't take as well to either the smell of diesel, or the presence of sharp chains and cork boots, it definitely handled the challenging road conditions much more efficiently.

By mid December, we were logging in substantial amounts of snow. There were plenty of places where the drifts measured four feet, but generally we found ourselves trudging though knee-high, dry, powdery snow which squeaked like baking soda under our boots. It was quite a contrast to the annual coastal snowfall I was used to, which during most years didn't even exist. I kept telling myself that things would eventually improve. I couldn't take much more—the cold, the isolation, and the constant discord in camp—I wasn't cut out for this lifestyle.

To conserve my energy I resisted the urge to verbally express my serious concerns, many times over I had decided that maybe we'd bit off more than we could chew, kind of like the greedy brain-dead yellow jackets back at camp. Besides our inability to get along, our excavator and dozer were continually having one issue after another, mostly due to cold weather. Even when we pampered both pieces of equipment, it was common for a hydraulic hose to burst or a fuel problem to arise. Due to the steep terrain on which we were working, the steel belt-like tracks which allowed the machinery to lumber along were occasionally peeled off, which frequently brought our logging operation to a screeching halt. I came to expect bad news at work every day—it was just a matter of what the disaster might be. Huge wrenches, our trusty come-along, a sledge hammer, and chains became our main arsenal for the continual repairs. Keeping the equipment running that winter proved to be finger-smashing, argument-provoking, strenuous work! Those delays made it even more difficult to reach our goal of producing one log-truck load of logs per day in order to make ends meet. As we worked tirelessly on the monstrous equipment, I imagined Lady Luck watching us from a distance but not willing to shine upon our foolish decision to be there.

Regardless of what happened on the mountain, seven days a week we always put in a full day's work, starting at 4:30 a.m. and not heading home until dark. As the hours of daylight began to wane, it was because of our payment deadlines that we always found ourselves in a race against the darkness, at times even working with the aid of our truck's headlights. Every couple of weeks I'd take a step back to catch my breath with hopes of gaining a little perspective. Even though I could see that we were making decent progress, I became convinced that this massive project would eventually do us in. I vividly remember telling Tom at least once a week that when this project was over, "We are done!" Marriage over! I kept watching for a light at the end of the bleak tunnel that I had been wandering through since I'd moved to Oregon. It felt to me like we hovered on the brink of disaster every waking minute, and I was in a continual state of exhaustion. In contrast, true to our starkly contrasting personalities, although Tom spent plenty of time grumbling, he was not yet convinced we had a single problem. Time after time he would explain that he wasn't mad at me…just trying to get things done. Whatever the case, it was during his frequent tantrums when I would poignantly remind him, "And this is *exactly* why I will never go to Alaska with you!"

As determined as Tom is, I should've have known that I would one day eat those words!

7

A Special Gift

As miserable as I was at work, I was glad that at least our new place provided a cozy refuge at the end of the day, even though according to the old timer's we'd met, the canyon in which our new home was situated was referred to as the coldest part of town, out of the winter sun's reach.

Our life had drastically improved since we'd arrived, but it was still primitive in many ways, though, because we were off-grid. It was due to the steep rocky terrain that existed between our house and town that the utility company estimated it would cost over $100,000 to get regular power to our property. Adding insult to injury, soon after, we were notified that a simple phone line would be just $7,000! And that was only if we performed all the digging of the mile-long trench required for the installation. Consequently, our power supply for the house consisted of a solar panel with generator backup, which had plenty of hiccups of its own for the first year. We could never find cell phone service, so during the first couple of months, in order to make a simple phone call, we got in the car and drove to town. Eventually, out of pure desperation, we engineered a tedious setup that allowed us to use the cell phone at the house—it worked on most good-weather days and only caught on fire one time!

As for our heat, we planned for a future wood stove, but in the interim, our heat source was a propane wall heater which worked fabulously. On the other hand, our private water supply required constant management, mainly because we'd never experienced such long-term freezing temperatures and deep frost. In more private matters, we weren't privileged with the use of an indoor restroom until February, which meant a porta-potty graced the front stoop for six long months. In the worst of winter weather we often rested our haunches on the snow-drifted toilet seat, compliments of Mother Nature. The blowing snowflakes continually filtered in through the plastic vents of the unit. During that stint we were only home after dark anyway, and thanks to my overactive imagination along with my experience with the snoopy nocturnal rats in the barn, I felt I had good reason to avoid the unlit porta-potty facilities at all costs.

Despite our hardships, we made good progress logging on the mountain. In the bitter cold weather, it was vitally important that we kept moving to stay warm. Frozen toes and fingers were an every day occurrence. We stopped only momentarily to snack throughout the day in order to avoid getting chilled in the freezing temperatures. I always bundled up in multiple hand-me-downs, the last layer being my dad's old logging jeans. During one moment of inattention, the swirling chain of my saw brushed my thigh, instantly cutting through all five layers of clothing. In my mummy suit of cotton armor, I miraculously sustained only a scratch to my flesh. I duct taped my clothes shut for the rest of the afternoon and vowed to move along in a more alert fashion; lesson learned!

Life bumped along. It was difficult but rewarding, and I sustained only minimal injuries, for which I was grateful, considering my lack of previous experience. Sometimes a surprise smack to the face would come when I tried to set a choker in thick brush. A tangled limb would unleash its fury causing a brisk "thunk" to my forehead. That would beckon my attention! After many harsh lessons, I felt lucky to have come away with my cheek bones still intact.

In the midst of that time I was still desperately grieving the loss of my golden retriever who'd passed away a year earlier. Licking the large metal mixing bowl coated with cookie dough leftovers had been one of his favorite pastimes. During my evening baking sessions, the clank of my spoon against the metal bowl was like a gong that aroused my emotions. The tears of sadness that developed would create plump droplets that perched on the brim of my eyelids, waiting to fall at the slightest urging. My gentle weeping for him was nothing like the tears of desperation that I'd shed when I'd allowed myself to be rudely transplanted in eastern Oregon; those had been sobbing tears of regret! The frequent sighting of a dog on a cowboy's truck regularly reminded me of the companionship that I missed so dearly. Even though I tried to hide my overwhelming grief, Tom finally insisted that we find another dog to fill the void. I resisted his offer for a while, not only because my loyal companion could never be replaced, but also because I knew that caring for a dog would interrupt my necessary focus at work. I felt I couldn't afford to add any more responsibilities to my already jam-packed schedule. As it was, I was exhausted from my duties, and any puppy we brought home would have to be my constant shadow in order to remain safe in the woods.

Just before Christmas a farmer was advertising in the local paper for a batch of Border collie puppies, available for pickup on December 18th. When Tom got done reading the ad he made his way into the kitchen, tossing the paper on the counter before me. "Come on, let's go!" he said, when I finished reading. That evening, after calling for directions, we left for the country, taking the same turns toward where we bought the wretched camp trailer four months earlier. The closer we got, the more I wanted to pay those dishonest people a visit, letting them know about the hardships we'd endured in recent months. By then I was pretty certain they had supplied the rats, too, as some sort of a package deal! Instead, we turned off just before their place, down a driveway to a modest mobile home. When we pulled in, Tom announced that he was staying in the car and made me promise to come back with one, and only one, puppy. There were nine in the litter, and he knew my tendencies.

It was dark outside when my knuckles rapped on the door. A teenage boy answered my knock and led me out to the unlit barn. A flick of a switch turned on a single bulb that was dangling from the lofty ceiling. Instantly, my heart warmed at the sight of all the energetic, loving faces that were milling about. Some were chasing each other, at times somersaulting over bales of hay. Immediately, I knew I would never be able to choose. I apologized for my crying as I wiped the tears from my cheeks, telling the kid that I'd lost my dog to bone cancer not too long before we'd moved to Oregon.

He left me alone for a bit so I could connect with one of them. The rowdy group almost didn't notice my presence as I sat quietly on the smelly hay-strewn floor. Ultimately, I was hopeful that one of them would choose me. If so, I wouldn't have a lifetime of guilt for leaving the perfect angel behind.

At last one came to sniff my knee. The visit was brief, and the puppy returned to his playful party of eight. Soon, another black fur-ball meandered in my direction and climbed into my lap. He immediately made himself comfortable, putting both paws over the crook of my left arm while viewing the playtime activities of his siblings. I wasn't sure what he looked like in the face, but it didn't matter, he'd stolen my heart. He was the biggest of the litter, which was perfect, since I'm partial to bigger dogs. About then, their petite mother greeted me with a gentle lick to my cheek. She wiggled with joy, presumably sensing that I might be lightening her more-than-full load. After I paid the young man, I strolled to the car like a proud new mother with my delicate bundle of joy gently cuddled in my arms. I became overwhelmed with emotion again as I nuzzled my face in his silky-soft fur. I couldn't see what the rest of him looked like, but his paws and his fluffy curly-cued tail appear as if they had been dipped in white paint, just barely. We bonded immediately. As I look back now, from that moment on we became inseparable.

When we got home, I lovingly looked him over. As a Border collie with fairly typical colorings, his mostly-black body was highlighted with a pure white ring around his neck. The snow-white fur spread onto his front chest like a bib. His face couldn't have been cuter! On his forehead and snout, the evenly proportioned bright white markings were complimented by a shiny-wet jet black nose. There was no mistaking, I was in love!

"Pup" became his popular nickname and a new routine began. Pup rode to work cradled in my arms, even though there was plenty of room beside me on the bench seat. Throughout the work day he perched studiously on my lap while I operated the machinery. I narrated as the large metal teeth of the equipment would grasp each log.

"Got one," I'd announce each time. His brown eyes watched carefully as the "boom," or long arm of the equipment would reach out for one log after another. As the cab spun around with each load, his drool, which disbursed with every bark, was magnified in the bright light of the morning sun. From early on, it was obvious that my co-pilot was intent on learning the ropes. He never tired of his duties.

Three months passed and our logging project progressed. At work, my new puppy napped in a duffel bag that I toted around to each cutting area. Tom would work a short distance ahead of us, cutting down large groups of trees before moving on. Once the fallen trees were free of snow, the resident deer had begun to gather around the fresh food source. Each day, a large herd would follow Tom, cleaning up the now easily accessible moss that had developed in the upper regions of the age-old timber. Pup and I trailed the deer, a safe distance behind Tom as I de-limbed the downed timber like the Tasmanian Devil from daylight to dark.

After a few months on the job, we'd experienced just about every breakdown imaginable on the two pieces of equipment we owned. By then we'd worked out a solution to just about any problem that would arise. Tom and I had even ironed out some of our own differences. A log truck showed up a couple of days a week to pick up our piles of logs. Life was good again. Pup was happy. I was happy, and just like Tom had predicted several months earlier, we were making substantial amounts of money, which meant our loans and enormous fuel and equipment bills were covered. That alone was a tremendous relief. By spring, I felt like I was in an unstoppable rhythm, but we weren't out of the woods yet, so to speak. Our $28,000 bi-annual balloon payment was rapidly approaching.

8

Over the Edge

It was April when Tom and I re-evaluated our progress and decided to hire a crew of guys to help us finish the logging on the mountain. The main reason was that we had a massive balloon payment coming due and we felt that the two of us couldn't process enough wood in time. With their advanced equipment, they could process the logs much faster, increasing our profit margin, which essentially covered the expense of their wages. It was a win/win for all of us. Besides the extra machinery and man-power that would be joining us, the crew boss also had connections in the log market that would take all of our smaller wood.

Their newer machinery was computerized and could've been considered elegant in comparison to ours. The most important piece of equipment they brought to the jobsite looked a lot like our excavator, but it had a cutting head in the place of a bucket. With that amazing device the machine could grab the tree, cut it down, de-limb it, measure it, and then cut it to specific lengths, all in a matter of a minute. We couldn't compete with such efficiency, especially on the smaller wood which was worth much less at the mill.

With the logging crew on site, our work routine revamped itself. Tom didn't fall trees anymore, he worked on the dozer all day, and from then on Pup and I were stationed full-time on the excavator at the landing. By then Pup had grown too big for my lap and was far too hyperactive to sit, so he and I learned to share the only chair available inside the cab. He communicated his excitement by way of his incessant barking, growling and squealing. As I maneuvered logs around the landing, he worked every angle possible, utilizing both arm rests while I perched on the edge of my seat to run the controls.

There was no mistaking it. With the help of additional machinery and a full-time crew, we were cranking out the wood, producing ten log truck loads a day instead of one! Throughout the day, Pup got on and off the excavator with me each time a load was skidded in because part of my duties was to unhook the chokers after each load of logs was delivered to the landing. After the dozer took off for the woods again, I walked down the length of the logs with my chain saw to clean up whatever limbs or knots got missed. The instant I shut the saw off, Pup would run for the excavator, knowing full well that it was time to sort and stack logs again. I'd climb in behind him, and then we would move the logs to their appropriate piles.

A month after Tom and I began working together with the crew, a serious mishap brought about a change in our routine. It was 10:00 o'clock in the morning and I was on the Washington coast dealing with the possible sale of our house when I received an unexpected call from Tom.

"Hi," he said when I answered.

"Hi!" I replied. "What's wrong?" I asked, after a short pause. Tom didn't normally call during the daytime.

"The dozer went off the cliff."

"What?" I said, plugging my opposite ear.

"It's gone," Tom said.

"What happened?"

"Well, when I was unhooking the choker, the dozer started to roll and on the slope there, and uh…it just kept going. It took out a big fir tree, too! Actually, the logging crew thought I went over with it because I was running along side of it clear 'til it went off."

I pictured what he meant; he could have been killed.

"Where did it happen?" I asked. I knew the property well and I couldn't think of a cliff in that vicinity. He explained the exact location in more detail and told me that at one point his glove got caught on the shifter handle when he was trying to get the dozer stopped. I was grateful he hadn't been injured in the process, either by being run over or getting dragged off the cliff.

I felt myself drift off for a moment, deep in thought.

"Now what?" I asked. It was hard to be a good seven hours away from what seemed like such a life-changing problem. I wanted to be there to help.

"Are we insured?" Tom asked.

"Don't know, hope so," I said. We still owed $35,000 for the machinery we'd purchased on a contract less than a year ago.

"Who do we call to find out?"

I gave him my best answer, which was "The equipment company we bought it from."

"I'll call you back," he said, and we hung up.

The devastating news took a few minutes to sink in. Where could that have happened? And how? What do we do? We had a huge deadline coming up for our property payment. No matter what, we had to keep trudging onward, or we'd take the chance of losing it all.

To fill the equipment void at the jobsite, the logging crew brought in another piece of machinery, along with an extra guy. Taking the place of our absentee dozer was a skidder. From then on, Tom ran the only equipment we had left, which was the excavator, and Pup and I stayed home each day where I worked on finishing our new house.

Instead of our project taking five years like Tom had originally anticipated, all of the logging we'd planned on doing was finished by the first of June. With the help of the four-man logging crew, we'd made short work of the logging project on the mountain; they'd been on site six short weeks. Once the hired help left, there were mountains of logs that still remained which Tom had to load on to trucks headed for the mill. He spent day after day loading trucks with the excavator. In the meantime, his fishing season was rapidly approaching. He worked feverishly in order to get the logs out before he had to leave for Bristol Bay.

Unfortunately, for the first time in many years, Tom missed the fishing season. Delaying the logs' delivery to the mill until late July when he normally returned from fishing was not an option we could consider. It was of utmost importance that the wood was delivered right away in order to make our dreaded balloon payment at the end of June.

I knew a rough winter lay ahead due to the fact that his Alaska fishing endeavors have always been "the fix" that keeps him going. Being in Alaska is not just a six week event; it is something he talks about all year long. He's always cherished his time up north, but this year somehow he'd have to manage without it.

By the time the logs were all shipped out, it was the end of June. We returned our focus to the damaged dozer which was still upside down on the mountain hillside, two hundred feet below the road where Tom had been working that tragic day. Luckily, as it turned out, we were insured, but only because it had been required on a loan of that nature. Thank goodness! The fifty dollars a month we'd been sputtering about had actually saved our hides!

After weeks of waiting, it was officially determined that due to proposed expenses, the equipment company couldn't profitably recover the dozer, not even with the last of their available options; an army-style helicopter. It was destined to remain on the mountain indefinitely! As far as they were concerned, it was ours to do with what we wanted.

Following their decision, Tom and I re-visited the crash site. It truly was a disaster! Bent parts were flung everywhere. Tom was optimistic that if we could get it turned right-side up then we could possibly ease it a couple hundred feet down the side of the mountain by pulling it with a cable attached to our excavator bucket. It was "iffy," but we didn't have much to lose; it would cost us only the price of some cable and our time.

With a little ingenuity, and a full day of hard work we were able to retrieve the dozer off the mountain. Once it was home again, Tom went to work on the massive repairs. Within a month, it was in working order and we put it back to work right away.

9

Implementing the Alaska Dream

Eastern Oregon
September 15, 2008

Tom and I had spent four action-packed years in Oregon where we'd done extensive logging, sold property, built two homes, and in addition, Tom had even gone partners on a fishing vessel in Bristol Bay, Alaska. Looking through Tom's eyes, I thought we had "arrived." In our new home, we enjoyed the constant exposure to world-class elk, phenomenal deer, and year-round wild turkeys, all from our dining room table. He seemed thoroughly satisfied with our lifestyle, except for one small detail that was still missing: property in Alaska. He wanted it all and more!

Once again, Tom began working more earnestly on the "Alaska" dream again, which really meant he began "working" on me. As he quizzed me about Alaska this September morning, there was something different about his demeanor. His quiet suggestion gave me reason to believe that his dream of making it to Alaska was becoming more about necessity than desire. Or was it just his crafty approach? Now that I think back, he did seem overly convincing as I listened to his ideas about the different kinds of spectacular fishing he wanted to do, and of course, the cozy, rustic cabin we could build together. As he spoke, the increasing twinkle in my eyes probably urged him on. He knew that projects of this nature were irresistible for me.

At first, I wanted absolutely nothing to do with being stranded somewhere

53

in the wilderness, trapped in a far away land. Even though Tom didn't see it that way, that's definitely how owning property in Alaska felt to me. After my difficult, frustrating, yet somehow gratifying experiences during our logging operations, I was less than excited about another long drawn out project with Tom by my side. However, it was the wicked devil's advocate standing tall on my shoulder who would point out that Tom and I had made it this far, so how much worse could it possibly get? After all we'd been through months of severe heat, rats galore, lengthy isolation, terrifying danger and never-ending arguments. Add to that, we'd also labored in freezing temperatures, I'd suffered injuries of all kinds, all while teetering on the brink of financial disaster a good share of the time. The last four years we'd spent together had definitely been no picnic. So, in response to the devil's advocate I thoughtfully replied, "Exactly, how much worse could it possibly get? I mean, really!"

My dear husband was forty-six years old when the "Alaska" idea once again reared its ugly head. I was forty-two. For me, Alaska meant deep, dark waters, unfamiliar boating activities, wild bears and the intimidating unknown; each of these would easily qualify as one of my greatest personal fears. Besides my own insecurities, one of my primary hesitations was because of Pup. He and I had become nearly inseparable over the past four years. His suffering from occasional seizures had been an ongoing problem since birth, so it was of utmost importance to me that his comfort and welfare be carefully considered. Therefore, as far as I was concerned, there were two important requirements to meet before I could consider a full commitment. First, the commute couldn't involve any commercial airplane travel. Flying him in the belly of a plane was absolutely out of the question. Because of my first request, the second requirement was that the property had to be as close to home as possible, keeping our driving time to a minimum. I had absolutely no desire to drive for days on end just to get to Alaska. After expressing my desires, I was hopeful that my strict requirements would somehow deter him. After all, this transition meant hours upon hours of driving resulting in days of wasted time; a well known pet peeve of his. Instead, Tom immediately responded to my less than accommodating requests with a cheerful "that's fine," without even an ounce of hesitation! His quick reply reminded me that he would do anything to be able to get to Alaska, even if it was temporary.

After studying a map, it didn't take long to figure out that the closest Alaskan soil for us to consider would be Ketchikan. Still, the whole concept seemed highly unlikely. For one, I couldn't imagine how we'd ever pay for the whole excursion. But right away, Tom began to sort out travel details to determine which route we might take and what our expenses might be. The most economical course, he concluded, would be to drive up through Canada to catch a ferry in Prince Rupert. From there it was a six-hour ferry ride to Ketchikan before we'd officially set foot in the state of Alaska. Upon our arrival, if we actually managed to make it that far, we'd build a cozy cabin in the woods, just off the water's edge where we could not only fish but live happily ever after….for six weeks at a time, anyway. After what I'd been through already, I considered that maybe I could endure a brief spell up north.

On second thought, had I lost my mind, I wondered? This was not a lifestyle that I even partially understood. However, fishing had been in his blood from the time he was a young boy. He'd grown up on the coast of Washington a mile from the beach where he fished year round with his dad, uncle and grandpa. They explored the rivers and the ocean where they spent countless days together, drinking pop, telling stories and catching fish, rain or shine. When he wasn't fishing, then he was hunting; not just deer and elk but ducks, coyotes and the elusive black bear. Following his high school graduation, he worked in the Bering Sea on a crab catcher/processor during the harsh winter months where his small stature was almost instantaneously transformed from boy to man during the treacherous months of hard labor. During the off-season, he worked on local crab vessels in his home town of Westport and even then, much of his spare time was devoted to every other kind of fishing-related endeavor. In his early thirties he was introduced to the more forgiving lifestyle of commercial fishing in the bay.

As a striking contrast to Tom, I had never fished before in my life. Our family didn't tell fishing tales, own fishing poles, or plan fishing trips. But like Tom, my dad also regularly spoke of his longing to live in Alaska. During my childhood, my father had even drawn up his own plans for a fabulous log cabin he thought he might build in the wilderness one day. For years, he dreamed of an escape to the wild frontier, but for one reason or another, he'd never actually made it there. Even though I thoroughly enjoyed the outdoors, my father's fantasy of making it to Alaska had never interested me one little bit.

Instead, my childhood passions had involved building forts under the mountain high blackberry bushes across the alley from where I lived. In my world of outdoor adventures it was all about making the perfect chocolate-mud-pie. However, I also diligently worked on a hole in the back yard which I was certain would get me to China one day. As I dug with my trusty table-spoon, pictures of upside down people living in darkness became thoughts that filled my head. Interestingly enough, my tedious excavating always created a fine dust, the exact ingredient my younger sister and I sought out for making the back yard confections. Without fail, I'd get sidetracked from digging after sifting my hands through the silky, soft "flour," and once mud-pie fever kicked in again, I would deviate from the original plan of tunneling to distant China. In addition, besides playing softball, climbing trees and roller skating, there went my whole summer year after year.

Even though I had also grown up on the Washington coast, I couldn't ever recall being on a boat except for an occasional ferryboat ride to Whidbey Island, Washington. Many of my parents' relatives lived there, so throughout the year our family made regular trips. Each excursion to the island destination first required a long drive toward Everett to the Mukilteo ferry. My younger sister and I looked forward to getting to the passenger line-up area just early enough to have time to get out for a treat, yet hopeful of a short wait time. Once we had our tickets and were parked in line, without fail, dad would reward the family with an orange-sherbet-swirl cone from the restaurant down at the dock. The ice cream always calmed my stomach, which was inevitably car-sick from the long drive in the giant, family-sized car. If the ferry boat was more than five minutes off-shore, my sister and I were permitted to walk down to the dock to observe fisherman and ferry workers while we passed the time.

As a little girl, I remember the flocks of squealing seagulls hovering over-head, watching for floating tidbits of food which were often stirred up by the incoming boat traffic. As I took in the sights, the odors of creosote, salt-water, and seaweed carried on the sea breeze unknowingly permeated my soul. She and I observed people from all walks of life as they lined the docks at the ferry terminal in hopes of catching something. The nets, ropes, fishing poles, and tackle boxes all appeared as nothing more than useless clutter from what we knew. But my sister and I intently watched all of the busy activities anyway, until eventually the big, rumbling ferry boat would pull in. The workers wearing fluorescent vests would unclip the safety chain and lower the dock's loading ramp onto the ferry. One by one, each car's engine would start with a different hum, and two by two, the cars slowly motored off the ferry with a "tha-thump," as their tires crossed the end of the metal ramp. It wasn't until the vessel had completely emptied and the cars in our line began to move, that she and I would sprint for the big, dark-green station wagon in which we had arrived.

From the time I was kid and then up through adulthood, I was overcome with nervous excitement each time I boarded the giant ferry. I remember listening to the creaking structure of the vast ship as it traveled through the water. The groaning noises it produced made the steel monster seem flexible somehow. On the old but well-kept vessel, the slightest broken seal on a window caused it to feverishly whistle a tune as it traveled into the headwinds on the open water. I remember leaving the warmth of the indoors to take in the sights from the upper deck where the bird's eye view of the dark, nearly black sea was almost paralyzing. Everything from the aging vinyl on the bench seats upstairs to the fumes emitted from the enormous idling engines, all were triggers which brought back one terrifying experience I'd had as a young child.

Etched forever in my memory is a time when I was held out over the railing and "flown" like an airplane above the water. Beneath my tiny suspended body spanned acres of nothing but turbulent algae-green water. A relative's hands around my rib cage were the only thing keeping me from plunging into the torture chamber below. I prayed he wouldn't drop me, and I found myself too scared to scream. As a helpless little girl, I imagined that once I hit the water, the gigantic metal fins would snag my clothes before swirling my small frame out of sight with no hope of rescue. Even after I was safely aboard the ship, the churning noises of the boat's enormous propellers enveloped my every thought.

As Tom and I continued to discuss Alaska, besides the long drive through Canada and the inevitable ferry commute, there were so many factors to consider. For one, the thought of buying property so far away made me extremely uncomfortable. The idea of starting over sounded fun, but only if the man I loved so dearly could get along with me. But what if we couldn't? Why would this excursion be different? Second, I experienced serious anxiety at the thought of being so isolated, separated from family and friends with whom I enjoyed daily communication, and I highly doubted we were going to end up with reliable phone service. Third, I dreaded the cold, damp, dark weather, and of course, the fear of bears came to mind, which now that I think about it, should've actually been moved the top of my list of worries. Above all, as we spoke, I could see how excited Tom was about the idea. I loved him and I didn't want to be the one to crash his party.

During the initial property search, I learned that gorgeous waterfront property is never cheap—at least until the magical word "remote" was unveiled. Remote, waterfront property was quite inexpensive compared to the real estate we'd priced on the banks of Ketchikan….and for good reason.

In hindsight, the word "remote" should've been my first giant red flag, but denial immediately stepped forward to convince me that a project of this magnitude might actually never take place. From my perspective, once again, the whole plan which Tom was completely on fire about seemed pretty farfetched!

"So if we buy remote property, how would we get there?" I questioned.

"By boat!" Tom shot back at me like it should be obvious.

I spent a moment in deep thought. From my perspective, the idea of a boat being our only mode of transportation seemed outrageous!

"So we have to buy a boat, too?" I quizzed.

"Yep," he replied without further explanation.

If gaining access to the property was the first issue, then second, there would be no power, no sewer, and no garbage service on this property that barely even offered an address. We'd be on our own, much like when we lived in the canyon in Oregon but on a much larger scale. It felt to me like we'd be cut off from the world, which was a huge negative as far as I was concerned.

As it turned out, due to our budget limitations, all of the properties we ended up considering were remote access only. There were no roads, only water. I couldn't get my brain wrapped around that concept. The deeper we got into the project, the more I felt I'd sacrificed enough already and living in the remote Alaskan wilderness might be pushing it off the charts!

"I don't know, Sweetie," I said with serious apprehension about my most recent concession. I was already getting cold feet.

Tom, however, had been given the green light and I don't think he heard another negative word once I'd uttered, "Okay."

After his intense search for affordable property, he contacted a realtor and organized a meeting; Tom and I would fly to Ketchikan and hire someone with a boat to cart us around. In order for Pup to avoid the plane, for this trip he would stay at Grandma's on the Washington coast. I schemed that once we were in Alaska, Tom and I would shop around, and then I could say, "Sorry Sweetie, I tried!" That comment had a familiar ring to it!

Well, even though I was full of anxiety, in just a few days the plan was coming together. Before Tom and I left for the airport, we made arrangements with a charter boat captain in the Ketchikan area who agreed to escort us around in his skiff for a day, "weather permitting." Red flag number two shot straight to the top of the flagpole with mention of weather issues, but still, I agreed to forge ahead. I naively pictured this daring escape to 'The Last Frontier' unfolding against an ever-present canvas of beautiful blue color which would only take place under the blessing of unending sunny skies. In that perfect world, Tom would always be patient, and Pup and I would be eternally happy. Whatever!

We made plane reservations right away. And in spite of the red flags, I actually began to get excited for our short trip up north. Now after hearing so much about Alaska, I couldn't wait to see what this magnificent land was really like.

Once we boarded our plane in Seattle, Tom's much anticipated project of exploring property in Alaska was just two hours away.

How am I going to get out of this one, I wondered?

10

Testing the Waters

It seemed like no time at all before our plane landed in Ketchikan. We met up with both our realtor and the hired guide to go over the information on a number of different pieces we'd hand-picked to investigate. After loading us into a van, the charter boat captain chauffeured us along the waterfront on the busy two-lane road which eventually led to the dock at the end of town. Once there, we boarded his small boat. I was a little nervous about the outing. After all, we were a long way from home, heading off into the unknown with a stranger we'd just met. For one thing, I was hopeful that he was a competent captain. But judging by the way he speedily readied the vessel, I could see that water travel was routine for him, and right away I felt confident in his abilities to transport us across the open water.

As we headed out to look at property, the atmosphere was identical to the snapshot of my mental picture. The gentle breeze was warm, and the surface of the deep turquoise-colored water was smooth. We experienced beautiful weather the whole day while we combed over several potential beachfront locations where we could build a cabin. This wasn't so bad, I thought.

With maps in hand, we investigated property in both George Inlet and Carroll Inlet which are just outside of Ketchikan. Out of all seven parcels, only one piece of property boasted the easily accessible, flat beach Tom had predicted would be most suitable for our adventure. Satisfied with our choice, we returned to the dock in Ketchikan where we took a more serious look around town to determine what supplies were available in the event we actually did decide to go through with a real estate transaction.

Following our search for property, we did as much investigating as we could do while on foot, checking out the nearby fish and game office, grocery stores, and lumber yards. We noted that the town was limited on fast food joints but otherwise seemed to offer a wide variety of services to the 7,500 townspeople who, according to me, appeared to be trapped there. It was hard for me to comprehend that there were actually no roads leaving Ketchikan. The short stretch of pavement that exists abruptly terminates at each end of town, so I'd heard.

Our second day there, we rented a car in order to expand our discovery area and check on property details at the county offices. On our way there, we noticed that the Coast Guard station appeared to be in full time operation, judging by the many docked vessels and the active parking lot. Heading back through Ketchikan, we quickly interpreted the quaint but recently vacated shops to be the heart of the shopping area for the cruise ship passengers. The cruise lines had just finished their busy tourist season only days earlier. At the far end of town we located a Wal-mart and the typical car dealership or two.

Tom and I made our way to the newly constructed dock where the smell of creosote planking and saltwater filled the air. All of a sudden, the fond memories of childhood flooded my head, causing my heart to beat a little faster than normal as I stood there watching the seagulls and other shore birds energetically circling and then landing on the water. The deafening growl of sea planes taking flight momentarily grabbed my attention. Watching them fly off one after another kept me busy for a while, wondering where they might be going and why. To work? Sightseeing?

Gravina Island located across the water from Ketchikan on the west side of the Tongass Narrows provided the airstrip for commercial airplane traffic which was landing and lifting off regularly. Off in the distance we watched the hoards of airline passengers milling around. Their plane had landed only moments earlier. From there, the luggage toting passengers would be forced to wait for the shuttle-ferry to transport them on a five minute ride over to Ketchikan, just as we'd done the day before when we had arrived. As I stood there, I felt a sense of limited freedom, if there is such a thing. Although Ketchikan and its surrounding region offered an unthinkable amount of area to explore, for the average person, the only way to escape was to buy a ticket out of town. Travel to and from the city was apparently "pick your pleasure: plane or sea." I could tell that if I were to choose to live in Alaska, it would definitely be a different lifestyle. It would be quite a transition to move from the parched Oregon summers to the breezy Alaskan waterways; I really wasn't sure I was ready for the drastic change, even if it was temporary.

After a full day of research, we returned to our hotel. By then we were well-stocked with maps and pamphlets of the area. All afternoon, we contemplated the pros and cons of buying remote waterfront property. I couldn't see it happening, but if buying something would give Tom something to do for a few years—then maybe we should make an offer, I thought. Better yet, we'd make a low-ball bid, and then if it was accepted, it was meant to be!

Astonishingly, our conservative offer was eagerly accepted before our plane even touched down in Seattle. Up popped red flag number three, which should have been all the warning I needed! Was someone anxious to get rid of it? Did we make the right decision? Much like the flu, this sinking feeling filled my gut with a touch of buyer's remorse. Reality was setting in because now we were financially committed to another project, and I knew it was just a matter of time before we would officially own property in the great state of Alaska.

The transition from "no way" to "okay" had all happened so fast! It had only been one short week since I'd agreed to finally give the Alaska project a chance. Now, Tom's lifelong dream of owning property in the Alaskan wilderness had come true. As we headed out on the long drive home from the airport, in the back of my mind I clung to the hope that he would draw plans for the ultimate cabin and eventually tire of the idea. On the contrary! Instead, within five minutes of the property being recorded in our name, he was on the phone about a permit. Reality snapped its fingers and I abruptly awoke. I became aware of Tom's determination to steam full speed ahead. I don't know why, but it was hard for me to comprehend. I should have been able to recognize the pattern. Somehow I had let this happen again!

I sensed that we were headed out on another wild journey, and I was terribly afraid of what was around the corner! With our new land acquisition located so far away, we both knew that we were going to be in for quite a challenge. There were so many questions to answer, not only for ourselves but also for our friends and family who quizzed us non-stop about our newly hatched plan. The concept was a crazy idea, no doubt, and every waking hour of the next few months was spent imagining the best, planning for the worst, and then talking day and night about how it might all play out. I remained hesitant during the months following our real estate purchase, hopeful that somehow our bigger-than-life plans would fall through. On sunny days, which are plentiful in eastern Oregon, I could almost visualize the plan successfully coming together. But when the snow fell day after day during the dead of winter, I pictured more realistically the potential struggles of building a cabin in a frozen, isolated land.

To offset my dragging heels, Tom became the fire behind the entire project! He went right to work looking for a boat, pricing materials, as well as doing lots of organizing. The deeper we got into the details, the less excited I was becoming about the potential "trip from hell" experience. Not Tom; he wasn't the least bit discouraged by the daunting tasks that lay ahead. We had a new "baby." So for him, there were hours of preparation that transpired over the winter months. Because of the cost of goods in Ketchikan, he determined early on that it would be well worth our while to buy materials locally, and then have them shipped to Alaska all at once. After extensive research, he found that it would prove most economical to load all of our supplies into a shipping container stationed in Seattle, Washington, which would then be sent by barge. He ordered trusses from the lumber yard near our home and metal roofing from Washington State. From what I could tell, this plan was developing into a lot of loose ends; piles of junk all needing to be carted hundreds of miles before finally being shipped. I instantly knew by the wide-ranging lists of items we needed to round up, that gathering it all in one place was going to require making several long trips back and forth to the Washington coast. Oh, what fun!

Tom's intense planning continued. He learned that once the cargo left the dock there, the container barge would take exactly one week to arrive in Ketchikan. If his calculations were correct, the timing should work out perfectly. He estimated that if we loaded the container in Seattle on day one of our trip and started driving on day two, by the time we drove through Canada and caught the ferry from Prince Rupert to Ketchikan, we would arrive in Alaska around the same time as our container, give or take a couple days.

We scheduled our trip as a pre-summer adventure in order for Tom to be back in time for the Bristol Bay salmon fishing season in June. But that was about to change; this year would be a little different. A short time later, Tom landed another fishing job in Togiak, Alaska, and the employer requested that he report to work in late April—six weeks earlier than he'd originally planned. Due to the schedule adjustment, it became necessary to bump the departure of our Alaska trip from late April to mid-March. I began to rethink my commitment. The month of March is still winter on my mental calendar, especially when thinking about Alaska. If we forged ahead, deciding to leave that early in the year, the winter weather might very well be unbearable. However, if we chose not to chance the cold trip in March then we'd be waiting until August, almost a full year after we had become owners of this coveted real estate.

By then Tom's dream of living in Alaska was so close he could taste it! It was understandable that he was not interested in the further delay of plans. The months quickly passed. Before I knew it, Christmas, New Year's Day and Valentine's Day had come and gone. Our departure was right around the corner. To mentally prepare ourselves for the frigid temperatures, we began watching weather reports for Ketchikan and comparing them to our own snowy forecasts in eastern Oregon. Since we planned on living in a tent at first, we were hopeful we could brave the cold Alaska weather for few days while we built a cabin. After all, in previous years we'd endured feet of snow while we'd logged through the winter, but we'd also had a warm shelter to escape the plummeting night-time temperatures. We knew we wouldn't be afforded that privilege for our first week in there. Could we hack it? And then, what if we couldn't?

And as we thought about bears, maybe a tent wouldn't be a very good idea. Tom and I weighed the pros and cons of sleeping on the deck of a small boat while it was safely anchored just off-shore near the property. The fears I had about being in a tent in bear country far outweighed my other concern: drowning in my sleep. However, our floating hotel idea wasn't the perfect solution for someone with a history of sleepwalking issues…..and as a child

I'd had a history! So as we spoke at length about the idea of either sleeping in the tent with a loaded gun, or on the boat with a life preserver under my arm, I carefully pondered which choice might be the safer option.

Without a dock at the new property, Tom decided that a flat-bottom boat would enable us to pull right onto the beach for convenient parking and ease of unloading. With the project moving forward, we bought a used aluminum boat a month before we were planning to head for Alaska. Our newly purchased ride was eighteen feet long with two engines, one large, and one small. It offered a tiny windshield at the steering station but no cabin. Unbeknownst to me, he immediately had big plans for our latest purchase!

Lucky for us, Tom's extensive exposure to boat building had begun during his grade school years. He had spent many months helping his dad build a homemade craft in the family's back yard. When the boat was completed, Tom proudly commercial fished the vessel with his dad at first and then by himself as he got older. In high school, he'd landed a job at the shipyard for a company that built yachts. Since I'd met him, he'd completely refurbished a twenty-eight foot commercial fishing boat, so I knew he was no stranger to work being done in that field. Therefore, I shouldn't have been surprised that immediately following our purchase, the vessel was completely gutted. Original aluminum parts were cut off, compartments were built in, and new hardware was added on. In addition, it was Tom's theory that in order to protect both us and our new electronics from the inclement weather, he should build a cabin which would be situated in the middle of the boat where the steering station was already in place.

Once he explained his vision, a boat cabin sounded like a good idea. We were counting on the additional protection being able to block the freezing wind and rain, which would keep us from chilling to the bone during our wintry travels to and from the property. I had confidence in Tom's ability, so I questioned nothing about his thought processes in that department, and in no time our vessel was becoming more personalized for our upcoming adventure.

Then the question was, "How do we get the boat there?" We desperately wanted to avoid dragging the monstrosity on the long journey clear through Canada, so it was equally important that the boat's new addition was exactly short enough to fit into the shipping container along with all of our other belongings. Tom measured carefully. The boat itself would easily fit inside the container, but the boat's trailer measured a couple inches too wide. To solve that dilemma, he reconfigured the trailer so that the fenders and axles could be removed. Soon, narrow scaffolding wheels were bolted to the frame and with a car-jack and a wrench the entire package could be easily transformed to slide into the container. It was ingenious! It reminded me of an invention straight out of a James Bond movie, which Tom enjoys watching all too often. When the work was finished, the new structure was just tall enough for us to stand in, resembling some sort of school bus-stop shelter with a slant roof.

Next was the task of figuring out how much room we needed to ship the boat and materials all in one load. To determine the length of the container we would need, we began to estimate how much room our cargo would require, and then how we'd stack the supplies to best fit the space. During our lengthy discussions we not only looked over long lists of what would be sent, but we also calculated how long it might take us to load the container before it left from Seattle: hours, days—we didn't know.

With our shipping plan thoroughly processed, we began earnest conversations about what to do once everything made it to Ketchikan. Since the property was located in a remote inlet, we conversed at great lengths about how we might get our cargo transported from the boat launch to our property, in other words, from one shore to another. Tom was pretty certain we could successfully transport all of our materials in our own boat during many trips over the course of the week. As he spoke of his idea, my imagination created vivid color pictures of each load; the worst one was the sixteen-foot-long triangular shaped trusses, eleven of them to be exact. His strategy was to strap the trusses to either side of the boat's cabin. I was hesitant at best and very much aware of the awkwardness of a truss. I had packed plenty of them around the job site, up ladders and so on. The suggestion of eleven trusses being strapped to a boat which I might be a passenger on was causing me a great deal of mental anguish. I couldn't safely picture it, wanted no part of it, and deep down I knew that I had no intention of going along with such a risky plan. In my head, the image was dangerously top-heavy, and that very scenario had already put me at odds with Tom in the months leading up to our trip.

Personally, due to my lifelong fear and utmost respect for open water, I was all for towing both the trusses and the lumber in the water behind the boat. Of course he thought my idea to be equally out of line! I did agree, however, that a large majority of the cargo could be safely transported in small amounts, but I knew that until the time actually came to move the larger items, we'd be in complete disagreement. Nothing new there!

"Here's an idea, how about if I just stay home," I suggested to him more than once.

"Well, I couldn't do it alone," he said. "It wouldn't be any fun to go by myself. Just trying to get the stuff unloaded, putting the boat in the water, figuring out the cabin….I need you there to help me!"

After those invaluable admissions, I made him promise to be very nice to me on the trip, and I frequently reminded him that the "good attitude" clock would start ticking the minute we left the driveway in Oregon, or else! This was not my dream, this was a favor.

As we began to pin down the perfect departure date, it was still Tom's desire to leave in early spring, or late winter, as I called it. And as far as I was concerned, it was the winter weather which opened the door to increased risk and possible failure. Surviving the cold and fighting to be productive in the snow were my initial concerns about the next stage of the Alaska dream. However, if we stayed in a warm hotel, not only would the cost of lodging quickly dwindle our tight budget, but from there it was no quick jaunt to the property; there would be a lot of time wasted just traveling back and forth. And also, with possible rough weather issues we might be held hostage in town for days at a time, at which point nothing would get done at the property. After all, building a cabin was the entire reason we were going. If we actually did get stuck in town, then the majority of our time in Alaska might be nothing more than standing on the dock waiting for the foul weather to subside, which didn't appeal to either or us.

All fears aside, in earnest, Tom continued to gather the final supplies and plan for our departure. In contrast, besides our lengthy conversations, I had only set aside a few clothes and dishes. Despite my hesitations, he continued to forge ahead, securing all of the final details of our trip. During that time, there were many changes in our original program. For one, even though Tom had spent considerable amount of time altering the boat trailer to fit our container, once our ferry tickets were purchased we completely changed our minds about shipping the boat. We realized that if we sent the boat along with our cargo, then we'd be sitting in Ketchikan with nothing to do for four days before our container would arrive. In our opinion, that would be fruitless. At least if we towed the boat through Canada, not only could we count on packing many more supplies, but also we could motor out to the property during our four day layover while we waited for the barge to show up. That sounded more sensible.

As our plans evolved, each scenario had several options, rated usually by their financial gain or loss. But most of all, we liked the idea of having access to the boat upon our arrival to Ketchikan. We felt that being able to familiarize ourselves with the area for a couple days might be the best idea even though it was a bit more expensive.

By the first of March, thanks to Tom, the challenging pieces of our complex puzzle seemed to be coming together. He and I were each nursing a separate set of nerves. I knew this adventure was out of my comfort zone, but I had full trust in him. I was trying to be strong in regards to both the scary water and the bears. I was dreading the cold weather and isolation, but I convinced myself that this adventure wouldn't last forever. We'd be returning home before I knew it and I could recommence with my familiar routine.

Unlike me, Tom was extremely excited about the adventure, but he was very unsettled about getting across the Canadian border in a timely fashion. He couldn't bear the thought of missing the ferry. He also had absolutely no desire to be stranded in Canada for four days waiting for the next boat that sailed for Ketchikan only because we were late for our departure. To him that would have not only been an unforgivable waste of time, but also money.

In spite of all our worries and planning….at last, the time had come! With much nervous anticipation we packed our final bags and checked our lists before locking up the new house in order to leave on our adventure to Alaska.

Even though this giant undertaking was another step toward Tom's lifelong dream, I acknowledged that we were headed out on a journey which had all the ingredients of a catastrophic event that might test our marriage to the limit. I was hopeful that I was up for the challenge.

11

Journey through a Foreign Land

On Friday the 13th of March, of all things, we anxiously departed from eastern Oregon with full intentions of making it to Ketchikan by the following Thursday. It had been just six short months since our initial Alaska property search. I couldn't believe the winter months had passed so quickly and we were actually on our way to Alaska. Leaving on a superstitious date didn't seem like the brightest idea, but in order to get everything accomplished in the time frame we'd established, it had become the logical day to depart.

We nervously set out on the first leg of the journey: an eight hour drive to Westport where Tom's parents lived on the Washington Coast. Since Westport was much closer to Seattle than we were, Vern and Nancy had generously allowed us the use of their garage and in previous weeks it had become our official staging area for the Alaska trip.

For the last transport of goods from Oregon, Tom drove his pickup towing our fully-loaded boat. The bed of his truck was packed full, right up through the lumber rack and beyond. As for Pup and me, we followed cautiously in the Durango, which was crammed with all of the personal items we couldn't live without on an outdoor adventure of this kind. During the entire road trip I was on high alert, keeping an eye on Tom's cargo, which appeared to be bursting at the seams. Even though it was smooth highway driving, in my car the loosely packed lanterns and dishes rattled like the contents of a covered wagon on the bumpy Oregon Trail. The commute was slow going, but by evening we'd successfully arrived at his parents' home where we unloaded the final shipment of miscellaneous materials.

By then the components of the cabin had more than begun to take over their garage. There were heaps of odds and ends such as old blankets, used tools, plumbing parts, and life preservers. A closer look would have revealed an antique propane cooker, old fishing poles, mismatched rain gear, and ropes of all lengths and colors. At first glance, our stash of important supplies appeared to be the perfect ensemble for an upcoming garage sale. But then with the stacks of pre-cut lumber, trusses and windows completing the picture, it was obvious that this was more than just a sale; there was a serious plan involved.

Our confirmed ferry tickets cemented our departure from Prince Rupert, B.C. in just six days. We were so relieved to have the first leg of the trip behind us, and it was just a couple of days before our reservation at the shipping-container headquarters in Seattle. We knew that there would be no turning back once we'd left for Alaska, and we still had a lengthy list of tasks to complete, so we were hopeful that we had allowed ourselves enough time to collect the remainder of supplies needed for the cabin.

We'd purposely delayed the final purchases which consisted of the bulky items such as the enormous bundles of insulation and cumbersome fiberglass shower stall in order to minimize our growing junk-pile in Vern and Nancy's garage. After rounding up those items, we shared a sigh of relief knowing that we were finally ready to be packed, strapped, and shuttled for the three hour trip to Seattle.

Besides our final purchases, the other important detail we needed to accomplish before we left on the trip was to take our newly remodeled boat for a test drive. Even though we'd bought the craft over a month earlier, we still hadn't taken it out for the pre-trip assessment. In eastern Oregon, ice and snow is the norm for up to six months a year. In March it is common for the local lakes and ponds to still be frozen over, so at home we had nowhere to properly try out the boat and its engines before we'd left. Instead, in order to evaluate our engine's general health, Tom had tested each of the two motors by running them in a large tub of water. But even then, we still wanted to see how the boat was going to handle, especially with the new cabin he had installed.

It just so happened that now that we were on the coast, the unfriendly winter weather persuaded us to skip our test drive. If Tom was on edge about boating in bad weather, he never let me witness any of his apprehensions. In Westport that day, the less-than-perfect conditions seemed to be more of a time consuming inconvenience for him. He was disgruntled about driving to the dock, unloading the boat, and getting fully drenched in the process; he didn't have time for such nonsense.

For just a fleeting moment, I wondered how the same unruly weather would affect us once we got to Alaska. But even though it seemed vitally important, it was only one small detail on my long list of worries, so my concerns about the boat's ability to maneuver in rough water quickly faded. At this stage, the commute through a foreign country was foremost on our minds, and there were more urgent matters to attend to other than taking our boat for a leisurely spin. We still had to transport our massive mountain of supplies to Seattle in time to be put on the barge, and finally, the long, wiggly stripe on the map which represented our path through Canada was a huge unknown. How long would our journey take? Would we encounter snow and ice? What if the car broke down and we missed the ferry? And so on.

Our ideal scenario for the commute to the big city would be to transport everything in one trip. However, by then, we'd acquired quite a large heap of "must haves," causing us much doubt as to how we'd actually get it all delivered in one load. The day before, during the final loading activities in Westport, it had become apparent that our cargo transfer would have to be a two-trip event. We were already aware that the container in Seattle was scheduled to be loaded onto the barge the following night, which meant the entire day's travels would have to go perfectly in order to make the 5 p.m. deadline. We were also quite certain that we couldn't count on driving swiftly through Seattle's bumper-to-bumper traffic. We contemplated renting a large U-haul van, but that would've required us to unload the cargo yet another time from our already packed vehicles. After seeing our frustration, Vern and Nancy graciously offered to join the caravan. In no time, we had their vehicle and trailer also loaded to the hilt. Their generous offer to help really bailed us out.

With everything packed, we assembled the troops early the next morning.

It was dark and raining when we made our final preparations to leave for Seattle. During the commute, the traffic was heavy but not jammed, and we made it to our destination in a reasonable amount of time with only minor delays. As we pulled through the unlocked gates of the giant shipping yard, a quick survey in every direction noted endless rows of metal shipping containers as far as I could see. The monumental stacks of metal boxes were equal to the size of large buildings. For me, the sights were intimidating. Right away we made our way to the head office for further instructions. From inside the towering office full of windows, the bird's eye view resembled what my perception of an air traffic controller's desk at an airport might be. While we studiously filled out the paperwork for our shipment, we could easily discern that our "once in a lifetime adventure" constituted a very routine, "business as usual" event for the shipping yard. This provided us an unspoken reassurance that all of our carefully selected cargo would actually reach its intended destination of Ketchikan.

From inside the lofty building, we were directed to the location of the relatively small, lime-green metal box which Tom had reserved over the phone a month earlier. Once outside, we slowly maneuvered all three vehicles and their trailers through the maze of white, green, and brown containers. Once we were parked, we got out to size up the situation. Our container looked comparatively small; it was the shortest length available, measuring just twenty feet long. At one end, two large steel doors swung open to allow easy access to the empty space.

The drenching rain we'd arrived in continued to pour down as we loosened the many straps securing our loads. Without delay, we began unloading the cargo from our vehicles and then, per Tom's stern but well thought-out instructions, we began methodically organizing all of our belongings into the shipping container. As the space started to fill, the contents resembled a jigsaw puzzle. Now, handling the materials again it became evident just how enormous some of the cargo would be in comparison to our miniscule, flat-bottomed vessel. We had twenty foot lumber and sixteen foot trusses to transport in an eighteen foot boat for fifteen miles. For a moment, I imagined myself in the boat with some of the larger cargo like the shower stall, for instance and I found myself quite agitated about the upcoming shuttling events. But that hurdle would have to be jumped at a later date. Maybe once we get to Ketchikan, the property won't be as remote as I remember, I silently consoled myself. Whatever the case, ultimately I knew that if the transportation situation appeared too unsafe, Pup and I would be happy to wait at the dock for Tom's return!

At the shipping yard it took just two hours of highly concentrated efforts to fit everything into the container. I was both relieved and exhausted, and when it was all said and done, not a crack was empty or a slot left unplugged. With great satisfaction, we closed and then padlocked the heavy, steel doors. Our imaginations flashed ahead to Alaska when we would see our belongings again. With the loaded container ready for the barge, next on the itinerary was to return to Westport where we'd make the final preparations for our drive through Canada the next day. We still needed to load our personal items into the car and secure the boat for the long road trip. The journey was expected to be a long, uncharted adventure.

Our master plan to efficiently navigate through Canada was to drive as many hours as possible and nap in our car as little as necessary while enjoying the scenery along the way. Once we were on the road, our first concern would be to ensure that all of our documents were in order for the upcoming border crossing. And even though we had checked and double-checked the required paperwork such as passports, Pup's shot records and car insurance, we were fearful that we might end up being the unsuspecting travelers held up at the border. To botch the whole trip, all it would take was one border-crossing agent in a bad mood.

Our second concern was to make it to the ferry in time. From the Washington border, Prince Rupert was approximately 900 miles away. We checked mileage charts and maps, estimating our arrival at Prince Rupert to be in plenty of time for our ferry boarding if all went well. At this point, reaching our destination in two days appeared to be very achievable. Our penny-pinching travel plans were to sleep in our car the next couple of nights. In doing so, we could also protect our belongings, which would be exposed on the open deck of the boat during our commute. After all, we couldn't afford items such as our crab pot, chainsaw or tool box to go missing while we were fast asleep inside a motel in a foreign country.

Fortunately, Tom and I had tried to sleep in our car once before only to find out how cold it was despite being in the best of conditions. We'd discovered that even with the car's heater running, the hard surface in the back of the car had sucked the body heat right out of us. For the upcoming road trip, I was hopeful that we were prepared. Before we left, we'd purchased a travel trailer mattress from a supply catalog. We were optimistic that a four-inch-thick, queen-sized foam mattress should provide adequate insulation from the cold while we slept. And even though the mattress we stowed had no chance of lying flat in our car, we were hopeful that the cushion would be able to get us by, allowing us to snooze wherever we might have the need.

With all the junk in our trunk, I felt that our trip had all the indications of a very labor intensive project which might hardly be worth the trouble. I'd spent some time grumbling about all the wasted time, but this wasn't a concern for Tom. Regardless, we had both stored plenty of energy for the tasks ahead knowing that in order to have the luxury of a mattress it would require frequent unloading and restacking each time we wanted to pull over and rest. The mattress would not only serve as a bed during our travels, but it would eventually provide additional comfort throughout our stay once we made it to Alaska.

Our departure was near. By the time we finished packing, the car was loaded to the ceiling with all of the personal belongings which couldn't be safely transported on the deck of the boat we were towing. At last, the time had come! We left the coast just before noon, stopping right away to fuel up at the nearby gas station. We were both full of nervous excitement but not saying much. I was going over my final mental checklist: cash, boat keys, passports, phone charger, and so on. As I opened the back door, out flopped my expensive memory foam pillow which landed dead-center in the oiliest of mud puddles. Was this some kind of omen, I wondered? As I snatched it up off the ground, I quickly removed the soiled pillow slip before it had a chance to soak through. But it was too late; my luxury item from home was instantly heavy with moisture on one end. Off to a great start, I thought! For the next couple of hours, I continued to be sensitive to any other bad luck indicators, but all went well for the hectic freeway commute. It took just four hours to reach the Canadian border where we chose to cross. By then we were in Sumas, a small town north east of Bellingham, Washington. As we pulled up to the international zone, both Canadian and U.S. flags were confidently flying just a few feet apart. Right off, I noticed that there were multiple lines of cars waiting to cross in both directions, all of us creeping toward the row of manned booths.

We chose a lane and began inching forward in line along with everyone else. As anticipated, the suspense began to build as we approached the official border-crossing facilities. We didn't know what to expect. Every few minutes, a green light would flash up ahead indicating one of two things: another traveler had either successfully passed their interrogation, or else they'd been pulled aside for further inspection. Finally, it was our turn. We presented our paperwork. The agent sternly thumbed through our documents and began asking the necessary questions.

Fortunately for us, Tom was in the driver's seat. The booth attendant's inquiries were simple, but were fired in such rapid succession that if I'd been sitting in his place, I would have stumbled and stammered under the pressure. Within a few minutes the questions ceased. We'd been approved, at last we were on our way!

We felt privileged to be through the magical gates of the border patrol. As we began our explorations of beautiful British Columbia, we were able to experience perfect driving conditions that day—dry pavement and slightly overcast skies. I couldn't help but notice the huge drifts of dirty snow lining each side of the road as we moved through Canada, indicating the not-so-nice weather which had been there previously.

Hour after hour the mesmerizing drive continued. The interesting sights from one town to the next began to blend into themselves along the two-lane road. When darkness began to take over, it became increasingly difficult to navigate the poorly marked route. In fact, as we traveled farther north, many of road signs had all but disappeared under the enormous mounds of hardened snow lining either side of the foggy, unlit highway. Many miles would pass sometimes before we would be reassured that we were even still heading in the right direction through the frozen, desolate region.

The steep, winding roads through the countryside were sprinkled with traces of gravel here and there, presumably because of the icy circumstances that had preceded us. As a result, potholes and poor maintenance made for a less than smooth commute. By midnight of the first travel day, we surmised that it was the abusive road conditions which had put our boat trailer lights on the fritz, and even though we'd been minding our manners, our bum trailer light had prompted the Canadian Police to pull us over for a brief chat. Fortunately for us, a more important call came in on his radio, at which point the officer wished us well as he took off in a hurry.

We continued to snake through many sleepy towns until finally reaching the fairly sizable city of Prince George. According to the map, it meant we were about half way into our drive through Canada with about nine hours left to go if all went well. The previous week had been laced with fear and trepidation, but after making it this far, we were feeling more relaxed just knowing the most challenging part of the trip was behind us. Since the faulty running lights on the boat trailer were only required to be operational after dark, we felt that waiting until daylight would ensure that we'd avoid more unwanted delays. On that note, we decided to postpone the last segment of the journey until morning. Our plans for daybreak were to embark on the final stages of our trip toward Alaska.

It was well after midnight. We slowed several times in search of a suitable location to stop before finally pulling into a convenience store parking lot where we would spend the next few hours resting. Due to the crisp night air, our car's thermometer registered an outside temperature of a chilly seven degrees. A quick survey of our surroundings revealed old snow crusted on everything except for the pavement on the main two-lane road. As we stepped out of the car, the lone security light that shone across the parking lot of the small store offered only a small amount of visibility. Tromping ankle deep in snow, Tom and I spoke very little, as we swiftly moved some things from the car to the boat and vice versa, eventually unfolding the mattress for its first use. Because of our car's tapered interior, the mattress formed a much too cozy "V" shape near the back while flattening out nicely on the opposite end which would clearly be the head of the bed. With the bedding spread out and pillows in place, our car became a very inviting environment for a quick nap. After removing our snow-caked shoes, Tom and I crawled in on all fours and closed the door. But before we could get into our sleeping positions, our poor exhausted Pup had plopped down right in the middle of the main part of the mattress and was instantly out like a light.

Just for the record, Pup isn't spoiled, he's loved! At this moment, his loving, brown eyes were temporarily hidden behind their sleepy lids as he lay sacked out on our freshly made bed. Once we were all finally inside the car for the night, we started the engine and ran the heater to get the car warm inside. We scooted our sleeping Pup just a smidge, so we could each squeeze in on either side of him. As soon the car was warm, the engine was turned off, and we quickly fell asleep. Not too much later, I awoke feeling nearly frozen! I reached around the driver's seat to start the engine again, and then fell back asleep only to wake up scorching hot a short time later. "Engine off" and "engine on" went the routine until 7:30 in the morning. When we awoke for the day and stepped out of the car, we were greeted with bone chilling winds. Briskly, we transferred our frozen belongings out of the boat and into the car before getting back on the road again.

It was snowing heavily as we left on our drive this morning. The fresh flakes coming down were the size of cotton balls, which prevented us from seeing too far ahead. A few hours into the commute, Pup was refusing to eat anything we offered him. Ordinarily he'd at least eat something if I sprinkled his food with lamb starter, a powdered milk supplement meant for precious little lambs, but it was mostly likely due to our hectic schedule that he hadn't consumed anything at all since the day before. Since his lack of appetite often signals a seizure, I insisted we stop for a hot meal....for all of us! In the fast food parking lot, he was finally able to scarf down some mashed potatoes, gravy and a little chicken. We all felt better afterward as we headed out again in search of the finish line; today it was the town of Prince Rupert, British Columbia!

The closer we got to the town of Prince Rupert, the more magnificent the scenery became. Near the end of our journey through Canada, the winding road was taking us closer to sea level. Now, off to our left, the jade-colored Skeena River which we'd been following off and on for some time was drastically increasing in size. Chunks of melting glacial ice were clogging some areas, while other spots of the river were frozen completely over. Just before we reached Prince Rupert, the breath taking landscape which began at the river's edge began a steep ascent shortly thereafter, encouraging my eyes to follow the rugged terrain skyward to the majestic snow-capped mountaintops. From there, the gorgeous white peaks eventually punctured the puffy blanket of white clouds canvassing the entire panorama. What beautiful country!

As it turned out, only the first hour in Canada had been spent on the freeway. From then on, the drive had followed a scenic two-lane highway clear to the ferry. Upon entering Canada, Tom and I had been full of excitement, hopeful of spotting some wildlife. But in the end, the only big game we observed was a lonely moose which we'd spotted as he stood shoulder deep in the roadside snow.

With great relief, we arrived in Prince Rupert and much to our delight; we'd reached our destination almost a full day early. There was fresh snow everywhere as we coasted into town. We watched carefully for signs indicating the direction of the "Alaska Marine Highway System" where we officially checked in to pick up our boarding passes for the ferry. The clerk handed us our packet of information and instructed us to report back two hours prior to our departure time the following day. At last, another phase of the journey was complete. I was looking forward to relaxing. We'd almost made it to Alaska and I was relieved that we could finally rest for a bit!

12

Nostalgic Ride

To my surprise, even though we had arrived in Prince Rupert in a timely fashion, Tom was already nervous about catching the ferry which wasn't scheduled to leave for almost twenty-four hours. For the life of me, I couldn't understand the source of his anxiety; all we had left to do was to get on the boat and we'd be there! To calm his nerves we spent some time carefully scoping out the ferry line-up area in an effort to decipher exactly how the program would work the next day. With plenty of food and drink in the cooler, Tom thought we should hang out for the remainder of the day in the snow-covered parking lot near the ferry terminal, and as for the overnight stay, we'd just sleep in the car just outside the locked gates.

I whole-heartedly disagreed! According to me, we'd been driving for way too many hours by then, and as a result I had utilized every sitting position imaginable. After exhausting the regular travel poses, I had gone from feet on the dash, to cross-legged Indian style, and then side-saddle with my legs folded. My bones ached and my skin was sore. I was pretty sure bed sores had not developed in this short amount of time, but I was convinced they would be surfacing soon.

"Enough is enough," I said firmly. I made my case:

"Listen, we have been sitting in this car for twenty-how-many hours, and Pup still has to be stuck in the car on the ferry most of the day tomorrow. I can't do that to him! Plus," I continued, "we could actually stretch out, be warm, and have a good night's sleep. I've never had the opportunity to watch Canadian television, and I need a shower!"

I knew it might be the last one for a while. It crossed my mind that even though it was Tom's fantasy we were trying to fulfill, I felt he owed me this small debt of gratitude for getting to this stage of our journey. I wasn't going to budge.

After a lengthy discussion, Tom was still uneasy about leaving the boat unattended, but he reluctantly agreed to search for a motel as long as we could park the car and boat directly outside the window of our room. I would soon realize that Tom's whole issue wasn't just that the boat might get stolen. I discovered that my dear husband has a severe case of ferry-line-anxiety for which he should probably be treated.

Following a brief tour of the quaint Canadian town, I spotted the perfect accommodations a mile from the ferry terminal. Tom was certain that it wouldn't meet his high standards of security, but against his wishes he pulled in anyway so I could ask the clerk at the front desk if the corner room on the ground floor was available. To my delight, it was. Our ideal lodging enabled our car and boat to be parked just five feet from the motel window, and for security reasons we planned to leave it partially opened all night.

This was Pup's first motel experience, so upon entering the room, he was delighted with what he saw: two queen beds! I pulled back the hotel bed-cover and spread my favorite cotton quilts onto the bed. Without hesitation, he jumped up to lie down. For the remainder of the evening, while Tom and I watched television, Pup rested peacefully. Right away he began snoring loudly as he stretched out, taking up one whole bed all to himself. Later that night, Tom and I each enjoyed a well-deserved shower followed by a superb night's sleep.

In the morning, thanks to Nervous Nelson, we found ourselves waiting outside the locked gates, mind you, a full six hours prior to our departure. It was two long hours before the ferry terminal's gate was even unlocked. Besides the unmanned semi-truck trailers that were parked inside the secured area overnight, we were the first and only ones in line. As our departure time drew nearer, Tom became even more anxious due the impending doom of another border crossing, which would no doubt entail being interrogated once again.

By this time, I was becoming quite irritable with his uptight behavior and I found myself running out of patience, fast. My happy childhood memories of orange sherbet ice cream cones on the dock and the fun-filled ferry boat rides that followed were slowly becoming tainted by his dark mood. To avoid being overcome by the stress, Pup and I frequently exited the vehicle for walks around the parking lot. More than once in the next few hours we meandered over to stand on the dock overlooking the water. The salt-water, creosote pilings and seagulls were all present.

With video camera in hand, I recorded our surroundings in the snow-blanketed ferry terminal parking lot. I had already been documenting many of the highlights of our excursion up to this point, including our cargo loading frenzy in Westport, our rain-soaked trip to Seattle, the nerve-wracking border crossing into Canada, and the lonely moose sighting along the way. This morning, I continued by video taping our parking spot at the ferry terminal, and "Captain Crab" who was permanently planted in the driver's seat, as well as the vessel we would be boarding for our ferry crossing this afternoon. I was most worried about leaving Pup alone for so long, but in spite of my anxiety, my spirits remained high for the most part. Besides the ferry ride, I was excited to finally implement the plans we had only talked about for the past several months. I've discovered that I love it when a plan comes together, even if I don't like the plan!

Tom was monitoring all aspects of the parking lot from his permanent position in the driver's seat. Two hours before our set departure time, the booth attendant finally motioned us forward where we were subjected to another invasive line of questioning. We passed the test with flying colors, just as before, permitting us to move to yet another ferry-line holding area on the Alaska side of the fence.

During our wait, I watched as a group of pigeons flocked toward the ferry worker who obviously fed them on a regular basis. Pup and I wandered to the other end of the dock where several rows of smaller fishing boats were moored. There were various styles, sizes and conditions, each very unique. A large dilapidated boat listed to one side, while tarps covered sections of its cabin. I looked on as some fisherman worked on another nearby vessel. I could see that a wide array of tools covered the deck, and cords stretched from their tools to the dock's power supply, allowing them to cut and weld on their fishing equipment. Meanwhile, another boat loaded down with crab pots maneuvered carefully out of the cramped mooring area and headed out past the rock jetty into the open water before disappearing out of sight.

While we were parked in our assigned lane, Tom and I kept an eye on all the people moving about. Since our window was open for Pup, we could hear all the conversations going on around us. We were surprised at the family reunion-mentality of the many passengers waiting to board. Clusters of people leaning against their cars were discussing from where they'd come and why they were each headed to Ketchikan. Compared to the plain-Jane stories we overheard, our adventure actually seemed quite interesting. We calculated that if we could steer clear of the inquisitive travelers then we wouldn't have to explain our crazy idea to anyone else there. We made a mental note of who was asking most of the probing questions in order to ensure we wouldn't get cornered by "Sir Talk-a-lot" on the lengthy ferry commute. We'd encountered plenty of questioning in recent months, and I was looking forward to the anonymity that might be provided in what seemed like a whole new world. For sure, no one would know us in Alaska.

Eventually, one by one, the vehicles were instructed to load. And even though I'd carefully observed the ferry while it was docked at the terminal, it didn't seem as monstrous as it actually was once we boarded. Our thirty-seven foot long presence barely took up any room on the spacious steel deck. Once we parked, we thoughtfully resituated our belongings in the car and then gathered our personal items which would accompany us on the upper decks during the long commute. Not really knowing what to expect upstairs on the ferry, I packed food and water, pens, paper, puzzles and our phone. I also grabbed a pillow and blanket for extra comfort. I wanted to be prepared, knowing we couldn't return to the car until we docked in Ketchikan six hours later.

Once we were all organized, we stayed in the car with Pup until the last possible minute. When we said our "good-byes," he looked very content as we walked away. We hiked up the ferry's steel stairway and began to investigate all of the ship's amenities. The first revelation was a full restaurant-style cafeteria offering a wide variety of meals to all passengers. To my surprise, the well-stocked vessel was set up to permit passengers to ride for days at a time, not mere hours as we were doing. On the rest of our boat tour, we came across a computer lounge, movie lounge and a drinking lounge. There was also a reading lounge, cabins for rent, and public showers, all of which are necessary accommodations for the passengers making the long commutes in and around Alaska's many islands.

As I viewed the activities surrounding me, I noticed that many of the people seemed very familiar with the routine of ferry travel, making themselves just as comfortable as if they were in their own living room. Some got right to work on their laptop computers before we even left the dock. Their shoes were off and their feet were up! Others had chosen an area for their party to set up camp complete with sleeping bags, food, games and pillows—by all appearances, everyone was getting settled in for the long journey. Groups of squealing pre-teen girls scurried by from time to time as if they might be attending a friend's sleepover. Other than the occasional indoor disruptions, the ferry ride was lengthy but peaceful.

While Tom stayed inside with our belongings, I ventured out to the deck of the ship in order to take in the sights. A cold chill washed over me as I stood at the rail facing into the wind. The rain pelted my face and made splattering noises as it peppered the row of windows behind me. I wondered what the rest of the trip would be like, yet even in the bad weather, the pristine environment was absolutely stunning! A quick glance behind the ferry revealed the sights of town quickly becoming too small to see. The surrounding scenery, which our ship continued to move through, exuded the purest of natural beauty: blue-green water, tree-covered land masses, and endless miles of driftwood-laden shoreline. Hour after hour the gigantic vessel maneuvered between the groups of small and seemingly uninhabited islands.

After five hours on the ferry, the town of Ketchikan was slowly becoming more visible. It was dusk. From a distance, I could discern the town's tiny structures perched in tidy rows along on the steep hillside, many of them even hanging over the water's edge. Beyond the large, compact city which twinkled with thousands of lights along the shore, there was a thick, untouched forest extending clear to the top of the landscape which was not quite a mountain but more than a hill. As we approached the large island on which Ketchikan is located, we were able to pick out the boat launch we would be leaving from in our own boat the next day. And way off in the distance, we could barely decipher the mouth of the inlet we would be navigating to get to the property the next morning. It even looked sort of familiar.

Half an hour before our scheduled arrival, the flurry of passenger activity began to increase as the commuters anticipated docking in Ketchikan. Now at the end of our journey, Tom and I dined on cheeseburgers and fries as we rehashed the details of our next phase. Since we were planning on boating out to the property first thing the next morning, we were both a little nervous about our first attempt. After all, it had been six months since we had been there, and that fleeting visit had only lasted for a quick half an hour while the charter boat captain waited for us just offshore in his boat. We wondered if our new real estate would be how we remembered it, or had our imaginations developed it into something else in recent months?

Eventually I moved outside to the boat deck again in order to spend a few minutes observing the massive sea of choppy water which our ferry was currently gliding through. I couldn't help but wonder how our small boat might handle the same ride the next morning. I leaned into the wind as I took notice of how much snow there was on the ground in Ketchikan. Besides the snow covered roof tops, the entire forest was dusted in fluffy white. By then I was exhausted from our travels and already dreading the cold isolation we were bound to experience soon. The reality of that thought brought a tear to my eye. I kept myself distanced from Tom because I knew that if he'd spoken a word to me at this point I would have burst into tears. I truly felt like I was about to step into another world, one that might require more courage than I could muster.

I was unaware that I had drifted away in deep thought until I was rudely startled by the blaring announcement on the ferry's loud speaker. The woman's voice commanded: "At this time, all passengers with a destination of Ketchikan please return to your vehicles." By the time our ferry docked, the sky and water were both the same shade of pitch black. As a result, the glistening ribbon of twinkling lights reflecting on the water created the only distinction between land and sea.

Like us, many of the vehicles offloaded in Ketchikan, but there were just as many passengers that would remain aboard in order to continue farther north. Once off the ferry, we drove around town to find a suitable, well-lit place to spend the night in our car. At last we were doing what we had only talked about for so long. The opportunity felt surreal. Good or bad, the reality that we were finally in Alaska was beginning to sink in! We had made it, at last!

TWENTY-EIGHT DAYS IN THE LAST FRONTIER

13

Finally in Paradise

Day 1 in Alaska

As we awoke in our car this morning, with a few swipes of our bare hands, we attempted to defog the windows in order to get a clearer view of our surroundings. We were surprised to see that while we slept, everything in sight had been blanketed with several inches of fluffy new snow. We were hungry and a bit cramped as we contorted ourselves like pretzels in order to get dressed for the day's activities. Soon enough, we found ourselves swapping around our belongings from car to boat, and boat back to the car in order to be organized enough to drive downtown. Without a word between us, we scurried about our business. The shoes stay in, tools go to the boat, seats fold up, bags move to the back, covered totes move back into the car, and last, we checked for anything that might have fallen to the ground. We were becoming very experienced shufflers, so much so, that we didn't even have to think about the lengthy process anymore.

Before we could leave for the property this morning, the list of things to do included: getting our boat licensed as well as purchasing some herring bait for our crab pot which we were very anxious to set out once we arrived. Although Tom and I each had life jackets accounted for, we still needed to locate one for Pup. In addition, since there were restrictions on traveling through Canada with firearms, Tom's guns had been shipped and were still in transit; therefore, I was insisting on the purchase of two canisters of bear spray. Although Tom didn't see the need, I felt it was important. It would be our only line of defense for the next couple of days until the container showed up in Ketchikan.

Using only the information from the local phonebook, we successfully navigated our way around the unfamiliar streets of town as we took care of the necessary business. With our checklist completed, in less than two hours we energetically arrived at the boat launch at the far end of town. The excitement was palpable. It was snowing and very cold, but we were still in a hurry to get going. We were within minutes of embarking on our long-awaited journey to the new property.

In order to apply new stick-on lettering which would make us legal boaters in the State of Alaska, my immediate duty was to dry a small surface area on either side of the bow. It was bitter cold outside so my fingers were instantly numb. It was because of those freezing temperatures that the aluminum boat never did feel very dry. I contemplated the idea of possibly applying the letters on a better weather day. But Tom had informed me that the all-important lettering would identify our boat to the Coast Guard should the need arise; it was a legality.

While I carefully applied each letter, Tom was moving briskly about as he readied the boat for its maiden voyage out to our new property. He raised the VHF radio's antenna which had been locked in a horizontal travel position since we'd left Oregon a week earlier. He also removed the square of plywood that had been protecting the contents inside the boat's cabin the entire trip and then transferred the loose items to the car before reconnecting the expensive new electronics onto the dash of the steering cabin. As soon as our preparations were completed, Tom backed the boat down the ramp leading to the water. This was all new to me, so I watched carefully as the boat trailer, lights, tires and all were being submerged into the saltwater. Once the boat was afloat, he unclipped the vinyl strap which released the boat into the water. At this juncture, I insisted that Tom take it for a quick test drive, not only to reassure me that it remained floating, but also that it functioned properly both in forward and reverse. He was certain it would and was somewhat short with me for insisting that he waste his precious time on such a useless task, but I know how he is, the words prevention or precaution are not part of his vocabulary.

Just like that, off he went! All seemed well as I video recorded the boat's first outing. Once Tom returned to the dock, Pup and I suited up with life jackets and took a seat at the "stern," or the rear of the boat. Before I knew it, we were motoring away from the jetty as we set out on our journey through the open water.

I could sense that we were headed away from all civilization, so immediately I reached for my cell phone let my family members know that I'd be out of reach for a few hours. Now that the boat ride was underway, I noted that we were traveling in the choppy water I had observed the night before on the ferry. I was scared! Just minutes earlier at the boat launch, the water had been calm, of course, because we'd had the protection of the rock jetty. Besides my concerns about the turbulent water, it seemed to me that our vessel was floating too low, especially as we pitched and rolled from side to side with all the choppy wave action.

Maybe I hadn't been mentally prepared after all. I encouraged myself to breathe! Long before this moment I'd clearly understood just how small our new boat really was. The jet sled had been parked in our shop for a month before we left on our trip. In an effort to work out my nerves, during the previous couple of months Tom and I had engaged in numerous conversations about the boat ride out to the property. However, the experience wasn't turning out to be quite what I had envisioned months ago as I sat safe and sound in my warm, comfy home in eastern Oregon. To me, our boat felt like it had the buoyancy of porcelain claw-foot bathtub. As Pup sat beside me on the bench seat, his ears stuck straight out from the side of his head like the wings on a seaplane. Pup's "airplane-ears" indicated to me that he was also very concerned about our current situation. As I evaluated my circumstances, in my unprofessional opinion, our mode of transportation also seemed a bit undersized for the mission.

The farther away from the jetty we got, the worse I began to feel. The skies were gray. The biting cold air pushed against my exposed face as we traveled over the water. Now as a passenger on our tiny boat, I felt my gut screaming at me to return to land! Right then I couldn't have been more disgusted with my decision to be in Alaska, but I said nothing. I really should have known better than to have come in the first place. I knew that it was urgent that I somehow get a grip.

This was only the beginning! I knew from our pre-trip calculations that we had ten miles to go until we would reach the property, but from my perspective, the dark water looked like it could swallow us up without a trace. A quick look around revealed there wasn't another soul in sight. Even the locals were still snuggled in for the winter, I thought. Quickly, I'd need to dig deep and find a way to suck it up. I swallowed hard, pushed my fears aside, and began focusing my stares straight ahead toward the opening of the inlet across the way. Maybe I could make it that far, and from there it might get better, I convinced myself.

Tom, on the other hand, seemed very comfortable with our surroundings. He wasn't giving me any impression that something could, might, or would go wrong. I noticed that instead of wearing his life jacket, it remained safely stowed under the dash. With his lifetime of experience I guess I could understand why he felt so comfortable, but I made it clear that I disapproved of his choice not to wear a floatation device. I knew I would be of no help to him in case of an emergency. I could predict with full confidence that I'd be nothing short of a basket-case!

On this wintry day, my observations noted that our boat was not much bigger than our car. In contrast, the water covered a wide open area but not like the ocean, because off in the distance I could see land in all directions. Some of the land was in the form of individual islands. Other tree-covered masses were extensions that jutted out from other larger sections of land much farther away. However, as I tried to cope with my fear of the open water, the distant sights didn't stop me from imagining the worst possible scenario: death by drowning. And the visual which kept coming to mind was that of a lonely tea cup afloat in a tub of dishwater. All goes well for the tiny teacup if the water remains motionless. As we motored along, however, our teacup was being bombarded from all sides by the sloshing sea.

From inside the small cabin, Tom appeared to be experimenting with the power of the engine.

He would occasionally turn to ask me, "Is the engine spitting water?"

Each time, I would twist my bundled self around to peer over the back of the boat.

"It is," I told him on three occasions during the next few minutes, wondering why he cared. It was obviously running, and I found it impossible to ignore the racket which was comparable to that of an ancient lawn mower's engine.

As we motored along I heard myself making repeated involuntary moaning sounds as if I was getting ready to vomit. I couldn't keep quiet as the boat swayed and rocked, and the water slurped at my hand which was tightly gripping the side of the boat. Right that second, I knew that sea sickness was not the problem; doubt sickness apparently was. How did I ever let Tom talk me into coming here?

By then, we had motored past the jetty and were in the process of attempting to make our way across the wide open water. A few more minutes passed when all of a sudden, the deafening noise of the engine instantly ceased. Seated in the Captain's chair was Tom, who said nothing as he raised his hand to point at the smoke curling into the air above the motor. I noted that the relentless buzzing noise was instantly replaced with an odor of toasted metal. Judging by his calm demeanor, I figured he just needed to start the engine again, and then we'd be on our way. He's not freaking out, so I shouldn't either, I told myself. About then, Tom stood up from his seat and then bluntly announced with little fanfare, "We're screwed!"

I made eye contact in order to determine the severity of the situation. Did this mean we were done for, or just inconvenienced? He still wasn't grabbing for his life vest, but he did start fumbling around like he was on a mission of some kind.

"The engine has just burned up," he admitted, as he began removing its dome-shaped cover.

That made sense, I thought, as I carefully observed his facial expressions in my attempt to pick up some sense of what was really happening. I was in the process of digesting the bad news that our engine had self-destructed a mile from the boat launch when I realized he was on a mission desperately trying to get the other engine lowered into position; it had been tilted out of the water until this point. We had a backup motor; we'll be alright, I decided. Once it was in the water he began frantically trying to pull-start the tiny back-up motor. Over and over, he tried, but it only rattled. Soon he was out of breath. With wide eyes and a stern look on his face, he warned me that if he could not get the other engine started, we were, as he explained it, "in deep shit," as he yanked on the cord several more times. Oh man! My heart dropped.

So we've actually become the floating tea cup, I thought to myself! I couldn't believe it! All was quiet except for the sloshing splish-splash coming at us from all directions. As we came to grips with our circumstances, the boat randomly jerked about in the water. It resembled all the ducks I'd ever seen adrift in rough sea, rising and falling under the water's command. As the seconds slowly passed, I became more and more afraid. I may not have had any boating experience under my belt; however, I sensed that one unforgiving wave coming out of turn would've started an endless bailing frenzy. Come to think of it, I hadn't recalled seeing a bucket on board.

And while the boat radio chirped away in the background, I noticed the depth sounder was displaying numbers that were in the hundreds. "After six feet it really didn't matter, did it?" I questioned, sarcastically. I am only five and a half feet tall. Besides, I was pretty certain that the depth of the water probably isn't the issue when a person is freezing to death.

Along the water's edge I could see plenty of homes so I optimistically considered that we weren't lost at sea! But they were clearly too far away for a swim in the icy water. With any luck someone in those houses might eventually notice something awry out here, I began to desperately hope. And, I did remember spotting a flare gun somewhere.

As I began to collect my thoughts, the conclusion I came to immediately after the smoking engine was this: I would refuse to be part of any plan which involved our miniature boat shuttling large quantities of building materials anywhere, that I knew for sure! At this point, I knew that if Tom brought the subject up again, I planned to promptly veto the idea. For the time being I kept quiet. He had enough on his mind!

Even though I felt pretty unlucky at the moment, I was very grateful we hadn't gotten all the way out to "nowhere" before that old engine had decided to give up the ghost. As he continued to yank on the starter cord, I was hopeful that once the backup engine was running that it would even have enough "snuff" to get us safely through the rough water. It seemed pretty small. Above all, I couldn't wait to get back to solid ground!

Pup and I sat quietly as we took in all of the developments. At first, Tom was wiggling various parts and blowing on hoses. Soon there was tapping, which quickly escalated to pounding. In between moments of concentration, his eyes scanned the horizon in all directions.

"There's the Coast Guard," he announced, leaning a bit to his left to peer around the steering cabin.

"Are you kidding?" I quipped, as I jerked my head around to see more clearly in that direction. Staring into the foggy haze on the horizon, I could see a boat out there now that he had pointed it out, but I certainly never would have guessed Coast Guard. However, with Tom's boating experience, he could easily discern the silhouette to be just that. Thankfully, a few minutes later our smaller spare engine was barely sputtering as he motioned the Coast Guard over to within earshot. As they were passing by, Tom hollered out to them, double checking which emergency channel they monitor in case we needed to call them for assistance.

"We're having a little engine trouble," he jokingly yelled toward across the water. My ears funneled his understated assessment straight to my brain. My eyes instantly bulged.

"A little? Uh, how about more like major engine trouble!" I muttered as I cleared my throat. It was fried!

Without hesitation, the Coast Guard boat revved its engine to immediately turn their vessel around in order to follow us while we limped back to the dock. What a comforting sight it was to see them behind us until we reached the safety of the boat launch again, so I videotaped that too! Within seconds Tom became noticeably irritable and began to mumble his grievances. Once I sorted out a few words, I soon learned that with the Coast Guard now on our tail, some sort of an inspection would soon follow. I considered this a minor inconvenience….at least we were safe!

As we each pulled up to opposite sides of the dock, I couldn't keep from noticing how big and shiny the engines were on the Coast Guard boat. Plus, there was not just one but two of them mounted on the back of their top-of-the-line vessel. We could really use one of those, I dreamed jealously. Maybe then I wouldn't be so scared.

Now at the boat launch, the men on the Coast Guard vessel quickly tied up. All four of them were smartly dressed in a striking orange uniform as they stepped single file from their boat onto the dock. They looked very professional and qualified to be on the water. In sharp contrast, there we were: a mismatched, stocking-capped, low-budget carnival show!

Thankfully, Tom had insisted that I take the time to get our boat's identification applied before we'd left just minutes earlier. In a very businesslike manner, one official took charge asking questions while carefully inspecting every aspect of our boat. By the time the officer finished his detailed investigation, he would validate that except for an emergency whistle, all of our required emergency apparatus was in order. I have to admit, this surprised me, because the Tom that I know is famous for functioning with the barest of necessities, at best. Nonetheless, the soft-spoken official handed him a complimentary plastic whistle. With his shiny metal clipboard in hand, he began to fill out paperwork. While my husband was being entertained by the head honcho, I felt compelled to ask one of the other men a few questions of my own.

"If you were me, would you go out in this boat with the water this rough?" I quizzed. His answer wasn't quite what I had in mind. He told me that it was indeed safe enough, but it was really a matter of each individual's comfort level. So, I concluded, Tom isn't as crazy as I thought moments ago. Just like when we worked in the woods, I knew that, once again, Tom's brainchild was going to present a huge learning curve for me! I was optimistic that if I could outlast this excursion in Alaska, I would most likely be better for it in the end.

Fifteen minutes had passed before we received certification documents confirming that we had been boarded by the Coast Guard of Ketchikan, and the "golden ticket," as the gentlemen referred to it, would allow us to avoid future boarding inspections for one year. The officer delivered the news like it was an announcement which should've provided us some sort of great relief, but quite frankly, another inspection was the least of my worries right then; we didn't even have reliable transportation at this stage of the game.

Without further delay, all four of the Coasties boarded their vessel to leave us to our misery. It truly would have been interesting to hear what they must have said amongst themselves as they pulled away from the dock. Not only did we probably look like a couple of goofs with our dog, but as they were leaving, Tom was cranking our boat back onto the trailer when the strap on the winch suddenly ripped in two. That misfortune caused our boat to slip back into the water, and I was certain that we looked like complete idiots.

Afterward, we realized that during the nearly sixteen hundred mile journey to get from eastern Oregon to Ketchikan, Alaska, the shaft that supports the boat winch had unknowingly come loose and slid out of position. That modification made it impossible for the boat's crank to function correctly; therefore, it had torn the strap. Following the mishap, Tom and I remained visibly composed, while at the same time we kept wishing under our breath that the Coast Guard would speed clear out of range before anything else could go wrong. Fortunately for us, their boat did continue to pull away, allowing us a moment to recover from the events that had just transpired.

Right then, Tom turned to me and said, "We are probably going to have to hire someone to get our materials…"

"Fine with me!" I interrupted.

Even though we'd scraped every coin we could find just to get to Alaska, at this moment, I didn't care what the cost might be. I was terrified, and therefore, willing to pay just about any price to transport our goods.

"Now what are we going to do?" I asked Tom.

"Well, we'll have to get a new engine," Tom replied.

The first, brief trip was terrifying for Pup and me. The water was much rougher than I'd anticipated. We had attempted the ten mile commute in a boat with a less than sufficient engine. The wide open area of water we had only begun to navigate across made me sick to think about yet another go of it. The water wasn't as friendly as I'd remembered it when we first looked at the property six months earlier in September. Perhaps I wasn't conscious of much then because I knew we'd been in the hands of an experienced charter boat captain. Up to this point I'd been aware of the extent of Tom's boating experience, but as I began ponder his track record, all of what I knew was only because of what he'd told me; I had never actually been with him on a boat. I flashed back, remembering, but the month of September also didn't feel as much like winter either. More than anything, I just wished I was home. This trip was beginning to feel like one gigantic mistake.

I recapped the events of the day, trying to put it in perspective somehow. We'd arrived in Ketchikan by ferry late the night before, but since we planned to be up very early the next morning, we'd opted to sleep in our car again. In those dark hours, plenty of mischievous-looking traffic had come and gone from the parking lot in which we'd chosen to set up camp. The uneasiness about possible theft or vandalism had kept us on edge the entire night, making Tom extremely cranky as we had begun our day. All this time he'd been so worried about his prized boat, which I had since discovered, wasn't so spectacular after all.

As I processed all that had transpired, I continued to be amazed at how disgruntled Tom was: this was his dream after all! I rewound our conversations we'd had in previous years in which he'd always told me, "It'll be different if we are in Alaska." So far it wasn't the least bit different; he was still as grumpy as ever. The upbeat mental picture he'd given me several months earlier was of a smiling, happy, and patient Tom, who'd be living out his dream in paradise once he arrived. I was beginning to wonder if and when that personality might show up.

Well, I pondered, at least we've made it this far. I can honestly say "I tried!" It was noon, which meant we'd been in Alaska less than sixteen hours, and already we were at an absolute standstill. I wondered if leaving on Friday the 13th had brought all this about.

14

Back To Square One

After months of planning and days of travel, we suddenly found ourselves inconveniently stranded ten miles from our final destination. We had huge problems. Our boat had a fried engine and we had no other means to get to our property.

First of all, if we didn't find another engine, then for sure we'd be going nowhere—except straight home! If we decided to go home at this point, we would still have to deal with the contents of our shipping container which would soon be arriving in Ketchikan. Second, if we continued to forge ahead, we'd be hiring someone with a vessel much larger than ours to transport our materials for us. As soon as possible, we would need all the available information to make an educated decision about what should happen next. We determined that we should head out immediately in order to come up with answers to some of these burning questions. Dragging our dead boat behind us, we humbly left the boat launch in search of a boat shop that could give us a quote on a new engine.

The heavy snow we'd woken up to this morning had almost melted away. By then it was raining but still cold as we wove our way back through town on the sloppy, two-lane road in search of a boat shop. We gingerly motored past a gas station, a market, and a lumber yard and other businesses until eventually we spotted a potential source for boating supplies and immediately slowed to pull over to the curb. Across the street a small, storm-weathered business on the main drag became our first, and quite possibly, our only option. I have to be honest; by the looks of the sagging structure, I didn't have much hope.

Tom waited for a gap in the traffic before he trotted across the road. After a few minutes inside the tiny family-run store, he returned to the car with news that the boat shop did indeed have an engine which would be the right size.

"Yeah, but how much is it," I said, wincing as I braced for the bad news.

"Oh, $5,800 or so," I heard him say.

Oh man, that seemed high. But this was not the time to scrimp! For a few minutes we tiptoed our way through a discussion on money. After some financial juggling, we found a credit card to use for our unexpected purchase. It would be a huge risk, but we schemed that if all went well, the engine could be installed the following morning. The only mechanic, however, was recovering from surgery on his right hand, which would require Tom to assist him during the engine mount. This was no problem. Tom had installed engines before. In fact, if we'd just brought the necessary tools, he could have done the work himself, he told me.

But was it the right thing to do? As we mulled over the facts before us, Tom and I reminisced about the special care we'd taken to keep the boat's engine from being harmed during the process of our long commute. We scoffed at our protective behavior toward the useless junk we had carefully toted the nearly sixteen hundred miles to Alaska. The rough roads through parts of Canada had us clenching our teeth at times as the boat bounced along the poorly maintained highway. Then we'd recalled that when we'd boarded the ferry, more than once, the steep ramp at the dock had made contact with our precious propeller as it scraped its way down to the parking deck. Then there's the sleep we lost while keeping watch over it in the dark parking lot, which in hindsight, was also a complete waste of energy.

"It would've been a blessing to have been stolen," we chuckled to ourselves; our insurance would've paid for a new one under those circumstances.

Nevertheless, plans were made to get the new engine installed the next morning. But due to the space limitations, this particular establishment didn't have a shop to work on boats. We'd noticed that many of the buildings in Ketchikan boast a beautiful waterfront view, but unfortunately, due to the prime location, they are extremely limited on parking space. Therefore, in order to have a chance at getting the work done the next day it would be necessary for us to show up very early. Upon our arrival, we'd occupy one of the two curbside parking spots available in front of the store.

With our information collected, the visit to the engine shop left us feeling rather apprehensive about such a large, unforeseen expenditure. Before the trip we had anticipated a snag here or there along the way but not this grand of a snaffoo, especially right out of the gate. But now with the engine debacle partially solved, the next mission would be to find a company to transport our materials to the property. Initially, we weren't very optimistic because Tom had already researched extensively before leaving on our trip. But as hard as he'd tried from home, a simple phone directory hadn't been too helpful. Having connections with the locals was what we needed. Today it was our good fortune that the boat shop was able to give us a promising lead on a transport company that might be able to provide some assistance. They spoke of a father/son team who owned a large vessel and were in the business of transporting supplies.

To understand our mind set, in the months that preceded the adventure, Tom had spent countless hours strategically planning each phase of the project. He'd estimated each step of our progress from the time we were scheduled to arrive in Alaska, until the cabin was built. Since we'd be on generator power at the remote property, Tom had pre-cut, then bundled much of the framing lumber, ensuring that the cabin's assembly would move swiftly.

The first week's schedule had been expected to go like this: after our arrival in Ketchikan Thursday night, we'd travel to the property Friday to locate our legal corner markers. We would also spend some time clearing trees and brush to prepare the building site. By Monday when our container was available, we could start shuttling materials out to the property as needed. After a week of building, we were hopeful that we'd be able to get the cabin "roughed in" enough to camp in, at which point we'd have the worst phase behind us. From there it would all be down hill, we had thought optimistically.

Tom and I were both keyed up about the idea that if we could actually get our boat back in operation by the next day, then we could stay on schedule

The landing craft we hired to transport our supplies from town.

with our initial plans to start work on the cabin. From there, the main push was going to be during the first week, but being goal oriented we energetically welcomed the challenge. For the time being, of course, we were back to square one, waiting for an engine.

It poured down rain as we sat together in the car in front of the boat shop. This whole excursion we were smack in the middle of at the moment seemed like one bad idea after another. Rain, cold, winter, boats: all were negative aspects in my book. Tom used the cell phone to make contact with the transport company. A short time later, we met two men downtown where we scheduled the loading of our materials. A tentative delivery time was set for the following day in accordance with the tide schedule, weather permitting. I quickly realized that it no longer mattered what time we preferred to eat, sleep or travel because from then on, the tide and weather would dictate our lives. Now that we were in Alaska, the all-important concept was beginning to sink in: all schedules are subject to weather conditions and tides.

The most disheartening news in our turn of events was that we were about to spend a lot more money than we originally anticipated. "It's only money," we tried to reassure ourselves more than once as the day wore on. After compiling all the pertinent information, we returned to the boat launch to get a head start on disassembling the worthless engine responsible for getting us into such a mess. It was early evening by then, and the entire parking lot was vacant except for us: Jones—party of three. As we tromped around in the muddy snow for the next couple of hours, off in the distance, the deep orange glow of the setting sun provided a little cheer for which we were very grateful. In preparation for the boat work that would take place the next day, Tom removed all the old engine cables and dismantled the defunct motor. Once the prep work was done, we readied the car for the purpose of sleeping once again.

With everything in order for the morning's engine replacement, we spent the rest of the soggy evening carefully weighing our many options of what to do next. Above all, we were hopeful that we were doing the right thing. The debate continued as we snuggled into our miserable, makeshift bed again for the night. We knew if we left for home at this point, not only would our wild adventure of a lifetime be remembered as a major disappointment, but it would also be slated as a terrible financial loss. The fact was either way, we had already spent the money not only for our travel expenses, but also for a shipping container, our material costs, as well as the boat we had purchased specifically for the excursion.

Could we live with ourselves if we gave up now, we asked each other? The answer was a resounding no! Eventually we came to the conclusion that the ordeal was going to cost us money no matter what we decided, so we might as well make something of it. After a lengthy dialogue, we felt we had chosen the lesser of two evils; we planned to keep forging ahead. On this final note we drifted off to sleep.

15

Mother Nature's Lessons

Day 2

This morning, instead of snow, we awoke early to heavy rain pounding the car like a commercial carwash. As we got ready for the day we commented to each other that after sleeping on our decision to replace the boat's engine, we felt really comfortable about the choice we had made. At seven o'clock in the morning we pulled the boat into the coveted parking spot in front of the boat shop. With two hours of waiting until the owners arrived, Tom and I chatted about the chain of events up to this point. We'd certainly never anticipated a Coast Guard encounter during our stay in Alaska, let alone on the first day. Our hopes remained high that the engine failure would be the last of the drama on our trip. We were excited that soon we would finally be making some progress!

Just as promised, the bandaged mechanic arrived as the business opened for the day. He and Tom got right to work. By noon the engine was mounted, and the next logical step was to take the boat for a spin.

After our unfortunate outing the day before, I was feeling less confident in Tom's boating assessments, however right or wrong that was. To him, the previous day's events involving the Coast Guard were more of a nuisance—a mere bump in the road—because we didn't actually "need" the Coast Guard for anything, he told me. In my eyes, the gap between his comfort level and mine was becoming more of a canyon. So as we drove toward the boat launch,

I noted that the honeymoon stage of the Alaska trip was definitely wearing off. I could feel my passive inner-self beginning to find its own voice. At this juncture I was tired of being a good sport, and quite frankly, I was in no mood for what I felt was going to be another experimental boat ride.

Upon our arrival, I insisted that Tom make the trial run alone. By then I didn't care one iota if he thought he was wasting his time or not. As soon as the boat was in the water, Tom jumped aboard. The brand new engine started right up without a hitch. He carefully backed the boat away from the dock before quickly disappearing behind the gigantic rock barrier. Pup and I walked over to the beach just around the corner from the jetty, a location that provided a better vantage point from where I could critique the performance of the boat's new engine. Once there, I took a skeptic's pose. I knew very little about boating, and right then I knew that Tom would have a lot to prove to me before I could begin to trust in his abilities again.

After observing the boat as it paralleled the shoreline, I felt extremely encouraged. Compared to the previous outing, I instantly recognized a remarkable improvement in the engine's performance, even as inexperienced as I was. Before we'd left the boat shop an hour earlier, he'd been instructed that the new engine was supposed to be run at half throttle for a few days in order to break it in properly. Now, even at half-power, our new purchase was showing up the old engine, hands down. By the time Tom returned to the dock, I was ready to join ranks again. We were in full agreement that our engine purchase was money well-spent and I felt renewed hope and confidence in our decision to stay and repair the boat.

It was Saturday, and the well-behaved water had attracted other boaters who also were moving about. Seeing the flurry of other human activity made me feel much more at ease. We both expressed our desires to head out to the property right away, but against our innermost wishes, we determined it was too late in the day to safely make another attempt to reach the property. It was 2:30 p.m. Even though we'd been there before on one sunny September day six months ago, we still had some uncertainty on the direct travel time it would take to get to our place. Back then, we'd spent four hours looking around, which had also included viewing several other parcels. We felt it would be wise to allow sufficient daylight to not only locate the property, but also to find the corner markers, choose a delivery area and pick out a building site. It was decided that it would be best to wait until the next morning, weather permitting, before we would make another go of it, opting to regroup by spending a well-deserved night in a motel.

Day 3

Our motel lodging was located right on the water's edge, allowing us a front row seat to the Tongass Narrows, part of Alaska's majestic inside passage. As we awoke this morning, a quick weather assessment revealed sunny skies reflecting brilliantly on the flat calm water. At daybreak we watched an enormous container barge as it chugged through the picture-perfect waterway leaving huge smooth ripples in its wake. A tugboat was steadily guiding it along as it rumbled slowly through the channel past the motel window. The barge was not only transporting stacks of shipping containers but also chained atop the enormous cargo were school buses and dump trucks, all of which appeared toy-sized from our perspective. We couldn't help but wonder if it might be the very barge carrying our cargo.

Above all, we had big plans for the day, so anxiously we checked out of the motel, heading straight for the launch at the other end of town. Today will be the day, I hoped excitedly. When we arrived, the water was absolutely peaceful compared to two days earlier which put me at complete ease for the upcoming boating experience.

At the boat launch we sorted through the car in order to pack the boat with the necessities. We thought ahead momentarily to what we'd need once we got to the property. The crab pot we were anxious to employ was already in the boat. We definitely wanted to start setting up camp, so we made sure to have the tent, chainsaw, gas, food, and several duffle bags of clothes. We also unearthed an ax, a winch, and other tools we thought we'd use to clear brush and set up the tent. Next we took as much as possible out of the car in an attempt to start thinning out the clutter we'd have to weed through for our next stay in our "motel on wheels." We were planning to return this evening to sleep in the car one last time, so we left behind the mattress, most of the bedding, and plenty of clothes for whatever weather might arise during the following day's cargo transfer project. After carefully double-checking our load, we felt content with our choice of supplies which would be accompanying us on our first trip to the property this morning.

After we finished packing, once again we bundled up for the chilly commute before Tom backed the boat down the slimy, algae-coated cement ramp. I stood nearby on the dock, holding onto the bow line in order to pull the boat off the boat trailer as soon as it was floating. When Tom left to park the car, I tugged the boat in close so I could tie the bow line to the cleat on the dock. Although the concept of tying up a boat appeared simple, I knew I would have to learn the proper protocol for securing a floating vessel. As I fiddled with the soft rope it was obvious that I had no idea what the tie up procedure entailed. It didn't involve regular ol' knots, so I faked my way through a few figure-eight style wraps around the cleat before Pup and I donned our life jackets and stepped into the boat. When Tom returned from parking the car, he started the new engine. We were pleased that it purred like a kitten. I felt the emotions of both relief and excitement. Our immediate plans had all the indications of a spectacular adventure as we eagerly untied our vessel and headed out for our property on this promising day.

We sped across the water with the wind in our faces as we took in the amazing sights in all directions. Just as I'd hoped, the boat ride this morning was night and day different from our first outing. The new engine hummed so quietly. Because of the sufficient power available, the increased speed allowed the boat to travel more on the water's surface making for a much smoother, controlled ride. Soon we approached the mouth of the inlet where the water's surface improved yet again. Except for occasional areas along the shoreline, all the land we could see was packed with cedar trees in various stages of growth. The healthy green forest was dotted with spear-like remnants of weathered, decaying timber, many of which were still upright amongst the dense cedar forest. Traveling toward the property, we stayed to the left near the water's edge as we followed the contour of the inlet. As we cruised along, I watched behind us as the wake from our boat spread out evenly, and my eyes followed the ripple until it lapped against the rock wall that greeted the water's edge. I was delighted. I even asked Tom to videotape Pup and me during the ride, the water was that smooth!

The familiar sights were just how we remembered them to be during our first visit with the charter boat captain. We continued to buzz along at a brisk clip up the straight stretch of the inlet, around the bend at the rocky corner, then straightening out again as we headed toward the small island off in the distance. Its presence indicated to us that our property was located directly to our left in the small protected cove and would be the final marker representing the end of our journey this morning.

In no time at all we were closing in on our very own secluded beach. Slowly we came ashore and were a bit surprised to see the changes which had taken place. Since our initial visit last fall, all of the wispy, tender green shoots of grass coloring the shoreline had all disappeared. I should have expected as much; it was still winter, after all. We took notice of several inches of snow in every direction. The white blanket had been uniformly erased at the high tide mark, indicating where recent tides had come and gone.

"We're here!" I announced with excitement as we cautiously stepped into the shallow water, taking great care to plant our anchor securely in the sandy bottom. The extraordinary sights were extremely quiet and equally exhilarating. Safe on land, the crisp air filled my lungs which could now breathe more deeply knowing that we had made it, at long last!

As it was, the boat ride seemed like it had happened very quickly, and upon our arrival it truly was paradise, just as one might expect. The color of the sky was a perfect robin's egg blue with a ribbon of friendly white clouds standing by on the horizon. The bright orb of the sun overhead shone brilliantly on the pristine mountains, which were glistening in every direction as they displayed a majestic winter landscape I'd seen only in pictures. Add to that, the flat calm water of the inlet perfectly duplicated all of the breath-taking sights like a giant mirror. It was undeniably a gorgeous sight!

Tom baited the crab pot with herring and motored out to drop the pot into seventy feet of water to begin our search for crab. Later in the day, we were looking forward to pulling up a pot with some fresh crab inside. It was anyone's guess where the hungry crab might be, but we were hopeful they were close by.

We all three curiously scouted around the beach for a few minutes. Even in the fresh snow we were able to find our property's lower corner markers to be exactly where we remembered seeing them six months earlier. Tom and I commented to each other that the spectacular view was well worth the wait!

The serene water was currently about fifty feet from where our property started at the base of a fairly steep incline. From the edge of the beach, our newly purchased landscape continued uphill as far as we could see through the tangle of both large trees and thick brush. Everywhere we looked there was moss covered timber, reminiscent of an ancient rain forest. Without hesitation, we began our climb to see what else the property had to offer.

Now up off the beach, my eyes scanned skyward, trying to locate the tops of all the beautiful, tall trees surrounding me from where I stood. After hiking around a bit, we easily selected the ideal location for the cabin. A spot close to the beach seemed to be a practical choice. In order to build our cabin there we had some large trees which would have to be cleared; but otherwise, the site offered a great view of the water. Finding an area to set up the tent presented a slight challenge because the property was crawling with roots from giant trees that towered overhead. Timber and scraggily branches were looming everywhere, except for the location we chose just above the beach where the land benched. Although it wasn't perfectly flat, there was just enough of a clearing for a tent, and plenty of saplings stood nearby which would provide the necessary stability for our primitive canvas shelter.

Still stowed in the boat were the tent, cooler, and other essential items which would need to be unloaded and put to use during our first trip to a remote land. I got busy with those tasks while Tom started his chainsaw to cut down some trees in the area where we planned to build the cabin. Off he went, clearly on a mission.

Four years earlier during our logging days, whenever Tom was felling trees anywhere near where I was working, Pup would sit on my lap while I would narrate what was taking place. "There it goes!" I would say as the timber fell. When tree after huge tree crashed to the ground, I made sure Pup knew to be afraid of that sound. Now in Alaska, he was fearfully awaiting the big crash as he cowered quietly in the brush on the steep hillside. Oddly enough, the big crash never came. In our patch of timber, the limbs of each tree were tightly tangled with neighboring branches which prevented the all-out "ker-thud" as they slowly lowered themselves to the ground.

Once the logging session was over, Pup and I made our way up to the clearing Tom had just created. After his demolition party in the woods, he and I spent the next half hour working together erecting the army-green, canvas shelter. At the same time, we were watching the tide and listening to the birds overhead. All we really wanted to get accomplished today was almost done. Welcome to Alaska, I thought! This wasn't so bad. We slowed to a lazy pace, enjoying just being in the moment as we took in the breathtaking sights.

Meanwhile, all of the cargo I'd unloaded was still sitting at the bottom of the hill at the edge of our property. In order to move it out of the tide's reach, we made several treks up the fifty-foot trail that crossed the hillside above the beach, first with our five gallon containers of gas for the generator, then back up again with an ax, a tarp, and oil for the saw. It didn't take long to realize what a miserable hill we'd have to conquer each trip, but we took comfort knowing that neither the tent nor the future cabin could be washed away at high tide. By the time we finished hiking up and down the steep mossy hillside, a trampled path remained visible in the cushioned ground cover.

With our camp in order, we enjoyed the peaceful view of the water while we ate a nice lunch. It was a gorgeous day. On a regular basis, we took time to squat down and peer through the trees in order to monitor the boat's wellbeing down below. We paid careful attention to our only mode of transportation, not only to make sure it didn't float away, but also that it didn't get beached; it was a warning which Tom had mentioned to me on a couple of occasions already. I imagined how terrifying it would be to get stuck there, deserted in an unfamiliar remote setting.

The water was ever so quiet as the tide came in and soon began to sneak out without any cause for concern. After lunch, we hiked up the hill to stack the brush that Tom had cut earlier, both of us keeping a careful eye on the tide's progress while we measured and imagined where the new cabin would sit. All at once we became conscious of the fact that even though the boat was still floating, it was also completely surrounded by dry land. Despite our vigilant efforts of constant monitoring, it was now sitting in a puddle! We raced down to the beach in an effort to move the boat toward the water which was only a few steps away, but the mucky beach and exposed rocks wouldn't allow it to budge. The well-built vessel wouldn't move an inch, even after giving it all the heave-ho we had in us.

At first I felt a little panic-stricken. What did this mean, I wondered? Tom seemed uptight but he wasn't saying much. The small skiff we'd arrived in was now inconveniently stranded on our very own secluded beach.

As I stood beside our beached skiff, I couldn't ignore the radiating warmth of Alaska's bright winter sun reflecting off of my face. The intense heat on my cheek presented a sharp contrast to the brisk chill in the air, which was most likely exaggerated by the drifts of fresh snow blanketing the beach and beyond. Luckily, it was because of the chilly temperatures that we'd bundled up and were somewhat prepared for the outing. Deep in thought, I pondered how we would solve our current dilemma.

A short time later, I checked my cell phone during a short stint of cell service. It flashed two o'clock. I took a moment to consider what could actually happen; we could be stuck at the property until morning. After contemplating a few worst-case scenarios, I figured we'd be alright even if we did have to spend the night. In fact, for a moment it actually even sounded a little exciting: a night in the wilderness….with a big fire on the beach.

"At least we've packed enough stuff to survive," I reminded Tom.

"We're not staying here tonight," he announced. He wanted no part of that plan. I didn't ask why, but I assumed it had something to do with wasting his time. Somehow, he was certain we would be able to get off the beach during the evening tide. Nonetheless, for the time being, I understood we were going to be there a while. We spoke only briefly of our evening plan of escape which consisted of nothing more than leaving as soon as possible. The rest of the afternoon was spent waiting for the elusive tidewater to return to our boat.

Hour after hour, the water continued to recede. We kept constant watch on the tide's progress, wondering how far out the low tide mark actually was. By then, I knew it was going to be a very long wait before the water returned. Up until that moment, I'd never thought about why tides do what they do, but today I began to ponder their rhythm, their importance, and their magnificent power.

During our wait, we did some investigating. We found two types of clams available, mud clams and steamers. Besides clams, there was also an unending supply of navy blue colored muscles, and of course, plenty of unwanted barnacles. We knew we could look forward to enjoying a seafood buffet at any point in our visit, and we wouldn't starve to death if we ever did get stranded.

The beach was also generously scattered with beautiful white quartz rocks that were intermingled with truckloads of large flat, square stones whose edges had been filed smooth presumably as a result of years in the unrelenting surf. Further investigations revealed hundreds of miniature rock crabs hibernating under every object within the tide's reach. Also keeping us company were oodles of beautifully striped, cone-shaped shells. They resembled miniature Chinese hats and were stuck solid to rocks of all shapes and sizes. It appeared that there were signs of life everywhere we looked. The further out the tide went, the more life forms we found. At low tide there was approximately 350 feet of exposed beach. Wow! This was a lot of flat beach. Since the tide was in when we arrived, I hadn't thought anything about how it would be when the tide was out.

Our new discoveries seemed endless. As the hours passed and we waited for the tidewater to revisit our boat, I was becoming more convinced that we might actually be forced to spend the night in the wilderness. But after all, we had the tent set up, a new tarp, a flashlight and a fire. On the other hand, we had no idea what animals might be around, and our only available weapon was bear spray. Besides that, our tent sat too far off the beach, up a treacherous trail away from the fire. I'd remembered that we'd only packed one blanket, which wouldn't be nearly enough to stay warm unless we could huddle near the fire all night. Of course, we would've rather built a fire up the hill near the tent, but the several inches of snow covering the wet moss on the sloping terrain made that luxury unlikely. And the tent couldn't be set up by the fire, because once the tide was in, it would be flooded.

After a brief discussion, I agreed with Tom that we should get back to town tonight if at all possible.

As the day wore on, we realized that the resident ravens had taken it upon themselves to pack off the tub of butter I'd left sitting out after lunch! We recalled listening to their chatter all afternoon, but unfortunately hadn't realized what they'd been up to. Soon we noticed that the other half of my sandwich which I'd left atop the cooler was missing as well. Add to that, a full dish of Pup's food that was smothered in mashed potatoes and gravy. All of it, gone without a trace. What else have they taken, I wondered, even though it was the least of our worries right then.

We could see the feathered thieves passing overhead from time to time. We paid close attention to which direction the birds were flying, hopeful of eventually retrieving our stolen items. But the majority of the time, the ravens sat perched in the tall, leafy trees which lined the edge of our beach and they appeared to be thoroughly entertained by our mere existence. As we attempted to assess the meaning of the raven situation, the giant, black birds just stared back at us as if nothing had happened.

The delightful outing at the beach was quickly deteriorating. Our mistakes were mounting and I was feeling defeated again. Just getting here seemed difficult enough and now, even though we'd barely begun the adventure, we'd beached our boat, been robbed by the ravens, and didn't have possession of a simple tide book. I desperately wanted our bad luck to turn around!

Time was running out. The sun was on its way toward the horizon. It was starting to cool down considerably, and the tide was still out a good distance. By five o'clock, I'd started a camp fire, just in case we did end up getting stranded for the night. The beach would be the perfect location for a fire, we decided, and it provided some logs to sit on as well. I collected all the small twigs at first, and then dragged in the larger water-soaked branches scattered on the beach. With a good fire going, I picked up all that was available in the surrounding area, which eventually turned my standard-sized campfire into a roaring blaze.

By then we both had familiarized ourselves with our new beach front real estate. We'd already carefully investigated the massive collection of large, decaying cedar logs which had accumulated at the edge of our property. They'd most likely floated in during high tides in previous winter storms, we surmised. A closer look at the logs revealed how frosty they really were, probably not good for sitting on after all. Tom busied himself by cutting a path through the frozen wood at the base of the hill. The improvement allowed access to our trail without having to straddle the huge, inconvenient frosty barrier each time. Once the path was created, he began chopping the heavy ice-coated cedar rounds into firewood wedges, some of which went straight into my fire. From there he was quick to cut everything in sight, including the beautiful cedar bows that draped down onto the beach. I pleaded with him to let a few small trees and the pertinent branches remain along the edge of the property. In my opinion, the drooping branches conveniently disguised the unsightly mess of stumps and rotting wood; our property blended in with the surroundings that way, and I also liked the natural, untouched style it offered.

It wasn't too much later before Tom returned to the boat where he discovered that the remaining herring had been plucked from the package; the empty foam tray lay tattered from the assault. It was no doubt a revelation that added insult to injury. As I stood there on the desolate beach with my newly purchased bear spray hanging from my belt, I came to realize that the biggest pest we might face on the trip were birds, not bears.

Around seven o'clock in the evening, we were feeling a little frenzied and we were up for trying anything which might allow for an earlier escape. More than once, we found ourselves just staring at the boat for an inspiration of some kind. "Think,"….we urged ourselves. With the small logs lying around we decided to make an effort to point the bow toward the water. After all, the boat had runners on the bottom. If we could get it turned around then maybe we could winch it, we thought. Soon it was aimed toward the water and we found ourselves attempting to persuade it forward. Unfortunately, there was nothing but soft sand in which to secure the anchor, and as a result, the anchor resurfaced immediately.

With daylight quickly fading, our upcoming trip to town was most likely going to be a race against darkness. After a long quiet gaze into the fading fluorescent sky, a frantic feeling washed over me. We really needed to get going soon. Tom kept kicking himself for not picking up a tide book this morning. I was beginning to realize the extremely valuable information it would have provided. This whole trip had been dotted with harsh lessons. According to me, one by one, they had added up to one big disaster and at this stage of the game I was becoming overwhelmed with regret!

After scanning the beach with a critical eye, we came up with one last idea. Besides the mammoth logs where Tom had cut the path, there were also smaller logs littering the beach. Just like cavemen we could get the logs under the boat in order to roll it toward the water, we schemed.

Tom began cutting up one of the smaller diameter logs into manageable lengths. He jammed one end of it under the boat to pry it up out of the sand while I quickly inserted one of the small logs under the bow. In no time, we were both out of breath and tiring from our efforts, but I felt renewed hope as we scurried around. Why hadn't we thought of this sooner? We repeated the process and soon had another log in place near the stern. Then we stretched the boat's anchor chain in the direction of the water again. For additional le-verage, we completely buried the anchor in the sand this time and piled large rocks on it to hold it in place. Like "king of the hill," I stood atop the rock pile for extra resistance, balancing myself as Tom once again ratcheted the winch.

Regrettably, our valiant efforts proved futile. Even all of the additional weight didn't provide enough leverage. When we tried to winch the heavy, aluminum Red Sled toward the water, it might as well have been set in con-crete. Our last-ditch effort had failed. It became agonizingly evident that we were trapped on the beach at the mercy of the tide.

16

Denial Meets Reality

The atmosphere on the beach was eerily quiet. Darkness was on its way. The looming reality of a perilous ride back to town was upon us, and as a result, the mood in camp was a sober one. By 7:30 p.m. the water had finally returned to within twenty feet of the boat. I wished for daylight to hold steady. I never imagined the water taking so long to return. Tom and I continued to watch intently as the incoming tide inched its way toward us, silently encompassing each rock one by one until they had all been covered. Now the water just needed to flood the sandy pit which had held the boat hostage for the day.

The deep orange color of the winter sun was only barely visible above the distant hills as we mentally prepared ourselves for our long-awaited trip back to town. With my cell phone in hand, during the last few minutes preceding our departure, I crisscrossed the beach in search of a signal which might offer a few precious minutes of cell phone service. It was our good fortune to be able to get a scratchy call out to Tom's parents to inform them of our circumstances. I spoke with Tom's dad, who was less than excited about our decision to leave for town this late in the day. I reassured him that I would call immediately upon our arrival to the dock to let them know we'd made it back.

As darkness continued to overtake daylight, we could still decipher the nearly black silhouette of the sprawling forest against the pastel colors of the vast night sky. We discussed the fact that the visual aid made a big difference because the contrasting colors would be a good guide to get us partway to town. By dusk we could no longer distinguish between the water and land. The dark hues of the forest and the water were now too similar.

I thought ahead. What if we were forced to abandon ship somewhere along the way? Unlike our property, most of the landscape up to that point in the inlet did not offer an easily accessible beach. From what I remembered seeing earlier today, in most places the inlet resembled more of a canal where the sheer rock cliffs met the water's edge. If we did have to make an emergency stop, I imagined how difficult it would be to get ourselves out of the boat and onto dry land, especially in the black of night. We were in unfamiliar territory.

There were plenty of islands scattered about further up the channel, but the land mass directly in front of our property was the first one up to that point of the inlet. It exhibited the same features as much of the inlet, appearing as if it had erupted straight out of the water. Jagged outcroppings of rocks were exposing themselves here and there at the base of the island. Its solid presence reminded me of a large wisdom tooth protruding from the gum line. From what I could tell, the thick growth of trees which grew there magically had their stronghold in nothing but solid rock.

In our discussions about the trip, we were optimistic that if we could make it as far as the mouth of the inlet, we'd be able to see the distant lights of town to help us safely navigate across the open water.

"How long do you think it took us to get here this morning," I asked Tom.

"I don't know, maybe twenty-five minutes or so," Tom replied. But since we hadn't kept track of travel time earlier today, it was only a guess that if everything went right it might take us forty-five minutes to reach safety, even if we traveled cautiously. It was a less-than-ideal scenario, especially with the overwhelming fears I had about traveling through the dark waters, but we were low on available options as we hesitantly resigned ourselves to forge ahead. Perhaps I could swallow my fears for forty-five minutes.

Just for good measure, I elected to wear my survival suit over my life vest. After pulling the survival suit from the bag it where it had been stowed, I sat down on the floor of the boat, first cramming one leg then the other into the stiff outfit as I fought the resistance of the pre-formed rubber, basically threading myself into the suit inch by inch. After my feet and legs were inserted and it was up around my waist, reaching behind me I gripped the collar and then tugged it up around my shoulders, while at the same time forcing my arms in to their appointed spots. Next, I pulled the front opening together. Once I had the full-body suit on, the giant-sized bulbous fingers allowed very limited use of my hands. At that point, I employed Tom to close my zipper, which ultimately left only my eyes and nose exposed. It was a clumsy outfit, but I felt prepared.

Once I was suited up, I shuffled like a zombie toward the stern where Pup was waiting. He was already buckled up in his bright yellow floatation device. It was only the third time he'd worn it, but he was already telling me by way of his drooping eyelids and limp ears that he despised everything about it. Tom, on the other hand, wouldn't put a life vest on. And because of my nagging about his lack of a floatation device, I'd heard more than once in recent days that he found a life jacket very cumbersome. But this situation might be different, I thought. It's almost dark, and we're in the wilderness, I considered. "Why don't you just put it on?" I finally asked.

"I never wear one," he declared.

That's a bit crazy, I silently advised myself, but obviously, he's the experienced fisherman who's done this before, so who was I to say anything! But I also knew that if something were to happen to Tom while we were on the water, I would be called upon to maneuver the vessel on my own. I wasn't the least bit prepared to deal with that yet, so the subject of his life jacket was creating quite a chip on my shoulder. However, I also determined from his lack of eye contact during our conversation that he wouldn't be engaging in any more negotiations. Further discussion at this point would have been a waste of my precious energy. For the time being I spoke no more of it.

At last, a thin layer of water had inched its way closer and was finally touching the bow of the boat! As our departure time grew near, we continued to sit, impatiently waiting for the water level to rise. Interrupting the silence, a wafting noise overhead beckoned our attention. We all three looked up just in time to see Mr. Raven flying past with one of our herring clamped crosswise in his large, hooked beak. It just so happened that we weren't in the best of spirits right then. Tom and I rolled our eyes as we glanced at each other.

"We'll have the last laugh, you dumb bird!" Tom uttered. His shotgun would be along for the next trip to the property, at which point, he planned to take care of the pests at first chance.

"Isn't there a poem called 'The Raven'?" I quizzed.

"Coulda been," Tom replied.

"I wish I knew what that poem said about 'em, like if they are a bad omen or something," I said in deep thought, trying to transport my brain back to high school English class. I could recall the author, and distinctly remembered where my desk sat on the third floor of the old high school twenty-five years earlier. I could even hear the teacher's voice saying, "Quoth the raven, nevermore." But was there a hidden meaning, I wondered?

Together we watched quietly as the water crept ever-so-slowly, eventually filling in around us. I did one more mental check. Did we have everything? To prepare for the possible misfortune of being stuck somewhere between the property and town, I'd brought the tarp back to the boat, along with the lighter, and our cooler full of food. I'd also grabbed our lone blanket as well as our large flashlight which was stationed next to me on the bench. The video camera was also on board, ready to capture the upcoming event, although I didn't know how I would operate it now that I was entombed in rubber! We had one last safety precaution in place. Just for such an occasion, before we left on our trip to Alaska we had purchased "Spot," an emergency notification device. The hand-held emergency locator had already been zipped inside my vest pocket for safe keeping. All in all, I felt fairly prepared as we waited to leave.

Finally the boat began to float and it came time for us to push off. Because of the shallow water, the engine couldn't be started yet, so Tom stood at one side of the boat with an oar, poking at the sandy bottom and the barnacle-covered rocks as he pushed us along, guiding the boat between the groupings of larger rocks here and there. Since our beach was quite flat, we scraped across the bottom for two hundred feet perhaps, before finally launching into deeper water where Tom could lower and then start our engine.

Once the motor was running, we still moved slowly, because just as we began our uncertain journey toward town, dusk began fading into darkness. I remained optimistic because I still maintained a good visual of the immediate area. I could easily decipher the small, rocky island flanked in jagged rocks which was directly in front of our property. Just ahead there was also the floating buoy which marked where the crab pot had sunk to the bottom when it had been put out earlier in the day. As we motored around the buoy, Tom instructed me to keep a close eye on our immediate surroundings, ensuring the buoy line wouldn't tangle with the propeller now that the engine was running. Two minutes from launch, we passed on by it without any trouble while Tom steered the boat straight ahead at first, and then gently to the right as we headed in the direction of the dock at the edge of town. I took a deep breath, partially because we were finally on our way and also because we were actually off the beach! It wasn't all relief, though. The big breath also signified the start of what might be a marathon boat ride. I felt unsure and wary about the upcoming voyage in the dark across unfamiliar waters. Were we being wise in our decision to leave so late in the evening?

Needless to say, I was going to be very relieved to get back to town for the night, and I was so ready to put the long day behind us. And then there was Tom. He was not showing any signs of fear or anxiety, as if this excursion was a silly routine for him. He was silent, but his electronic device made a high-pitched "blip" as he activated the screen. It displayed a map which would help us find our way back to town in the dark. I could see a small boat on the monitor which represented our position in the inlet. Using that, he began to steer us through the water accordingly.

Only ten minutes passed before sundown threw a cloak of darkness over our efforts to navigate the inlet. We'd hardly made any progress in that short time. I became keenly aware that the less I could see, the more I could hear. As I stood very attentively just outside the boat's cabin, on occasion, I'd peer over Tom's shoulder at the screen he was using to navigate. Pup was by my side. I noted that even though I felt warm and dry in my orange, rubber jumpsuit, within the first few minutes of travel I found the lapping noises of the black, cold, deep water to be quite bone chilling. Because of the darkness, we moved slowly, and then even more cautiously, until the sky turned an inky black color, and we were barely inching along. Because of our deteriorating conditions, it had quickly become too dark to see whether logs or other debris might have been floating in our line of travel. We did have our flashlight though, so I flashed it occasionally to light our path.

The extreme absence of illumination on our vessel had suddenly become crystal clear. Up to this point in my life I had never thought about lights on a boat, nor had I imagined I'd be in a mess of this magnitude. In the midst of our dark silence, the VHF radio was chirping away with scratchy, garbled voices of distant boaters. Judging by the unidentifiable dialect, it sounded like the racket could be coming from another continent, or the moon for that matter. Tom sat inside the boat cabin studiously examining his brand new navigational equipment. The unit, on which all of his attention was focused, looked similar to a small color-television. As cartoon-like and user-friendly as the electronics had appeared to be in the light of day, they proved equally intimidating and unmanageable in the blackness of night. From where I stood, I could see the bright dash lights reflecting off Tom's face. All the while the boat's engine noise was barely audible as we moved forward at a snail's pace.

"We'll never make it to town at this rate," I calculated out loud.

"Just be patient," Tom instructed.

I frequently turned around to gauge our progress. Behind us off in the distance, I could still make out the flicker of flames from of our dying campfire, but over the next few minutes even that visual began to slowly disappear out of sight.

From what I could tell, we were traveling into a black hole, and now that the campfire was undetectable, I was truly terrified. Black water, black trees, and black silence completely engulfed us. I took some comfort knowing I could still barely discern the outline of the treetops against the night sky. In my own mind I felt confident that we could navigate the next few miles without feeling lost anyway. Where is the moon, I wondered? And I'd also noticed almost simultaneously that the boat was starting to turn too much to our left. We weren't traveling toward town anymore. In spite of my concerns, I remained quiet. Tom has to know, I thought. We were definitely not moving in the direction which I imagined we'd be taking to get back to civilization. In fact, we were heading straight for the shore clear on the other side of the inlet….completely opposite our property. Politely, I uttered my concern to the captain.

"Sweetie?" I asked.

"What!" Tom replied in an irritated whisper.

"We're turning too much!"

He didn't answer.

For a few moments I gave him the benefit of the doubt, keeping my unwarranted comments to myself. I don't need to harp, I thought. My eyes squinted into the night sky. I'm sure this is wrong, I processed, but I wasn't confident. Soon I began to express my growing doubts in our progress. I wasn't basing my opinion on some innate sense of direction either; I could still see, just barely. Without saying a word, Tom leaned to one side to allow me a more optimal view. He pointed to the electronic screen, showing me his brightly colored map. Was that maneuver supposed to convince me that I was wrong, I wondered, because the monitor was marked with black dots and scribbles which appeared like nothing more than a two-year-old child's artwork on an etch-a-sketch? On the beach I'd already been schooled on the idea that those specific marks indicated the return path we would need to follow in order to make it back to town.

"I'm following these crumbs right here," he said with confidence. "I made them on the way out this morning."

"Hmm," I replied.

Tom reassured me, "We'll be fine."

Even though I was full of suspicion, I patiently stood by, hopeful, but at the same time doubtful that he actually knew what he was talking about.

In the past, I had heard talk of these so-called "crumbs" which are commonly displayed on the screen of a high-tech navigational system. Before the trip, he and his dad spoke of relying on them to get through dense fog during their various fishing excursions. It was my understanding that with that foolproof trail of debris present on the navigational screen, one could easily get back from whence they came. Based on what I was witnessing, it didn't seem like this plan was working. But what do I know, I questioned?

To keep from panicking, I began a broad mental search in an attempt to put the evening's events in perspective. Before the day our engine blew up, I had recalled many successful ferry-boat rides. At that instant, my brain was scrambling for some sort of comforting experience to hold on to, but then again, I knew our boat was certainly no ferry. I desperately wanted to trust Tom, but as we continued to turn sharply to our left, my concerns were mounting, and rightfully so. I couldn't make sense of what was happening. Can't he tell that we are going the wrong way, I wondered?

It wasn't long before I gruffly announced, "Sweetie, you know you are turning way too much!"

After a brief discussion, it became obvious to me that my view of our trip from outside the cabin greatly differed from his via the electronic screen. In usual Tom fashion, he spoke more quietly than I, as we spent several minutes arguing in the dark about our lack of progress, or not. I kept my eyes strained for any clues as to where we were. Then, out of nowhere, I couldn't believe it! I blinked real hard. In a split second I rewound my memory. Without any doubt I could clearly distinguish an outline of a tree covered mass approaching. I was 100% positive that I recognized this very mass to be the small, round, rock encrusted island located directly in front of our property. This same island, which we had passed a while ago on our left, was rapidly approaching straight ahead on my right. My mental map was absolutely certain that this same island should have been long behind us.

Instantly, my personal alarm system was fully engaged, causing my voice to ramp up to a much higher pitch. My stubborn husband was still in total agreement with his navigational equipment, and therefore, not listening to me, whatsoever.

While he sat calmly on his soft swivel chair inside his newly built cabin he arrogantly insisted, "I'm getting it worked out, alright?"

"No, it's not alright," I protested.

My heart was racing. I noticed that by the time I'd finished speaking, that our blessed campfire, which had been on my right as we headed for town, was currently glowing on the distant beach to our left. How could this be true, unless we'd turned completely around?

This recent discovery was all the confirmation I needed before I began my rampage. There was no mistaking it. We were going the wrong direction.

"Sweetie, we're going the wrong way; we're spinning in circles!" I screamed.

My arm had abruptly outstretched itself in the darkness, just about coming unhinged at the elbow as I tried to point out the obvious facts. "Listen to me! Look with your bleeping eyes, there is the bleeping fire," I shouted at the top of my lungs. Only I wasn't using the word "bleep" at this point in the argument.

Unlike Tom, my eyes had adjusted to the darkness, and he was refusing to listen to my advice even though in reality, I was the only one who could actually see anything. Panic had definitely set in because the more he kept turning, the more certain I was that we were heading straight toward the small, rugged island! Before long, we'd be slamming into the jagged rocks, unless he either turned, or stopped.

"Stop!" I begged. "You have to stop. I mean it!" I said as my voice echoed into the night air.

I could feel Pup leaning heavily against me, probably feeling fairly uncertain about both of us. Soon I could see nothing again as the fire disappeared from my sight. I altered my relaxed stance as I braced for impact. I wondered if I should be contacting the Coast Guard. I groped in my vest pockets for the emergency device. It was still there. Is this bravery or stupidity, I asked myself more than once? It was beyond ridiculous! Tom was still following his beloved electronic map, so according to him, we were just fine. But it wasn't fine, not at all! Instead, we were making giant circles in the pitch dark and I was having no more of it.

"Take me back to the beach," I pleaded.

The intense fear came over me in waves. I'd had faith in Tom's abilities when we'd left the beach, but at this stage of the game my trust was fading! Then he'd speak with quiet confidence and I'd believe what he said for ten more seconds. We went back and forth for several long minutes while I tried to contain my frustrations. But once I realized that he wasn't going to trust me in return, it was over. It was every man for himself. The idea of "stand by your man" had taken on a new meaning for me, and from this moment forward I was consciously removing that worthless statement from my vocabulary.

"I hate water," I mumbled, followed by a loud groan!

Tom once again insisted, "Will you just let me get this figured out and we can follow our trail back to town."

Maybe that line would have worked the first day we were in Alaska, but we'd been through enough drama in the previous two days that I knew better than to believe everything he said. Oh how I wanted to, but something inside me had convinced me otherwise!

I was over that idea! No way was I going to allow Tom to talk me into taking another huge risk with my life. Continuing on toward town sounded like a bad recommendation that would only guarantee a dreadful outcome. I had naively gone along with him up to this point, but now I wanted off the ride! Another round of loud discussion ensued. I was reaching my breaking point. I was so angry that I contemplated throwing the video camera straight over the side. I was done with this trip! I'd had enough!! From day one this so-called adventure had been riddled with disasters and disappointing events. Now he was refusing to either stop or turn around. This was not going to end well, I could feel it.

My heart was pounding as I seriously contemplated a jump-and-swim-for-the-beach scenario. Like Mr. Magoo, Tom was steering us though the dark water unaware of our impending danger as all the while I looked on as we headed straight for the sharp rocks! What if we were ejected on impact, I processed?

 Soon he reluctantly explained what the problems were: Tom had only used this specific device once before, which happened to be on the way out to the property this morning. And second, he was trying to read it in reverse, because during the last minutes of daylight, he hadn't taken the time to figure out how to make the screen read properly. Genius! Not only were we lost in the pitch dark in the middle of a mile wide inlet, but Tom was trying to steer the boat down the chart while we were actually headed up. It was an awful feeling to be a passenger trapped on a boat traveling in circles in the dark. We are going nowhere, I processed!

Instinctively I knew we'd never make it to town and now my ultimate desire was to be back on solid ground.

Maybe I'll jump overboard, I considered. But what about Pup? I couldn't leave Pup. I knew that he had enough sense not to dive into the dark water. Frantic thoughts developed, one after another. At times, when I could still see a fleeting glimpse of our campfire, I could tell where we were. On second thought, jumping was probably not a good idea, I'd realized. Even though I would float in my suit, we were much too far away from our beach to swim in the icy water. Plus, what if he ran over me?

"Take me to the beach, now!!" I demanded.

"You just aren't going to be able to do this, are you?" he said, with complete disgust in his voice.

On the verge of tears I yelled back at him, "No, I'm not. Now take me back!"

Now on high alert, my eyes had become giant saucers as I tried to recognize any light source or familiar shape during the next while.

"What's that?" I screamed all of a sudden.

"What's what?" Tom said, in the same tone as an irritated parent.

"Those lights!" I snapped.

"What lights?" he nonchalantly answered back, completely annoyed by another disruption.

"Those blinking lights right there. Where did they come from?" I stomped.

"Don't you see 'em?" I asked, in a panicky, confused state.

He groaned, finally standing up from his chair, so he could figure out what I was squawking about. Off in the distance, he could also see a series of bluish-white lights which were coming on and off in a sequence like on a tower of some kind. In a split second, they were gone again!

"Where'd they go?" I screeched in complete hysteria, as they must have disappeared behind the silhouette of the island again. I sensed we were moments away from crashing!

My gut instincts about staying on the beach were so very right, now why hadn't I just listened? Instead of blindly trusting Tom, I should have been looking out for myself and then stuck with my gut! I would have kept a good fire going instead of letting it peter out. Faith is why. Faith in my captain had put me here right now. Yes, I'd be on the beach in the dark, no doubt terrified and steaming mad, but on solid ground where I would have a higher survival rate than on a tiny boat with no lights and a stubborn captain, I reasoned. "Never A-gain!" I told myself, as I filed the recent events into my overwhelmed memory bank.

After what seemed like an eternity, my eyes once again caught a faint glow of our campfire off in the distance. It was now behind us once again. Under my direction, thankfully, Tom turned the boat around once more. I was very relieved to be heading back to our property. Focusing my eyes on that tiny, orange beacon of light kept me very quiet until at long last we neared the shore. As we came into the cove again, we knew our boat would be approaching the floating crab line attached to our pot. Tom asked me to flash the light periodically to make certain we would not tangle in the buoy line, but due to our recent hour-long tour of darkness, for some reason, our flashlight battery was almost dead!

As we came up on the buoy, at last Tom's voice was very tense and his words were clipped.

"Careful! Don't let us run over that," he blurted frantically in a strained whispery voice.

Finally! I sighed. It's about time he started to worry!

We both knew that if the crab line had gotten snagged in our engine's propeller, we'd possibly be stuck there for days until help could arrive. I flashed the light once more. The faint glow produced only a small amount of precious visibility, but it enabled us to avoid the mess of floating loops—then it died! No more light! Now what?

Soon enough, we managed to scoot safely around the buoy. I took another deep breath knowing I was almost back to shore, once again. At last, we were approaching the isolated beach with much discussion about what to do next. We both agreed we should tie up the boat and try to get the fire going again.

I experienced a rush of renewed hope when I felt the boat hit bottom and I knew that we'd made it back to shore! Right then, I was aware that the glow of our campfire may very well have saved our lives! It wasn't long before the vivid reality overcame us: we would be forced to spend the night in the dark, frozen wilderness, a thought that hadn't sounded so awful when the sun was shining earlier in the day. But we were on the beach where I was confident we could survive a cold night in remote Alaska. We had food, fire, water to drink, and a tarp to keep us dry, if necessary. Right away I stripped out of my rubber jumpsuit and tossed it back into the boat for safe keeping. Although it would have continued to keep me warm, the over-sized rubber feet were causing me to stumble. I knew I had a lot of work to do if I was going to make it through the night.

My thoughts returned to Tom's parents. I knew I needed to get a message out to them, even though I couldn't get service on our cell phone no matter what I tried. On our emergency handheld unit there were three options to choose from. One button read "911." If activated, it would have beckoned emergency assistance. Even though I felt like we were indeed in an emergency, I couldn't bear the thought of seeing the Coast Guard again after what happened just two days prior when the boat's engine had blown up. A second button labeled "help" would notify our previously chosen contacts to send help ASAP but not emergency aid. The third button would calmly email our friends and family that we were "here and ok." A fourth button, in my opinion, should have been available on which I could take out my frustrations. I wanted to send out a message which would indicate that "this whole entire idea is insane," but unfortunately for me, there was no such button!

After a brief evaluation, it was decided that the selection which most appropriately indicated our situation was "here and ok." We certainly didn't need the expense of an unwanted helicopter search party on top of everything else that had gone wrong in Alaska. Using the dim light of my opened cell phone, I paid careful attention to select, before I activated the correct message button on the communication device. Although I had much more to say to his poor parents who were probably worried sick at this point, I was hopeful that once they did not receive our pre-arranged phone call that they would check their email to verify that at least we were still alive. I could only hope!

Above all, I knew it was urgent that I focus my remaining energy on surviving the night in the Alaskan wilderness.

17

Checking in at the Hell Hotel

The damp March air felt especially cold on the dark beach as I fondly recalled the friendly blue sky and beautiful winter sunshine which we'd been enjoying all day. Heavy moisture which seemed to be hanging in the air was raining down almost, and due to the chill that was settling upon us, we felt it would be wise to retrieve some additional clothing from our bags in the tent. While Tom secured the boat to the giant log, we plotted about the inevitable trip up the hill in the dark. The dim moonlight cast a few shadows here and there on the open beach but definitely not up in the woods. Soon we found ourselves on hands and knees, both of us carefully scaling the steep, forested terrain. We were on high alert. To avoid a serious mishap, we used occasional flashes of light from the cell phone to prevent a misstep off the edge of the trail. At least the phone was good for something, I thought, as I held the source of a faint bluish light outward above our path.

Instinctively, Tom and I both knew that we wouldn't be using the tent to sleep in that night. The most obvious reason was because we were in possession of only one blanket and one tarp in which to cover the sloping iceberg currently serving as the floor of our shelter. Even though we'd planned on spending the night there eventually, we anticipated bringing out quite a few more supplies before then. I wasn't the least bit interested in huddling for eight or nine hours in the pitch-black anyway; I longed for the light of a campfire which might actually provide some mental stability in the dark wilderness.

With a small amount of moonlight beginning to peek out, the beach and even the woods seemed difficult to navigate until we stepped inside the heavy canvas shelter where we could really see absolutely nothing. No reflections, no shadows, only pure blackness. With outstretched arms and flat palms we patted our way around the pile of our belongings, unzipping zippers to locate the heavy sweatshirts and extra pants. We were both shivering a bit as we rummaged through our duffle bags stuffed with spare clothes, all of which had begun absorbing moisture from Alaska's damp environment. In order to avoid another risky trip up the hill later, we figured we should grab the chainsaw and fuel while we were in the vicinity. Once we gathered our items from the tent, utilizing a backward crawl, we carefully made our way back down the hill to the beach. Now on flat ground again, under a small amount of moonlight we quickly pulled on our extra layers of clothing before suiting up with the final layer, our heavy duty insulated coveralls.

I went straight to work on the fire, or what was left of one. First I regrouped the partially burned wood back into a tight heap in the center of the mound of ashes. From the kneeling position I blew on the remaining coals and begged for a flame to emerge. A brief flicker would look promising at times, but over the next few minutes, the hope of a lasting flame eventually faded away.

Unfortunately, my many desperate attempts to rekindle the fire were unsuccessful. We'd been gone too long; consequently, after we had been on the beach about thirty minutes, we came up with a new plan. It might be a better idea to sleep in the boat while it was tied up to our crab pot buoy just a couple hundred feet off shore. We'd already spoken about the subject at great length before we'd left Oregon, and we had considered it a viable option. Of course, I'd optimistically pictured the fullest of all moons providing the optimal lighting for our peaceful stay on the flat calm water. After all, spending the entire night on a dark beach in the wilderness didn't sound too brilliant; our primary concern was being attacked by wild animals. I'd rather drown than be viciously shredded, I had decided after thinking it through. Besides, we did not want to be stuck on the beach again in the morning. We had made the all-important arrangements to meet the landing craft in Ketchikan around noon the next day in order to load their vessel with our belongings. I had no way to contact them in case we couldn't get there, and we certainly didn't want to foul up that darned schedule of which we were so proud. As it stood, we were still right on track with our original plans, even though we were living on Main Street in Blunder-ville!

Staying overnight in the boat would keep us out of reach from any dangerous animals, we schemed. Tom untied the boat and we once again piled into it before pushing ourselves away from shore. Pup was being such a good sport—loyally following our lead. As we motored unhurriedly out to the crab pot buoy, I opened my cell phone again to be able to see and then grab the line floating in the water while at the same time, taking great care not to drop my phone into the drink. As we approached, I carefully scooped up the line and handed it over to Tom so he could tie up.

There we sat, resigned to spend the long, dark night in the boat. The atmosphere was deathly quiet, but at last, I felt I could start calming down for the night. It seemed fairly safe out on the water, despite the fact we were afloat in a pitch-black silence only the remote wilderness can offer. For the next fifteen minutes, perhaps, we blindly resituated the items in the boat to prepare a place to lie down. First we cleared the deck in front of the steering cabin. It measured approximately five feet by seven feet and was the largest space available. Next, we spread out our spongy survival suits for a mattress of sorts. Then, after groping around, eventually we each found something soft on which to lay our head, and then we scooted apart as far as we could in order to allow Pup to cuddle between the two of us. For warmth, we spread our lone blanket out over us, and then unfolded the new tarp. We tucked both layers under our feet….then our hips, and finally around our shoulders, essentially pinning the tarp to the deck.

After several minutes of obnoxious crackling, the racket of the tarp quieted. Ahhh! At last we were situated for the night. We were going to get out of this mess after all! A gentle wind blew ever-so-slightly as we rested comfortably on the deck of the boat.

"There is much more space here than in the back of our car," I happily commented, and Tom instantly agreed.

We stretched out comfortably while we observed the beautiful night sky which was chock-full of stars. The crystal clear constellations twinkled against the charcoal-colored backdrop resembling a plush, black velvet curtain. As we rested peacefully, we observed all of the heavenly scenery which presented itself in a pure and flawless state. At long last, I was experiencing some much appreciated relief from our disastrous day.

Under the current circumstances, I was aware that we could be experiencing a very long night ahead but at the same time, it didn't feel like a good idea to let myself drift off to sleep….though I could have quite easily. I was silent for a time as I recounted the events of the day. What unnerved me even more than being stranded at the property today was the fact that I should have known better than to be in Alaska in the first place. Somehow, even though my instincts had warned me from early on that a six-week stint in the frozen wilderness would never end well, there I was anyway, about to give it a whirl. How did I allow myself to get talked into this situation? Love is not only blind, I concluded, it's also stupid.

At one point, I noted the stars were all but gone, and I realized that the clouds must have drifted in while I'd been rolled onto my side for a spell. Up until then, their presence had been a good target on which to focus my eyes. Now, in complete and utter darkness it was becoming difficult to keep my sanity. I could see absolutely nothing and I was even beginning to question which way was up.

As we lay in the darkness, adrift in our boat, I knew we weren't really anchored in such a way that the boat would hold steady. There was plenty of play in the line, so I knew there was a distinct possibility that we were drifting in circles, and that was probably why I felt like I was on some sort of a miserable merry-go-round. Or was it my imagination?

"I wish we could just watch the stars all night," I muttered.

It was eerily peaceful with only the soft sounds of rippling water interrupting the breath-taking silence. By then I'd convinced myself that as long as nothing changed, I'd be fine here for the night. When I popped my head up to locate the simmering pile of coals on the nearby shore, I noticed that they had finally started to produce an intermittent flame. It not only provided me with a visual reference, but at the same time I noted that our correlation to the shore was still a safe swimming distance, if necessary.

In the meantime, Tom and I spent our spare time conversing off and on about the activities we'd arranged for the following day. We also organized our timeline of events for the upcoming week so we could be most efficient when it came time to build the cabin. All the while I kept trying to get a call out to his parents. Finally, after many failed attempts, I gave up, tucking the phone inside my jump suit to keep it protected from the damp night air.

I snuggled back under the blanket once again and situated my head in a comfortable position. Regardless of all that was wrong at the moment, I was grateful that our clothes were still completely dry and I was looking forward to getting some well deserved rest.

The plywood deck of the boat had a three-inch gap between it and the boat's cold aluminum frame; consequently, the wood itself wasn't too cold to lie on. But within fifteen minutes of getting settled, a very light sprinkle had started to fall.

"Is that rain?" Tom asked disgustedly.

His remark was more of an acknowledgement than a question. I'd heard it as well, but had chosen not to mention it out loud. In a matter of minutes, the increasing sprinkle on the tarp had become a serious pitter-patter which began filling my heart with dread. The wind soon joined in, and with each gust, a slight chill traveled down my spine. Before long, a steady breeze was coming in at my neck and I was getting colder by the minute. Every subsequent blast of air became a little stronger and eventually began to lift the tarp off my shoulders each time, forcing me to have to repeatedly resituate our only protection from the elements. I said nothing as I willed myself to endure the discomforts of sleeping in a small boat afloat in the wilderness. It was exactly like I had expected it to be, only darker!

Pup was huddling against me inside my partially opened coveralls; his warm body was next to mine. At first, he'd settled in with his head resting on my shoulder, his back to me while I cradled him against my chest. As time went on, Pup was up, then down again as he kept trying to make himself more comfortable. I tried to explain to him just how sorry I was. He licked my cheek as an acceptance of my apologies before he flopped his head back down onto my outstretched arm with a thud. I reasoned with myself that as scared as I was listening to the waves starting to lap more vigorously at the boat, it was still a far cry from the fear I had dealt with earlier this evening during our hellish attempt to get back to town. At that moment, I began to understand the relevance of knowing when high tide might occur on any given day. Not having the most basic of details had given us false hope, which in turn had put us at a huge disadvantage; as a result, we were stuck in the cold wilderness all night without a good fire.

By then I had already started a Christmas list of what I wanted for our boat in the unfortunate event there was a "next time" we were stranded in the wilderness: a set of wheels that could roll us toward the water were first and a full array of sodium lights was second. Scratch that! As long as I was dreaming, how about a plane?

In spite of all the unknowns we'd been forced to sort out, we'd regrouped, and finally, with the tarp stretched clear up over our heads now, rain or not, we were all resting comfortably again under the makeshift shelter. As I laid there in the dark silence thinking about tomorrow's events, the faint sounds of small gurgling noises began to register in my ears. And although I didn't want to acknowledge the bubbles, eventually it developed into something I couldn't ignore. Soon, the noise was beckoning my full attention. But I was exhausted. Maybe it's nothing, I hoped. It sounded like an empty pop bottle filling with water after being forced to the bottom of a deep bucket. Or a better example might be a fart in a bathtub. Whatever the case, the flow of tiny bubbling noises I could hear definitely mimicked leaking water. With all my imagination I tried to associate that sound with something besides a sinking vessel, but sadly, I could not. Were my circumstances finally getting the best of me? I tried to tell myself there was nothing to worry about; I might be over-reacting. After all, I was still on high alert from the horrible evening we'd experienced already. Every few minutes I would sit up to pat my hand on the deck of the boat, just in case. I wanted to make sure that if water was leaking in, it wasn't up over the plywood floor yet. That would have been all the encouragement I needed to jump and swim for shore.

Each time I laid back down, I rewrapped my shoulders, breathed a sigh of relief and closed my eyes. But no matter what position I chose to rest my head, it always felt like a tether ball on the end of a long rope that was being swung around in large, sickening circles. Is the boat spinning or am I completely losing it? Holding on to my sanity was becoming more and more difficult as the minutes passed. In order to keep my head from swirling, I'd resigned myself to lie with my eyes wide open the rest of the night. Even if I couldn't sleep, at least I could stay warm. Under the circumstances, it sounded like a pretty fair compromise.

"Man, I wish the stars were out right now," I said.

"Yeah, I know," Tom answered regretfully.

Over and over, Tom and I repositioned the tarp to protect ourselves from the miserable, wet, cold weather that seemed to be giving us so much trouble. Forty-five minutes passed perhaps, and the boat was starting to bob around in the increasingly rough current. If I'd been on dry land and I hadn't been afraid for my life, the gentle rocking motion would've begged me to fall asleep, encouraging daylight to arrive soon. Off and on, my mind wandered to a warmer place where I was being cradled in a swinging hammock which was hanging from a majestic oak tree. But instead I was here—here in Alaska.

The gurgling noises continued. I sat up again.

"Do you hear any bubbling noises? I finally asked Tom.

For the longest time I'd been afraid to mention it. I wasn't sure I really wanted to know the real truth. He replied that he couldn't hear anything but also couldn't think of what it might be. In the meantime, Pup had become completely irritated with my inability to lie still. Now, instead of staying put when I sat up, he sat up, too, so I had to convince him to lay back down with me each time. Soon, without notice, the wind began to blow much harder. As the wave action began to get more and more turbulent, I eventually heard less of the bubbles until at last they were finally gone. What a relief!

After the change in the temperament of the water, it wasn't long before we acknowledged that the weather was clearly deteriorating. We debated whether it might be best to venture back to shore. We'd probably never be able to sleep with the violent rocking that was no doubt on the increase.

I could tell by the boat's movements that Tom had gotten up. He said nothing. I felt him crawl over me and begin fumbling around, eventually making his way to the steering cabin where he started the boat's engine. In no time we were scooting toward the beach where the small orange glow of coals barely glimmered in the winter breeze. As each minute passed, the waves grew stronger and more consistent.

"Do you think a storm's rolling in?" I questioned, in an effort to make conversation. Since I couldn't see his facial expression, maybe I'd be able to gauge his concerns by the tone in his voice.

"Must be," Tom replied in a less than enthused tone. He sounds disgusted, not scared, I thought.

The storm's arrival was sending relentless waves pounding onto the beach. I couldn't see them but as we inched toward the beach I could hear the crash… …crash…..splash as they rolled ashore. From observations made earlier in the day, we knew we would have to keep the boat from slamming into the jagged rocks off to the right of the campfire. However, the gusting wind continued to drive us straight at them with a strong rhythm and the waves just got worse and worse! By the time we approached our beach we were instinctively clinging to one thought: save our boat!

We must be fairly close to shore, I calculated, but due to the cover of darkness we couldn't discern exactly where the water stopped and the beach started. We could see the dying fire just thirty feet away, and in order to make an attempt to reach safety, we both jumped overboard into what ended up being fairly deep surf. I wasn't there long as I bounded toward the shore to grab the bow of the boat. With my coveralls on, I couldn't feel the water rushing into my boots yet, but a large splash engulfed me as I charged forward a few more steps. Depending on the wave action, we were in one to two feet of water, but each of us maintained a good grip on the boat as we battled to shift it away from the rocks. I leaned and pulled with all my might, while Tom pushed from the other side. Since we couldn't see a thing, our ongoing verbal communication was crucial.

"Whatever you do, keep a good hold," Tom boldly instructed over the crashing sounds of the waves. He was sounding more desperate which was more in line with what I was feeling.

"I am!" I hollered back right away in a determined voice.

"We've gotta keep moving to the left and I'll get it tied up as soon as I can," he planned.

I was out of breath. Using the dying fire as our gauge, we worked as a team to move the boat along the shoreline, both of us getting soaked from the activities at hand. The bucking aluminum monster continued to violently jerk us back and forth as the boat kept attempting to beach itself on the jagged rocks with each huge wave. It was evident that we were both filled with intense determination as we tugged the sturdy aluminum vessel toward the flatter ground in front of the fire. I felt the need to be extra careful to avoid getting crushed against the rocks as it violently rode the waves up and down, over and over. Since I couldn't see the boat, it was all about keeping it at arm's length and being aware of its presence. I could feel my adrenaline spike as I fought against the forces of nature. We were intensely aware that our boat would be the only way out of this horror-filled adventure; therefore, keeping it from being punctured on the rocks was far more important than being dry right about then.

Now we were in another serious battle of survival, and the strong surf tugged and pulled at the vessel while we both remained very determined to keep the boat from getting away. At the same time I was noticing how slippery the rocks were, and the force of each incoming wave wasn't helping me in my battle to stay upright. Stumbling along, instinctively I kept my eyes opened as wide as possible, trying to find my way in the darkness. In the midst of the pitch black, my eyes were drawn toward a ribbon of glitter which had become visible as a result of the crash of each wave. Now I am so scared I am seeing stars I guess, I thought to myself. What is happening to me, I wondered? Was it glowing? There was no logical explanation as to how I could've seen the glitter if it wasn't glowing somehow. But everything should be black!

Once we finally got the vessel settled down in the shallow surf at the water's edge, I encouraged Pup to jump out, and then Tom secured the bow line to one of the huge water-soaked logs on the beach. Finally, safe on land again, we were both relieved and exhausted from the battle with Mother Nature. With multiple layers of clothing, it was difficult to evaluate just how soaked I was on the outside, but I was grateful that the water hadn't penetrated through to my skin as of yet. Right then, I told myself that getting wet didn't really matter, even though it should have. It was just my way of coping with the horrible chain of events. Above all I was extremely devastated by our deteriorating circumstances.

I honestly couldn't believe that this ordeal was really taking place! This is what happens in scary movies or books—not my life! I kept to myself for a while just trying to figure out what to think of it all. I concluded right away that my onset of depression would have to take a back seat or I'd never get through this ordeal. Tom spoke only of his leaky boot which by then had filled with water. He had known of the hole for months. In fact, we'd purposely shipped all of our "second bests" to Alaska for which he was now paying the price. I didn't have a scrap of sympathy for him. In my mind, somewhere in the middle of the dark boat ride earlier this evening, the theme of the day had become "every man for himself." My immediate concern, however, was that I couldn't find the cell phone. Apparently, in the midst of the scramble to get back to shore, I'd completely lost track of its whereabouts. Without too much thought I concluded that if I got out of this one alive, the phone could easily be replaced, and I quickly moved on to the next most important task at hand: getting the fire going again.

18

Fire and Ice

Our circumstances were surreal! We really were stuck on a remote beach in Alaska. In the midst of the black hole we'd be forced to call home for the night, it had become quite obvious that the small comfort of a fire would be the only hope of getting me through the horrifying nightmare I was living. Not only would it provide some light to keep my center of balance, but the warmth it might eventually put forth would become extremely important in offsetting the cold wind, crashing waves, and the frigid temperatures which were embellished by the previous night's freshly fallen snow.

Even though there were large groupings of cedar logs littering the beach, all of the available wood offered itself to us in a frozen solid state, which had come as no surprise. With visions of a warm fire, Tom and I began to collect bits of bark, wood or anything that might help get it going again. Unfortunately for us, all of the easy pickings that had been strewn about when we'd arrived this morning had all been burned up as a result of my diligent cleanup effort earlier in the day. Now, as I began to work on the fire again, the rain was barely sizzling on the dying embers.

As I fiddled around with the fire project, I'd come to realize that in the last thirty minutes, I had apparently changed my mind about how I would rather die. Moments ago, after feeling like I was about to drown, I must have subconsciously decided that I'd rather be shredded by wild animals instead, I guess, because here I was back on the beach. But after all, being back on solid ground seemed to be the lesser of two evils for the time being, considering the water's current temperament.

The sounds of a violent storm had taken over our quiet beach and it was safe to say I was a bit jumpy. There was no mistaking the fact that in the midst of this terrifying darkness, my mannerisms were starting to resemble those of a badger. As a result, my anxiety was causing me to lurch at the slightest detection of possible movement. My heart was pounding in my chest. It didn't help that Pup had begun a ferocious growl into the night air. I wondered what might be lurking just feet away as his eyes were in full concentration on something toward the water. I tried to keep from imagining what kind of nocturnal activity normally took place on the shore. Wolves? Bears? Badgers? I didn't know.

To calm my adrenaline, I focused my attention on the fire. Flames just may deter a wild animal, I thought. I scoured my clothes for my lighter, patting either of my side pockets, my back pockets, and then my chest. It was there! Don't lose it, I warned myself as I carefully fished it out. I knew somehow I had to get a fire going again. A few minutes passed, and after having no luck in the flame department, I searched through my clothing for used tissues or gum wrappers. One pocket contained just the trash I needed, offering a glimmer of hope. I crouched down on my hands and knees again and then I lit the small assortment of crumpled paper I'd found. Next, I carefully piled the small, ice coated branches over the tiny flame while also trying to protect it from the gusting wind. Finally, the small flame burst into a miniature campfire. Oh man, this is good; just keep burning I pleaded silently. Unfortunately, the freshly cut cedar limbs crackled vigorously for only a couple of minutes before they reverted back to smoking a short time later. With my face just an inch from the coals I blew and I blew. At last a small flame erupted once again.

"Stand back," Tom directed.

Right away he began tossing splashes of saw gas onto the frozen wood. Eventually, the fire held only a weak flame, providing a small amount of light and no heat.

The campfire on which I was continually working happened to be positioned directly under a precarious cluster of trees. Earlier that afternoon, I'd made some guesses as to how the trees were even still living, let alone still standing. One large cedar was growing in a horizontal fashion with a curtain of branches hanging off the lower side. They draped down onto the beach like a 1970's hairdo. The limbs were mostly straight with a uniformly curled swoop at the very end. That eyesore inconveniently intersected with an age-old alder tree that barely had its roots anchored in anything solid. Although I couldn't see it at the moment, I knew that the whole mess was directly overhead. Over the sounds of the crashing waves, I was trying desperately to listen for the possibility of falling debris. The whirring sounds of the strong breeze whistling through the sparse winter foliage and the creaking noises created by the two interlocking trees as they see-sawed back and forth were only adding to my anxiety.

After a long struggle of collecting and then daintily stacking the burnable tinder, the fire was beginning to gather momentum. Little by little I carefully set the broken bits of cedar branches over the growing flames. With the available light, Tom had started up his chainsaw again, and was on the hunt for suitable fire material. All of the beautiful cedar branches I had begged him not to cut earlier in the day were now being pruned without an ounce of regret. Why would I care, I thought; I was probably never coming back anyway.

For a while, the freshly cut cedar bows burned like sparklers on the fourth of July. In the beginning stages, the flames looked promising and I was optimistic that the heat of a fire was only moments away. But once the cedar greens had sizzled away, the limbs were reduced to nothing but frozen twigs and the fire quickly went out, once again. We repeated the process many times over, never giving up. Eventually it would have to stay lit, I predicted.

It wasn't long before I became incensed with being repeatedly poked in the eye by the curtain of drooping branches. As a result, my hands desperately clawed through the air, high and low, feeling for any available plant life which might have the opportunity to jab me in the face before I could break it off to burn. My feet were on a mission of their own as they searched for a safe path back and forth from the fire.

As I returned in the darkness with each arm load of debris, a large, water-soaked log jutting out just before the fire managed to repeatedly trip me almost without fail. It was invisible in the black of night, appearing as a mere shadow in contrast to the occasional flicker of the weak flames. On more than one occasion, running into the unseen obstacle caused me to lose my balance, which in turn forced my armload of tinder to be ejected into mid-air. It was impossible to safely catch my fall, so the bruises on my shins were piling up in a hurry. My toes also hurt from being jammed over and over after slamming into the undetectable barrier.

As the night wore on, I was becoming afraid to even move, but it was necessary for us to continue our hunt for anything that might be burnable. At this point, my toes and fingers were the only parts of my body that were numb. If I kept busy, I knew I could stay warm enough although the warmth of a fire would've been a huge boost. It was only when I remained inactive that I began to shiver a little. The current situation felt pretty bleak, but by then I had confidence that we could make it through the night. In an attempt to gauge my mental stability, I chatted with Tom about the sparkly water I had seen while dragging the boat to shore earlier in the evening. He told me that he had heard of the phenomenon before, which I learned had something to do with phosphorous in the water. I was relieved to know that was all it was and it didn't involve my already questionable sanity.

Even though we'd been stuck since 2 o'clock this afternoon, I hadn't considered that we were in danger until the daylight disappeared. Now I felt officially stranded.

It was perhaps four long hours into our battle on the black beach before the endless darkness had begun to wear on me. Our joint assumption was that it might be midnight. By then I was physically drained and emotionally exhausted. My husband seemed to be the logical person on which to take out my frustrations. I silently blamed him for the whole mess. Between the two of us, the beaching incident was definitely in his department. We spoke very little for the next couple of hours while we tried to come to grips with our current state of affairs.

Unfortunately for Tom, during the hours of lonely silence, my negative emotions were beginning to stir. The longer I dwelled on the reality of our situation, the more I resented Tom. I couldn't determine if our circumstances were a direct result of his negligence or just a horrible affliction of bad luck.

Maybe I'd been too naive and should have been paying more attention to my gut instincts. Either way I was leaning toward the fact that the whole mess just might be due to his error. Although I had been involved in some of the decisions in getting here, it didn't help that every once in a while he'd say, "Sorry, Sweetie." That indicated to me that he knew it was his fault.

During the previous hours Tom and I had spent together, I'd been too afraid for my life to even consider getting angry. Now that some time had passed, my panicky feeling began to dissipate and I was well on my way to being furious!! After the last three miserable days, all of which we'd spent in beautiful Alaska, I had come to the conclusion that we had absolutely no business being here, especially in the winter! If I'd thought for one second that I'd have to endure such a long list of unbearable circumstances, I never would have committed to this crazy trip in the first place. I was filled with dread as I thought ahead to all we had in store for the remainder of our stay, knowing that we still had more than a month of activities planned for the expedition. I wasn't sure if I could hack six grueling weeks.

By the time I'd finished processing the most recent events, it felt as if my eyes were ablaze and could've burned a hole in the atmosphere. It had been a slow boil, but the "feisty" in me had finally surfaced. Tom, on the other hand, remained cool as a cucumber. I began to compare our very different personalities, and I was now convinced that this well-planned adventure might well be my husband's dream, but this excursion had long ago exceeded my expectations of my personal nightmare! But what would arguing do for me now? Nothing, I decided.

It seemed like it should have been three o'clock in the morning, judging by how long we'd been shuffling around in complete darkness. The tide was still in pretty close to the struggling fire, so we were quite certain it couldn't have been that late. We figured that if low tide had been at five o'clock, then by eleven o'clock the tide would be at its highest point. That was about when we had come back to the beach. That sounded about right. Maybe it was one o'clock by now.

Since our estimations were that we had at least five hours before daybreak, Tom went to lie down on the tarp. Pup went with him at first, but wouldn't stay; he returned to my side, keeping me company as I kept prodding at our struggling fire. Although I felt some protection from the unknown just having a flickering light to stand behind, I still felt terrified. I was completely disgusted that Tom had left me alone to tend to our life line. And although I knew he hadn't given up, I couldn't figure out why he wasn't helping. Wasn't he cold? What about the team effort? Again, Pup glared into the night air toward the water. Did he see something? There was a little more exposed beach now; I could tell by how far away the sounds of waves were. Was something walking around on the beach, I wondered? His airplane-ears were out again as he growled ferociously while he backed up into me until he was leaning against my legs. In a frantic whisper I pleaded with Tom to please get up. If an animal was creeping around, I wanted his eyes and ears to be functioning too. He didn't answer at first, or if he did, I couldn't hear him.

"Sweetie!" I snapped again.

"What!" He finally muttered.

"Get up, please? Pup hears something again!" I ordered.

By then, the fire was steadily burning, but it had yet to give off any warmth. There was no doubt in my mind that under the current conditions, a fire could very well be the only thing that might preserve what was left of my sanity. It was maybe two o'clock in the morning when Tom offered to trek out onto the dark beach to get our cooler which was still out in the boat. I was still too wound up to eat and too mad to acknowledge that he had even one good idea, so I quickly declined his offer. As he disappeared from the glow of the firelight, I listened to his feet tromp through the puddles in the wet sand.

He came back a few moments later only to mention under his breath that when he had stepped into the boat, there was water up over his ankles.

"What!?" I yelped, as I turned to face him, instantly hopeful that I'd misunderstood what he'd just said. My closed fists had firmly planted themselves, one on each hip as I waited for some sort of an explanation.

He repeated himself ever-so-calmly. "For some reason, there are a few inches of water in the boat."

"How?" I demanded to know.

"I have no idea," Tom relied.

I could not believe what I was hearing. If he could have seen the look in my eyes, he would have run for his life right then. For the next few minutes my tongue began to impersonate Satan himself as I spitefully recited all of the reasons why we had no business being out here. At that instant I decided that he alone was to blame for this entire mess!

"This really is a ridiculous idea to expect we could actually come up here in the middle of nowhere, with snow on the ground and build a freakin' cabin! Not to mention," I continued, "we put our trust in a boat you never even put in the water, which had an engine you never tested properly which proceeded to blow up after seven whole minutes of full throttle costing us $5,800 we didn't have!"

I thought for another second. "Right then we should have gone home and never looked back," I snapped.

He murmured something, but I was in no mood to listen as I interrupted, "Follow that up with the beaching of our skiff, forcing us to spend this miserable night in the freezing cold weather," I paused. "And clear up in Alaska?" I said accusingly.

Well....this was his big idea, not mine!

I felt my vocal cords began to tighten. Tears were on the way, but I knew crying would have only made matters worse. Shedding even one droplet of my own salt water would have been a waste of my precious energy. I needed to stay strong.

"So, our boat does have a leak in it, and I did hear bubbling noises. We never would have made it to town!" I announced. "This is just perfect!" I yelled into the night air.

I couldn't wait to get out of Alaska right then. And I was never coming back! What a disaster!! I tried to sort out the recent events, only concluding that our far-fetched plan was completely insane! The thought crossed my mind that due to our possible boat damage, we might be there indefinitely. However, Tom's demeanor was letting on that it was just another minor setback. I knew quizzing him any further may have started an all out war because I was in no mood to hear another peep out of him for a while.

In typical Tom fashion, my sweet husband gave me several minutes of quiet time. I had calmed down some and was crouched by the fire in deep thought, once again.

"I hope the weather is better tomorrow so we can get our materials loaded," he said in a cheerful, upbeat tone.

"Are you kidding?" I snarled as I rose to my feet again. "Have you heard anything I just said? If I wasn't stuck here fifteen miserable miles from civilization, I'd be organizing a garage sale to get rid of everything we owned, followed by a direct flight back to Seattle so I could put this dreadful experience behind me." Knowing I had hours of terrifying darkness still ahead I opted out on further argument.

Following our brisk discussion, I once again resorted to silent stares into the flames of our fire. It was a relief to finally feel some warmth, which come to think of it, might have been from my own rage-induced adrenaline. I began to reflect on the gurgling noises I'd heard in the boat earlier this evening. Now it made sense that they'd disappeared, just like they do when a sunken bottle is finally full of water at the bottom of a bucket, for crying out loud!

What am I going to do, I pondered? I honestly couldn't visualize spending one more miserable day in Alaska. It felt like another long hour might have passed while I was in deep thought. At last with some real heat radiating from the hot bed of coals, all three of us clung to the fire. Tom removed his wet sock from his cold, shriveled foot. By then I'd come out of my temper tantrum, and I felt somewhat sympathetic but not yet overly friendly. I twisted it tightly to wring it out and then draped it over a stick which I'd propped nearly on top of the crackling yet almost cold winter flame.

Eventually the sock dried out some and Tom plucked it from the warmth of the fire.

"It's just gonna get soaked inside my boot again," he mumbled as he leaned against the log to reinsert his foot.

"Get a bread bag or something out of the cooler then!" I coldly suggested. That seemed like an obvious solution.

He slipped his wet boot back on to make a trip out to the boat to retrieve a bag from the cooler.

As the night wore on, our exhausted Pup kept whining, begging me to lay down with him. There was no time for that. I needed to stay vigilant. But in an effort to make him comfortable, I resorted to scrunching our new tarp into a pile at my feet which were all but planted in the flames of the campfire. With my encouragement, Pup collapsed against my legs and slid to the ground where he curled up under the continual shower of sparks, somehow confident that I would keep watch over him in order to prevent his thick fur from igniting.

Maintaining the fire had become an all consuming task. Once the frozen wood was cut and split, I found that it wouldn't consider burning until I had leaned each separate piece on end around the fire for at least an hour. That lengthy wait-time allowed each frosty segment of wood an ample amount of time to thaw. Only then, the sopping wet wood was able to be moved to the next stage, the attempted burning. Without occasional splashes of gasoline and streams of dripping bar oil, I'm certain that our fire would have had no chance of ever showing a single flame.

Due to hours of endless searching for fire material, my frozen hands felt stinging-raw after peeling bark from anything I could find. Plus, I had implanted numerous thorns in my right hand after mistakenly groping, and then trying to uproot the same devil's club, not once but twice. Prickly reminders of that unfortunate incident would plague my fingers for days to come. During one of my many searches, I had tripped so violently that I barely caught myself before almost landing face first onto the cold slimy rocks. At that instant, the fire just happened to be roaring from additional splashes of gasoline. The bright light currently reflecting off the wet rocks allowed me to catch a fleeting glimpse of my phone as it shot from my coveralls and clattered onto the beach. Before I could grab it, I accidentally kicked it farther forward as I continued to stumble toward the water.

"I found the phone," I cheerfully announced, as I regained my composure. That was the first sign I'd witnessed thus far which would indicate that our luck might finally be turning around.

Like zombies, we spent much of our time staring into the flickering flames. Tom and I continued to quiz each other on what time it might have been. We couldn't even venture a guess at this point. I continued to watch the skies.

"Are those clouds or daylight?" I questioned more than once. As we waited patiently, hour after hour, the sky eventually turned from a hopeless jet black, to a hopeful dark gray. I can't explain the relief I had when I realized that dawn was finally approaching. Just having a little light encouraged our moods to pick up tremendously. I could see again, even though it wasn't much at first. But as daylight began to shed light on our circumstances, we became very excited about the possibility of actually getting off the beach.

Even though the winter weather was cold and dreary, I felt grateful to still be alive that morning. Once we had enough visibility to find our way around, Tom unscrewed the steel plug in the stern of the boat in order to let the water drain before the tide returned. We were still wondering why the boat had filled up with water in the first place. We were hopeful that it wasn't going to be an urgent problem which would require extensive repair, ultimately keeping us from getting back to town. Had the violent crashing against the rocks punctured the hull?

Eventually, as the tide came in higher and higher, Tom began to notice that with each surge of the waves, water was actually squirting back into the boat again. I was in shock! I looked on as he frantically felt all around with his bare hands in order to pinpoint the source of the incoming stream. He shoved the cooler aside and quickly removed the lid to the battery compartment, and then, out came the battery with a thud. At last, inside the battery compartment he located the culprits causing the leak. There they were: four wide-open bolt holes left from where the old engine had been mounted.

"Are you serious," I bleated? Can this really be happening, I wondered? This unbearable ride is never going to end, I concluded! During this adventure in which I'd agreed to partake, I found myself just trying to endure the events by the minute, not by the hour or day, let alone the week.

Needless to say, the confusion I experienced was ongoing. I guess, since Tom was the lifelong fisherman in the family, I'd put all my trust in his boat preparations before coming to Alaska. I imagined it was not unlike the confidence he put in me to make sure we were warm and fed. Although many of the boat's key functions were in order, I'd become aware after the recent engine failure that our vessel didn't have even the most basic of necessities on board: a scoop to bail water. Giving him the benefit of the doubt, I considered that maybe this is how all fishermen operate, flying by the seat of their pants. In the meantime, my definition of trust was being re-evaluated. It was becoming quite clear to me that, ultimately, my life was in my own hands, not my husband's. With my personal destiny in mind, I consciously began to custom fit my thoughts in that direction! From then on I doubt I was very good company, but I didn't care! On top of everything else, I resented him most for not taking me seriously. A light bulb should've not only flicked on, but it should have exploded in his head when I inquired about the bubbling noises. He'd installed the blasted engine himself only two days ago!

Before long, Tom was able to plug the holes with some sticks he'd rounded up, and soon he was in search of a scoop to get the water overboard. As it turned out, it was a good thing that I had kept the ice bucket from the motel. With that, Tom ambitiously worked on bailing water until the tide was high enough to float the boat. After some discussion, I began to understand that the holes would not be an urgent concern as long as the boat was traveling at a reasonable speed; therefore, our trip off the beach this morning would not be hampered after all. Since the bow of the boat comes out of the water during travel, the boat's position on the water puts pressure at the stern, which more or less sprays the water away from the holes. The bolt holes became particularly problematic when the boat was just floating, and even more so with the lapping waves attacking it when we were anchored to the crab buoy where we optimistically thought we'd sleep for the night. In spite of it all, as soon as our ride was fully afloat, without hesitation, we loaded up to leave, knowing we had an appointment to keep that day.

The ride back to town was fairly rough, but nothing was going to ruin my mood after out-lasting such a difficult experience. A renewed personal strength had emerged from my lengthy spell in the depths of despair. I knew right then that even though our first three days in Alaska had presented quite a challenge; it was the previous twelve hours that would change who I would forever be. As we motored along across the frigid water, I clung to the new found feelings of self-preservation and determination in order to make sure they soaked deep into my soul. They would never be forgotten.

It took us forty-five minutes, not twenty like we originally thought, before we found ourselves paralleling the edge of town again. What a welcome sight it was to see our car in the parking lot as we motored toward the jetty. The night before, everything in my life had been at a standstill simply trying to survive. But in spite of it all, I'd found the will to make it through. As we were approaching the boat launch, just hearing the familiar noise of vehicle traffic as it traveled along the waterfront road seemed to be comforting while also reminding me of the fact that "the beat goes on." But it would take several hours for me to return to a relaxed state after experiencing the previous night's drama. I enjoyed being in the moment as at last we'd safely arrived at the boat launch. After pulling the boat out of the water, I called to make reservations at the motel where we would not only spend the night, but also take the next of couple hours to dry our gloves and get our belongings back in order for the next trip out.

By then, I was able to get some perspective on everything that had happened. It wouldn't be long before we'd be able to take showers and put on a happy face. Our plans were to meet up with the delivery service in a couple of hours and we certainly didn't want to appear as if we had been up all night struggling to survive in the wilderness. After all, we'd just finished experiencing one full dose of pure Alaskan paradise!

Before leaving the boat launch, Tom called his parents. They'd no doubt been up most of the night, worried sick! In two vague sentences he summed up the most horrifying adventure I'd ever been on.

"Yeah, it got too dark so we decided to stay the night there at the property," he said, nonchalantly. I turned to glare at him, listening in shock as he cheerfully minimized all we'd just been through. The dismay and utter disbelief of what calmly flowed from his lips took just a split second to register on my face.

"But we're in town now and we're going to get a motel room, and then get our materials loaded this afternoon. So I'll talk to ya later," he finished, and then hung up.

What?! I thought.

"That's it?" I snapped. "Well, that's not how I would have put it!" I interjected. The old saying must be true, opposites do attract, and I have definitely found mine. His name is Tom.

19

Surviving Camp Alaska

Day 4

After enduring a violent storm during a miserable night in the dark Alaskan wilderness, I chose to put the horrible experience behind me as we drove into town with our boat in tow. A new day offered new hope even though the weather this morning consisted of sheets of blowing rain that wouldn't quit. We were so relieved to make it to the motel. After sorting out the rude comments of the outspoken hotel clerk, I realized that Tom and I both smelled like a walking batch of smoked fish, obviously due to the intense odors we had absorbed as we were huddled around the campfire all night. On any other day I might have been offended, but her observations didn't phase me a bit after all I'd recently been through. Once we moved into our room, the first order of business was to start drying our boots and gloves. Then, while I gathered up all the wet, smoky clothes for the laundry, Tom called the father/son team who owned the landing craft in order to confirm our meeting time later today.

After a hot shower and a quick snack, I felt refreshed and began to feel renewed optimism about our proposed adventure. What a shift in my thinking! From inside the warm motel room it was much easier to imagine our upcoming plans being successfully completed. Even though I was exhausted, I was still very anxious to get to the dock to transfer all the contents of the shipping container onto the hired landing craft. Noon was the confirmed time we would commence with the transfer of our cargo, and the container transport company had already shuttled our shipping container from their facility to a spot over at the city dock where the noontime activity would take place. Our cargo was now positioned along side the railing near the crane, then when the landing craft showed up, it would be stationed in perfect position at the lower dock directly below the crane.

An hour before the hired help had been scheduled to arrive, Tom and I made our way to the dock to get a head start. It would be a little different this time. For the loading project in Seattle, our container had been sitting on pavement. But now in Ketchikan, our container was perched approximately four feet off the ground on a semi-trailer chassis which would require some extra effort on our part. We unlocked our cargo and I climbed up inside using the rungs mounted on the back of the trailer. After doing a quick inventory, it appeared that everything in the container had made the long trip without any obvious harm. Several bundles of insulation were heavy with water, but that damage had happened previously on our rain-soaked trip to Seattle.

Right away I began handing the cargo down to Tom. As I weeded through our supplies, I was comforted by the familiar sights from home. Regrettably, I couldn't ignore the lasting effects of my recent devil's club encounter which was causing me some pain while handling the heavy cargo. But I couldn't complain because at the moment, the appreciation I felt for being safe on land far overshadowed my discomforts of thorns and fatigue.

Tom and I energetically sorted and then set many of the larger items off to one side and within the hour the landing craft had arrived and was moored at the dock below. We spent a moment admiring their beautifully polished, all-aluminum vessel. It was forty-two feet long with a raised wheelhouse stationed at the stern. The captain's headquarters were located up high over the engine room. The remainder of the boat offered a spacious deck, which unlike our small boat, was purposely designed for packing substantial amounts of cargo in and around Alaska's remote areas. For ease of unloading, the bow of their boat offered a sturdy, hinged ramp which would be lowered onto the beach the next day when we unloaded our materials.

To get started, the younger of the two men came up on the dock to run the crane which would lift bundle after bundle of our supplies up over the railing, then down fifteen feet to their boat. The father stood by on the landing craft. As each pile was lowered down, he took charge of determining how to strategically stack the supplies. Once the bundle was in place, he would unhook straps and the crane would return to the dock where Tom and I would have another pile strapped up and ready to go. At that point, we would hook another load back to the boom.

Like robots, we repeated the unloading, strapping, and stacking process. The driving rain refused to let up, so the first wave of relief came when the shipping container was at last empty and all the main items were successfully stacked on the deck of their vessel.

Once the bulk of the load had been transferred, we began to focus on the odds and ends we had set aside earlier. This included the guns, canning supplies, a portable saw mill and chainsaw, and all of our plastic totes and boxes along with the windows. The weather sensitive boxes were going to be stored inside their engine room overnight to keep them out of the wind and rain, while the new windows were carefully secured to the back railing. But before we were able to get all of our personal items aboard, the landing craft was out of room; consequently, some of our belongings had to be crammed into the car and would have to be shuttled to the property at a later date.

It took two solid hours working at full speed for the four of us to transfer all of the cargo. At last we were finished. We headed back to the motel, soaked, starved and sleep deprived, but very happy to have gotten this difficult task accomplished. After we changed into dry clothes and ate lunch, we promptly moved on to the next mission: preparing to build the cabin.

We had the rest of the day to get organized for the next phase of the project, which entailed organizing our provisions for "roughing it" in a frozen land! Our first trip to the property had already given us a good idea of what to expect. We knew that once we left for the property the next morning there might not be an opportunity to get back to town for a few days. It would be of utmost importance that we gather the bare necessities so that we would be prepared to survive for up to a week in the great Alaskan wilderness.

During our isolation the night before, we'd had plenty of time for discussion, so Tom and I had already talked the next task to death. Without further conversation we each got busy. Tom's job was to sort the contents of both the car and boat to make sure everything necessary to start our building project made it to the property on the first trip. While Tom was busy outside, I was mostly inside with lists which were checked and double checked for critical components for staying warm and fed once we arrived on site. The bedding and clothing were readied. Batteries were charged and flashlights packed. Medicine, band aids, tweezers, lighter, paper and related items were scratched off the list. Just a block away at the grocery store I picked up enough food, drink and toilet paper for a week. The one good thing about the freezing cold weather was that we wouldn't need ice for our cooler. For cooking I would have the choice of either an electric griddle or propane burner. I was very much aware that eating hot, well-balanced meals would be an important factor for us making good progress in the frigid weather.

Once the preparations had been completed, we phoned the relatives to let them know we'd most likely be out of touch for a few days. By 7 p.m. our goals for the day were accomplished, so we gratefully climbed into bed. We fell asleep with everything in order, hopeful that we'd experience more cooperative weather in the morning.

Day 5

There was neither wind nor rain as we left the motel and headed for the boat launch this morning, both of us fired up to start our day. Once the boat was in the water, we loaded a few more items from the car. My heart was filled with mixed emotions when I climbed aboard this time. I was aware of how very lucky we were that it had all worked out like it did. We could've been half way to town in the dark when the storm hit the night before. Even worse, we could've had engine failure at some point during the dark commute in the midst of a winter storm. I still had just as much respect for the water, but I had more confidence in my coping abilities, and of course, I was now fully tuned in to my gut instincts!

The boat ride out to the property was pleasantly uneventful! What a relief! I wondered if today would be a better day. How could it not? Even though

A likely view; crab cooker and waders on the deck.
The beautiful stone walkway to the beach.

Portable sawmill after we'd finished cutting a slab of cedar.

Eco-friendly facilities.

Some spectacular colors of the evening sunset as the tide was receding.

A freshly cut stack of cedar lumber which was put to use as siding on the cabin.

Our cabin all buttoned up as we said good-bye following our first visit.

Tom breaking a sweat with the log peavey, rolling one of our
cedar logs to the water so we could tow it home.

Tammy displaying part of the daily catch after a fishing excursion in fall '09.

Our boat's first outing at the boat launch in Ketchikan.

One of the many brilliantly colored starfish on our beach.

The gorgeous sights from our beach one summer evening.
Our boat's haul-out line is visible in the water.

Drying out some of our clothes over the fire on our second day at the property.

An intriguing view from our beach while we were cutting lumber in the fall.

Typical-looking crab pot fresh out of the water during our summer stay.

Our refuge from the storm as seen from the beach.

Inside the cabin.

Rustic towel rack.

the skies were still a dismal gray, the storm had passed through and the atmosphere on the beach was calm and quiet now. What a difference. As we came ashore, I felt a new reverence for remote Alaska. It had been thirty-six hours since we'd unexpectedly fought to stay alive there all night….and won!

Right away, we looked around to find the best place for the delivery boat to unload. For an outfit who provides remote delivery service, the tide can be very problematic; therefore, planning around the tide is absolutely crucial. After getting beached ourselves two days earlier, we fully understood the consequences of bad timing in conjunction with tidal changes. We were all in complete agreement on what time the delivery should occur—we didn't want the landing craft to get stuck either. Since we calculated that it would take us about two hours to unload, the optimal time to start would be two hours before the morning's high tide. Since the water level would be constantly rising, the boat would be on its way back to town before the tide began to recede.

There were two other reasons it made sense to unload at that time. The higher the tide, the less distance it was for us to pack the materials to our camp. Also, it would give us a full twelve hours before the next high tide to move it all even farther out of harm's way. According to the tide book, the tides were going to get higher each day. In other words, any piles which were stacked at the high tide line today would have to be moved before the next high tide tonight or we'd take the chance of our supplies floating away. I began to understand that our new lifestyle was one that allowed no mental down-time, ever!

Before the transport vessel arrived, we unloaded our own boat full of supplies, which included our tools, groceries, camping supplies and a few boxes of the cabin's components which hadn't made it on the delivery vessel. The landing craft arrived shortly thereafter, and once on scene, the men agreed that our beach was indeed too flat for a safe unload. We ended up down the beach approximately an eighth of a mile where their craft could belly up to a rock cliff during the delivery process. Unloading at that location allowed a safe depth of water under their engine. Once the landing craft was headed back to town, we would begin the arduous task of transferring all of building materials an extra few hundred yards to our property. Some would be done by hand, but most of the lumber and plumbing, for instance, was loaded back onto our boat and dropped off on our beach. Unloading so far away from our camp was a bummer, but the main problem it solved would be well worth our extra efforts; the delivery company wouldn't have the chance of getting stuck on the beach" until the next high tide.

Once their vessel was in position, the ramp was lowered so that just the end of it was supported by the rocks near the steep drop-off. The quick unloading of our materials went very smoothly. The elder of the two men stayed in the wheelhouse to watch gauges, ensuring that their boat maintained a safe distance from the jagged rocks. While the three of us unloaded, we chatted about several topics that morning, one of which was the ravens we had encountered on our last trip out. We were noticing those same black birds over on our beach hopping around as we conversed. Those rascals appeared to be snooping around in the provisions we had unloaded from our boat just an hour earlier. But we weren't concerned. After our previous run-in with the culprits, we were already aware that the birds were terrible kleptomaniacs; consequently, we'd made sure that everything had been safely covered up. The delivery guys related a few raven stories of their own. We laughed out loud about what a nuisance the birds were.

Unfortunately for us, the laughing didn't last too long. Once the delivery boat departed for town, we loaded our own boat to begin shuttling our supplies over to our beach. As we came ashore we quickly realized exactly what the thieves had been up to while we were a convenient distance away. To our surprise, the card board box sealed with duct tape lay torn wide open with its contents exposed. Bags of household items were torn open as well as our toilet paper. The further we investigated, the more we realized that somehow the ravens had found a way to get into just about everything! The large, plastic-wrapped bathroom faucet package had been extricated from its box and then carelessly hurled onto the beach. Parts from the new bathroom sink were cleverly plucked from their package as well. The small plastic pieces were still in bags, fortunately, but randomly strewn about.

Even though I thought I had sufficiently covered our groceries with an overturned laundry basket weighted down with a box of goods, apparently I hadn't. Therefore, the groceries took the worst of the beating as the displaced laundry basket now sat off-kilter. A full case of pop had been torn apart and emptied with several cans punctured and leaking. The rest of the pop cans, which were rolled out from underneath, lay scattered in the rocks, peppered with beak dents. The soda box itself was so tattered it couldn't even be reused. As we began to gather the salvageable groceries back into the laundry basket, we noticed the twelve pack of pudding had been ripped open, and the entire contents had gone missing! Almost all of Pup's dog biscuits had disappeared from their package as well, and Pup's sandwich bag full of "lamb starter" had been tasted several times but not emptied. At this point, we were wondering where we had left our car keys earlier this morning, and what else might be gone for good. I stood with my hands on my hips and took a few deep breaths to gather my thoughts.

Honestly, I don't know why I was so surprised. This latest setback wasn't the first indicator that this camping endeavor wasn't going to be easy!

20

Alone in the Wilderness

Soon it became obvious to us that the ravens were not just occasional free-loaders. Tom's weapons were with us now, and the birds understood that it was to their benefit to keep their distance as long as he packed his gun. They were clearly experienced thieves who'd been through a similar routine before. Eventually, one raven slipped up, presenting Tom with an opportunity. One raven down. It wasn't long before the ring leader had rounded up another rookie to boss around, and after only a brief reprieve, the camp robbers were at it again. From then on, every waking moment became a battle to keep our belongings intact. Anything important was kept in a covered tote. At that moment, war was declared between the two parties!

After cleaning up the ravens' mess, we made numerous trips back and forth down the beach to shuttle the majority of our materials over to our property. There was a huge stack of plywood and lumber as well as our shower, water tank, and windows and our entry door. Bundles of insulation, two ladders, and our large pile of floor joists were also rounded up. There were boxes of nails, household supplies, a boot dryer and propane tanks. Everything but the trusses and metal roofing got transported to our property. Next, our focus became all about setting up camp.

Up the hill in our tent I got right to work organizing our clothes and bedding. Since the sloping, uneven hillside consisted mostly of ice covered moss, it would have been futile to set the bed right on the ground. So for the next few days, a piece of plywood would provide a flat surface for our mattress. While one edge of the plywood remained sitting on the ground, a stack of eight boards propped up the other side of our makeshift sleeping arrangement. That adjustment made the platform level, and as a result, one side of the bed was about a foot off the ground. With our foam mattress and a few blankets, it would be where we all tried to sleep for the next few freezing nights.

To compound the reality of our lonely existence, the less than friendly winter weather made it a rare sight to see any other boats out and about. If there had been other traffic, an outsider's observation may have been that we were the designated hosts of a three-family garage sale. Boxes and leaning stacks of junk littered the pristine shoreline, and judging by the large piles of materials at the base of the steep trail, we knew it would be many moons before we could walk up the hill empty handed.

The mess was unsettling at first, but we were aware that dealing with the chaos would be temporary. Our small yet sufficient cabin was destined to be sixteen feet wide by twenty feet long with a covered deck on one end, while the longest side facing the beach would have three large windows to enjoy the beautiful views. We were optimistic that the initial framing of the cabin would progress quickly.

The first day at the property could have been referred to as hectic, but not overwhelming. With the majority of our provisions on site, our focus would shift to building the cabin. Because of our past experience as general contractors, the building stage of the project was a minor detail. A simple cabin on flat ground would have been no problem, but a small cabin on an untidy, sloping forest floor in remote Alaska did pose a few challenges. Nature's mess had squashed any hopes of a clean, flat building site, at least in our short timeframe. Rotten logs which had fallen years ago were lying crisscrossed, now covered in a thick carpet of moss and snow.

Since we had done some logging before, dealing with the ever-present tangle of brush and decaying wood wasn't too discouraging either. Of course, we knew from experience that a piece of heavy equipment would have made quick work of the mountain of debris, but having machinery available was clearly a fantasy. It was obvious that instead of us being in charge of what was happening, it was Mother Nature who had the reins and we were going to do the best we could to work around her obstacles. All in all, there were two daunting challenges that we faced. The first and foremost would be surviving the bitter cold temperatures. The second was being in a remote camp where we couldn't count on the convenience of running for supplies at a moment's notice.

It was certainly chilly as it snowed off and on the first day there. We were excited to learn that the crab pot Tom had set out during the last visit had caught its first crab. To cook up our first catch, Tom boiled a pot of water he'd collected from the creek. I started the generator in order to get the electric skillet heated up. We consumed the lone crab, along with a deluxe hamburger and fried potatoes. Delicious!

That evening as I was cooking dinner on the beach, I tried my best to get a fire going. I envisioned how wonderful it would feel to sit near it to warm up while we ate. Optimistically, I'd thought that our horrible night had been a stroke of bad luck and our future experiences might be different. Unfortunately, it did nothing but smoke, and smoke, and then smoke some more. I refused to give in that easily, so I crumpled plenty of paper, snapped mountains of twigs, and fanned the short-lived flames. Nothing! Admitting defeat, I headed up the hill for the night. After the experience on the beach a couple of nights ago, I should have expected as much.

Since it was dark and we had no fire, we retired fairly early. The beloved tent, which our good friends had graciously loaned us for the trip, was an age-old canvas shelter. Although it was reminiscent of something out of an old war movie, for many years it had served as a suitable hunting refuge. The tent had the ambience of a snow cave; and as a result, it was not surprising that we could see our own breath as we got ready for bed. For us, its main purpose was to provide rain and snow cover, not warmth. For that, we unboxed the gifts Tom's parents had sent along: a propane heater and a lantern. Our first night there we put them to good use. The instant heat felt fabulous!

Even though a tarp and a piece of carpet were providing a floor for the shelter, our feet became wet and numb while getting ready for bed. Even with the extra precautions, we'd unintentionally tracked snow into our sleeping quarters. That evening, we sat on the edge of the bed for a moment with our legs outstretched toward the flames in order to absorb all of the radiating warmth. Following that, we put on dry socks before climbing into our frosty bed. As a luxury, we kept the heater glowing on high for a couple hours until the propane canister ran out. The unit didn't ever come close to warming up the tent, but it scared away the dampness from one edge of our pillows as we settled in for the night. With all three of us cuddled together, we eventually managed to get rid of the goose bumps and fall asleep.

The first night at camp we were understandably concerned about wild animals bothering us. There were worrisome gaps here and there along the tent's bottom edge due to the unmanageable terrain on which we were perched. Occasionally I glanced around the poorly lit sleeping area with lurking animals in mind. With the odor of food in the air, we weren't sure what might unfold, even though we hadn't seen a bear or any other animal tracks in the snow.

As we lay in bed, Tom kept his loaded gun beside him and I tucked the bear spray under my pillow. It was after I'd been asleep for a short time when I was awaked by a scratching noise. It sounded like the movements of a mouse. I flicked on the lantern, just to make sure that's all it was. Pup instantly caught a glimpse of the varmint and shot out of bed. He energetically began rummaging through our mountain of duffle bags looking for the critter he never found, which kept him busy most of the night.

My thoughts raced back to a time when we'd lived in the rat-infested trailer in Oregon. Back then, we'd always kept the car parked next to the trailer which was inside the barn. On one particular day I had been perplexed as to how several items of clean clothing had ended up in the filthy gravel underneath the car's engine. On hands and knees, the first item I had rescued had been a pair of socks. But there was more. I had been in shock as I pulled into view my fluffy fleece sweatshirt from which the entire sleeve had been removed. Simultaneously, a light bulb had gone on in our heads….rats! Tom had popped the hood of the car and had slowly lifted it skyward. In the engine compartment he instantly had discovered an eagle-sized nest complete with a curled-up, sleeping rat.

"Get me something!" he'd frantically demanded.

I hadn't been moving fast enough for him, of course. My initial reaction had been to shriek while Tom went into overdrive as he'd reached for anything close by which he might have used to trap, maim, or kill the rat. Like the Tasmanian Devil, he'd snatched a potential rat trapping utensil while keeping one of his eyes on the rodent. It still had managed to scurry over to the passenger side of our engine compartment, and down into a cavity under the hood's hinge. The next thing I knew, Tom had announced that he'd had the rat pinned with a broom handle. I'd heard him ranting about something, but he had been speaking too quickly, much faster than my mind had been able to process. I'd glanced briefly at the fluffy nest for which our camp had supplied the building materials. Yellow insulation was the most obvious, which had also been joined by bits of my recognizable clothing....but I was supposed to have been on rat detail at the moment, so my concentration had returned to that urgent subject. When I sorted out some of the words I'd heard him chattering, I'd been pretty certain Tom had been expecting me to reach my hand inside of the car's engine compartment in order to remove the supposed speared rat.

"What?" I had asked, hopeful I'd heard wrong.

"Quick! Reach in there and grab him!" Tom had ordered.

"You do it," I had replied.

"Just grab it by the tail," Tom had instructed, even though he had been still pinning the critter down.

"I can see that he's dead," Tom had confidently informed me.

"What if he's not dead?" I had processed out loud. Neither of us had been able to accurately determine the rat's condition no matter where we stood. All we had been able to see was the hind end and tail. Tom's idea had sounded like a horrible proposal. I had been less than eager, knowing that all of the skin on my right hand might be shredded during the quick attempt to pull it free. Now, in the heat of the moment, it had been necessary to collect my courage, which for the moment had fled to a safe place far, far away.

The frantic dialogue had continued. Tom had refused to let up pressure while at the same time he had tried to convince me that Ratty was dead.

"My hand is too big to get in there anyway," he had eventually testified.

I had thought logically for a moment. The varmint had not been showing signs any of movement, not even the tail. Reluctantly, I had donned a rubber glove and began the gruesome extraction project, inching my hand out of my sight, feeling a pathway toward the victim, at the same time wondering if its partner was in the vicinity waiting to retaliate. Finally I had hold of the hard cord-like tail. Tom had gradually released the pressure on his rat-killing wand while I had tugged the limp body out back out of the opening which I had threaded my arm through. The rat had felt heavy, but dead. Immediately following its extraction, I had flung it onto the ground with a screech.

Once it had been out in full view, curiosity had returned our eyes to the nest. We had inspected our shredded personal belongings, attempting to identify what we'd unknowingly lost. A cotton glove or two, parts of my severed sleeve, and one sock for sure had all been intermingled with the tufts of yellow insulation. Binding all of the ingredients together had been a mountain of shredded paper towels. Tom had flicked the nest onto the barn's gravel floor and had surveyed the car's engine compartment once more to see if he'd missed anything. With pure disgust, I had wondered how long we'd been driving around like that, escorting rats all over town. How embarrassing!

As my thoughts returned to the reality of my wintry bed in Alaska, I remembered that Pup hadn't been part of our family at that time so he hadn't been privileged to attend the rat-training seminars offered to us during that summer. But, after our gigantic rat encounters in the trailer a few years back, the tiny mouse invading our tent would've had permission to sleep under my pillow if only he'd asked.

Day 6

After a long, bitter cold night, thank goodness daylight finally arrived so we could get to work on the cabin. The construction activities would finally get us warmed up after several hours of freezing darkness we'd endured. For our daytime attire, we were both wearing three layers of heavy clothing over our basic clothes. The crisp winter air touched only the exposed skin on our faces. Our attire seemed adequate as long as we kept active and didn't sit more than five minutes to eat. When I went down to the beach to get breakfast started this morning, I noticed that despite all my failed attempts to get the fire going the previous evening, that somehow, every stick of wood had decided to burn up sometime after we'd headed for bed. Nothing remained except the twigs which were hanging off the outside edges of the fire pile. At least it was good to know, I guess, that even without gasoline the wood actually would burn there in the winter…if we were patient!

For breakfast we enjoyed fried eggs and potatoes which were absolutely scrumptious. The steaming plate of delicious food would have taken first prize at any wilderness cooking contest. Even amidst the disorganization we were living in at the moment, we were happy and eating very well. As long as the generator was running for the griddle, we could also charge the cell phone and all the rechargeable tools and flashlight batteries. We also made a point to utilize our boot dryer, a modern convenience that proved to be worth its weight in gold. The boots rarely sat on the dryer long enough to actually get dry, but the heat thawed them out a smidge before we had to put them on to go to work for the day.

* * *

Even though we had been in Alaska six busy days, it was only our second day at Camp Alaska. The scheduled event for the day was to get the foundation started. Our first mission was to find something firm on which to secure the foundation. We wondered how to best approach the project since the sampling of ground we'd dug into was pretty spongy. In our search, after several inches of snow and then moss, we came upon various layers of decaying material. Tom and I took turns digging and chopping through the nearly impenetrable substance. At first glance the dark, wet sawdust closely resembled dirt, but it wasn't. Beyond the shredded woody substance, there was dark purple-colored sludge, and the deeper we dug the more stinky black muck we found.

After an hour of intense efforts, finding solid ground appeared to be unachievable. It was decided that the two fresh stumps left from the largest trees Tom had cut down would be put to good use. With the chainsaw, Tom notched one stump to accept the beam where the rear of the cabin would be supported. Due to the slope on the property, the back wall of the cabin would be at ground level, while the front of the cabin would be supported over six feet off the ground. That priceless space under the cabin would soon become our beloved dry storage area.

The weather was sunny and very cold, but nice for working. Most of all we felt that we were making good progress. We'd gotten a good start on the structure. The foundation was done and the floor was on. At the end of the day, we spread tarps over the new construction as rain loomed in the dark, briskly moving skies overhead.

For dinner, we had rice smothered with delicious gourmet steamer clams. Having fresh seafood available was such a bonus! We hadn't seen one raven today, which gave us hope that maybe we weren't missing anything else. After dinner, we attempted to start another fire. It would have felt great to get warmed up, but instead, once again we were just smoked out. Tonight as we lay snuggled in our bed, the wind began to blow. Eventually we heard the snapping and crackling down below us on the beach. We could only assume what was happening with the fire. Unfortunately, it was burning without us once more, and we could do nothing, except laugh at our circumstances.

The wind not only affected the fire, it also caused the water's temperament to worsen. We could hear the waves getting rougher by the minute and soon they were loudly crashing ashore. Just before I climbed into bed, I made one last midnight security sweep of the beach to make sure that the items left above the high tide mark were far enough out of the water's reach. It was hard to get used to the fact that living on a remote beach was going to be an existence which required constant awareness.

Soon there were high winds causing our tent to flutter uncontrollably. As the hours passed, the weather refused to let up. A couple times during the night I made a point to step outside to flash the light down onto the beach to be sure nothing was getting swept away by the aggressive water. Besides keeping an eye on the boat, our large water tank was begging to be floated away. As we lay there unable to sleep, we discussed the plans for the following day. The first thing the next morning we planned on getting the walls of the cabin built. We remembered that we still had some of our building materials across the way on the other beach. It would be necessary to get them moved over to our camp before the higher tides moved in over the next couple of days.

We tried desperately to get some rest, but it was just too cold. The three of us snuggled under all the blankets we had. In addition to the several layers of bedding, I unrolled an area rug for extra warmth. For the final layer, we topped the heap off with a tarp, hopeful that it would keep the moisture in the air from penetrating our bed any further. After a couple hours of unrest, I got up and found some pocket warmers to thaw my hands. That helped some, but what I really needed was an electric clothes dryer to remove the cold dampness from our bedding and clothes.

There was no doubt that the cold weather was working us over. Tom's joints have never given him trouble, but that night his knees started to bother him. As a result, to my left there was Tom, who couldn't lie still, and snuggled in on the other side of our tiny bed, was Pup, who was snoring like an old man in church.

21

Rain, Rain, Go Away

Day 7

The howling, beachfront weather had kept us on edge the entire night. The miserable hours of darkness seemed to drag on forever, but somehow we'd endured the horribly cold wind and eventually the rain as we anxiously waited for daylight to come. For sure, a flimsy tent was no place to hide in a squall of this magnitude. Fortunately, the towering, decrepit trees hovering over our shelter had also outlasted the violent storm which blew all through the night. As for our campfire, just as we expected, there wasn't a stick left when we went down for breakfast—only ashes remained.

When we had arrived there a couple of days earlier, we could discern from the decades of debris lodged on the shore that the water would sometimes come in far enough to cover the entire beach. This meant that during the highest of tides, the waves would come clear up to the edge of our trail leaving everything on the beach at risk sooner or later. As a result, short of moving all the supplies up the hill, there was no escaping the threat of the powerful tide water. We would need to keep a close eye on the tides.

Even after we got moving for the day, Tom was really suffering because of his joints. The condition of his knees was forcing him to crawl backward down the hill in the same manner a toddler descends a set of stairs. He explained that if he were to try to walk down the hill like normal, he would've instantly gone into a forward roll which would've sent him tumbling all the way to the beach. Imagining a grown man in somersault mode like a heavy boulder in an unstoppable roll down the hill was a visual that made me chuckle more than once.

Unlike Tom, my knees weren't hurting, so today I did all of the packing while he took care of the building. It was a good team effort. By nightfall, the walls of the cabin were upright with two rows of plywood sheeting around the exterior of the structure. Trusses for the roof wouldn't be too far behind, but they were still sitting on the other beach where we'd unloaded the landing craft three days earlier. After dinner, we packed them over to our beach, so we could move them up the hill to the cabin the following day.

Our camp site was drenched due to the non-stop rain and blowing wet snow coming down today. We knew that once we installed the metal roof, we could get the water tank set up to start collecting all that precious water to use in the cabin. But until then, there was nothing good about the constant moisture falling from the sky. Due to the rain, our path to the cabin was increasingly mucky and nearly impossible to maneuver, especially while carrying a heavy load. Because of those conditions, the need for agility and stamina were ever-present. If it weren't for the tangle of exposed tree roots sticking up everywhere, we would have had no traction at all.

Since the trail from the beach was an obstacle course of sorts, falling down several times a day was not an uncommon occurrence. At the very beginning of the sloppy trail up to the cabin, a small alder tree provided a hand-up if our arms weren't already too full. Six steps into the climb, the trail narrowed drastically, forcing all hikers to continue upward in a quick, yet careful manner. The chance of a steep drop to the beach at that juncture reminded us to stay completely focused. We found it impossible to avoid the stubborn stream of water flowing down the hill from the left. Several attempts to re-route the persistent trickle were unsuccessful. Then, just before the landscape flattened out a bit, two over-sized steps up dared us not to sit each load down before continuing out of the danger zone.

We knew how to improve the situation. For the first stretch, it would've been ideal to have a nice set of stairs. As for the trail, there was a never-ending supply of flat rocks, which could have made the upper path much more stable.

But we were already exhausted from lugging around the building materials and supplies, all while wearing our heavy, water-soaked clothes. The landscaping project would have to be put on hold. At this moment in time, building a dry shelter was foremost on our minds.

The ongoing rain wasn't just drenching our pathway, our dry clothes were in short supply. With multiple layers of clothing having to be changed throughout the day, our pile of clean resources had quickly run out. In fact, we knew that if it continued to rain all day and into the next, we'd be in serious trouble. Due to the sideways showers pouring in at the neckline and around our faces, even wearing rain coats, we were getting soaked. It wasn't long before every stitch of clothing sat in one of two designated piles: either damp cold clothes which weren't dripping yet or hopelessly sopping wet clothes which for sure couldn't be worn again. We kept each pile separate just in case. By then, we'd started to have better luck with the fire; therefore, some of our clothing was able to be hung over the heat during the day, when it wasn't raining!

Besides our clothes, we were also experiencing a severe shortage of dry gloves which meant we were always trying to dry our favorite ones too quickly. Those prized possessions were lined with warm lamb's wool and were somewhat waterproof. We'd sent packs of gloves to Alaska. But the only gloves which helped us in this freezing weather had been a parting gift from our neighbors, and we only had two pairs a piece.

While attempting to dry our gloves, we discovered the problem that comes along with burning frozen wood: not much heat comes from the fire. Therefore, it was always tempting to drape our wet possessions directly over the cold flame, which was hissing with moisture instead of crackling with heat. In fact, I think it was the campfire's smoke which did most of the drying. Unfortunately, on more than one occasion our gloves ended up too close to the flames, and as a result, they'd developed multiple cases of crispy shrunken fingertips.

Up to this point, we were eating well and drinking a lot. Because the ravens had wasted much of Tom's pop, he'd been consuming more than normal amounts of my water; consequently, the bottled water was nearly gone. While cooking dinner, I took time to collect water from the creek to boil it for drinking, so we would have it available if the need arose.

No matter what we were doing, we could always see the ravens perched overhead watching our every move. We felt lucky to have slowed their destruction and thievery.

The weather continued to storm all day. By late afternoon, we were hopeful that the water would settle down enough to allow Tom to motor out to pull the crab pot. We were looking forward to eating more fresh crab for dinner! Finally a weather window opened up, and Tom found two more crab in the pot. We had another great meal and then shut down the camp for the evening.

Day 8

There was a fairly high tide which had come and gone as we slept last night, but the water had been very quiet, so I hadn't felt too threatened. In fact, the stormy weather seemed to have completely vanished by the time we awoke. The beach air was dead still and very cold. By then we were getting low on the food supplies. For breakfast there was nothing but spam to compliment our last four eggs. Tom likes spam, but I despise it, so it was a good thing I was really hungry.

After a hot but less-than-satisfying breakfast, we got busy on the cabin. This morning we knew that with any luck and a lot of hard work, we would be able to sleep under a solid roof come nightfall. Mice had interrupted our slumber once again, giving us just the incentive we needed. Because of the visiting fur balls, we planned to push hard all day in order to finish the walls and roof on the cabin. We were optimistic that we could at least get the bed moved inside before dark.

All day long, as fast as we could go, we packed lumber and nailed on boards; both of us remained extremely focused. To save precious energy, any and all dialogue was only out of absolute necessity. Any tasks which could wait until later were put on the back burner which resulted in our camp being a complete disaster by day's end. As we labored tirelessly, nothing got cleaned up or put away.

When the tide water got to the boat, we sped out to check the crab pot. Sadly, it had only captured one crab, which we enjoyed for dinner. While we were out in the boat checking the pot just offshore, a glance back at the beach revealed the ravens had quickly and cleverly swooped into camp. Those birds must have been watching while I had stowed Pup's food away before we left, because they knew exactly where to go. As we watched helplessly from the boat, one raven jumped up on the pile of totes which I'd tarped for the sole purpose of keeping the pests out. The head raven poked his commercial-sized beak under the cover, grabbed Pup's plastic dish full of food and tossed it effortlessly onto the beach. Next, he hopped off the tote, and then he and his partner began their dining experience. They took turns gobbling the food one piece at a time, all the while, glancing in our direction. I tried to distract them as I not only yelled, but also pounded on the boat with a hammer. Neither my racket, nor Pup's barking, bothered them a bit. Both ravens feasted until we returned to shore, and then flew off with full bellies.

Over the next five weeks, we got to know a little more about the ravens and their antics. They have three dialects. The voice they'd most often use with us was the one which tricked us the first day we were there. It had caught us completely off guard. It was a friendly, tropical bird noise, which made more of an echo than the other squawking noises the birds would use to communicate. I came to realize that this annoying chatter was how they alerted other birds in the area that they'd found a sucker! Sometimes their sassy retorts emitted a bit of sarcasm; as a result, quite often I felt as if I was being mocked.

This afternoon, Tom framed the bathroom walls, and secured the exterior wall structure for trusses. Next, we set the trusses on the walls and braced them in place. Then, to attach the metal roofing, we needed the horizontal boards nailed on to the trusses. Tom took care of that, while I packed the sheets of roof metal up the hill to the cabin. By evening, we were more than half way done with the roof. We could have finished it that night, but the roofing project was temporarily put on hold; the chimney for the wood stove would need to be installed first before the last four feet of metal roofing could be attached. We didn't have time for the chimney project before dark; as a result, the last pieces of roofing would have to wait. Thankfully, at this point, there was plenty of cover to keep the rain off our bed, so I was elated. The partial roof would provide shelter over most of the cabin. And even though the lumber and plywood were dripping wet, at least we were able to get out of the relentless driving rain.

With most of the roof on, our next mission was to block the steady gusts from whistling through the cabin. With much enthusiasm, we covered the outside walls of the structure with plastic house wrap. Without that barrier, the hurricane force winds would've continued to howl through the three huge windowless holes facing the beach. Just before nightfall, with great pleasure, we started moving a few things inside. We were officially moving out of the tent, which was a noteworthy milestone. Tom quickly stapled some insulation to the ceiling and walls of the six foot square bathroom area where we would camp for the night. The insulation barrier could potentially stop the incoming breeze and also hold in the heat from our small propane heater.

Getting in and out of the cabin was quite a hassle. Without stairs, the entrance to the cabin was less than convenient to navigate. The framed door opening was four feet off the ground, around chest level, so it took an enormous effort to maneuver ourselves inside. We made minimal trips in and out, but even though we'd been careful not to track in extra mud, the cabin floor was already filthy and wet. To cover the entrance, I threw a large area rug over all the moisture and I started heaving the necessities up inside the cabin. Once the bedding was in, I lifted Pup in and then hoisted myself inside. I spread some scraps of dry plywood on the floor on which to lay our mattress. It was a huge relief to know we had made it through the worst of the building project. Besides the visiting mice, we'd also heard wolves howling earlier in the day. The timing to get out of the tent couldn't have been more perfect.

By the end of the day we were thankful it hadn't rained too much, but it still didn't change the fact that we were out of dry sweatshirts. It was becoming urgent that we make a trip to town to do laundry. Even though the stormy conditions were causing the water to be too rough for safe travel today, we were hopeful that the weather would cooperate the next day for laundry, showers, and food supplies. Besides the three necessities, we also wanted to check on the well-being of our abandoned car which we'd left days ago at the boat launch.

By the time darkness had set in, our focus was all about getting a good night's sleep. Once we were inside for the night, we started the generator and plugged in a work lamp to provide some lighting while we briefly attempted to organize the mess before getting ready for bed. Inside the cabin we were still at risk of being smashed by a tree, but if one actually did decide to come down, we had a better chance of survival than being in the tent. I was very excited to be on a solid floor. At last, we changed out of our wet work clothes and somehow found enough suitable clothing in which to sleep. To keep the heat in our tiny room, we nailed one of our precious cotton blankets over the bathroom doorway.

It was finally bedtime. Tom climbed in first. He scooted over against the far wall as much as possible and claimed a pillow. I was next, rolling on to my side with the blankets held high, and then Pup plopped himself down beside me to rest his head on my shoulder. We tucked the blankets up under our chins. My stocking hat was pulled clear down over my eyebrows in order to provide a slight buffer between my long hair and the exposed insulation which surrounded us on all sides. Our temporary sleeping quarters were cramped, but because of the drastic improvement, I considered it cozy. The glow of the heater lit up the small room just slightly. Once we were all snuggled in, we joined together in a satisfying sigh of relief as we listened to the rain hammering the metal roof while we drifted off to sleep.

22

The Tides Are In Charge

Day 9

At last, thanks to our first night inside the cabin, we finally were able to experience a warm night's sleep in Alaska. The night passed quickly in comparison to the long hours we'd spent toughing it out in the tent. Once again, the propane heater functioned superbly inside our cozy room for three hours, at which point the small canister ran out of fuel. It felt wonderful to be warm and damp as opposed to the usual—damp with waves of goose bumps. Well into the night, I vaguely recalled hearing the plastic house wrap which crackled continuously due to the intermittent bursts of beach front weather. And neither the noise nor the itchy insulation which I nestled up against seemed to faze me a bit during my hours of much needed slumber. I was completely worn out.

We were delighted as we awoke to calm water and sunny skies with only a little rain here and there. Our camp was a disaster with our belongings spread everywhere both on and off the beach. There were space limitations on where to stack our materials due to the brush, trees and uneven ground, so by then the trail to the cabin was outlined with various supplies that had been packed part way up the hill but not all the way to the cabin. Piles of wet clothes, dirty dishes, building materials and construction leftovers littered the immediate area. But with a real shelter to work with now, I felt renewed energy as I went about getting camp organized.

Our main objective for the day was to get to town for supplies. We hadn't sent up nearly enough six-penny nails in our shipping container; as a result, some of our plywood was only tacked on. We were low on groceries and desperately needed to wash our clothes, and we were quite optimistic that our first trip to town would happen since the water appeared flat calm early on this beautiful morning. However, due to my recent experience with sudden weather changes, I began packing for a stay overnight at the motel, or possibly on the shore somewhere in between our cabin and town. If the weather wouldn't allow us to make it either all the way there, or all the way back, I wanted to be prepared. Flashlight, tarp, knife, paper, clothes, bear spray, pistol, lighter, dog food and water were the essentials. I also took a small fleece blanket, just in case. As a result, my emergency duffle bag was exceptionally heavy. In fact, I almost couldn't carry it, but I refused to be stranded somewhere without it.

Even though we wanted to leave for town right away that morning, we could not. We had chosen to anchor up too high on the beach the night before in order to keep the boat safe during the storm. As the boat sat high and dry again, I couldn't help but sing to myself the words of the song I'd heard on the radio years ago as a child. *The tide is high and I'm moving on…*, the words played over and over in my mind. I get it now! I thought. Without the high tide, you go nowhere, which is where we were going, again. That song became my motto over the coming weeks, since I couldn't remember the words to the famous fast-paced Gilligan's Island tune, which was perhaps a bit more fitting.

As we waited for the tide to come in, we puttered around camp. While I was rounding up all the dirty clothes and topping off my emergency pack, Tom carried the rest of our building supplies up the hill in case the weather wouldn't allow us to get back for a couple days. That undertaking was no small task. Obviously, Tom's joints were improving. This included four windows, an entry door, water tank, metal trim and shower stall and the last of the totes and tools. With all the supplies finally hauled up the trail, our beach was returned to its natural state.

High tide today was around three o'clock, which meant that it was urgent we leave as soon as possible in order to be able to return before dark. It was no quick jaunt to town. Unlike our first day there, we now knew that the boat ride took a good forty-five minutes on a decent weather day. Because the launch area didn't offer moorage, we had to allow time for pulling the boat out of the water, securing it for travel, changing out of our raingear and boots, and then transferring our laundry and other personal items from the boat into the car. Only once that was done could we start running our errands. In general, we'd be gone three hours minimum, so we were really anxious to get going.

After all of the camp chores were done, we still had plenty of time to wait before the water got to the boat. While keeping one eye on the tide, we not only installed the chimney, but also the last pieces of metal on the roof, as well as the ridge metal screwed onto the peak of the cabin. At last, the roof was done and the floor could start drying out!

It was one o'clock before the boat was floating again. The trip went well. While doing our errands in town, we spent every spare minute talking to family while we had good phone service. There'd been so much that had happened during our five days at camp that it felt like we'd been out of touch for a month. We showered at the public facilities in Ketchikan, which felt tremendously refreshing. The best part by far, was putting on the warm, dry sweatshirt fresh from the dryer! I would describe it as unbelievably awesome!

It was because of our late departure to town that we didn't get back to the cabin until about 6:30 this evening. The mountain of laundry alone took two hours. Upon our return, the tide was half way out, which meant it was necessary to hike a good distance through the rocky muck with all of the goods we had picked up from town. And besides our groceries, we'd also brought our plastic chest of drawers and two folding chairs which had been stowed in the car, plus propane tanks, gutters, and all the wonderful clean, dry laundry. What a treat it was to have it all there. It felt like Christmas to have dry paper towels again, chairs to sit on, new food and clean water. At last we could enjoy a fresh start.

Even though we were eating well, it wasn't long before we realized that we were craving sweets! The pudding we'd brought out initially had been confiscated by the ravens. So in town I picked up some snacks. Looking back, it was on that day we all three began our addiction to frosted graham crackers. They were a quick sugar fix, and with a little practice, Pup's nose became aware of them the minute they were frosted. In the damp Alaskan environment our crackers would be perfectly softened in less than thirty minutes.

Once we were home from town, the tide continued to recede, which meant we had no choice but to let our boat go high and dry on the rocks again. Because of the inconvenient location, we'd need to look after it around midnight, Tom calculated, because that is when the tide would be back to the boat's current position. We chose to go to bed right after we ate dinner. As soon as possible, we needed to get the boat to a better location where we could keep a closer eye on its welfare. If it remained where it was, too much could go wrong. If a storm came through and it was left unattended, rough water would most likely either sink it, or set it free.

Our boat required round-the-clock monitoring which was only one of many inconvenient facets of the new life we'd chosen for ourselves. I wondered if I'd ever adjust to the idea that nothing could be taken for granted. I longed for the feeling I had back home when I could put the car in the garage and be done worrying about my mode of transportation. Remote Alaska doesn't cater to that lifestyle. For the time being, we took a couple spare ropes to add on to our other anchor line, so even where the boat was sitting it could still be tied up to something besides a rock. More important, once the tide came in, we needed to shorten the line back to the normal length. If not, then while we slept, the boat would have the opportunity to float in too far. The tide book indicated that the highest tide in the coming weeks would be at 3:00 a.m. the following morning. If the boat were to float all the way in on such a tide, it was very possible that we would have been stuck for a month. With that outcome in mind, without fussing, at midnight we got up to deal with the boat situation before eventually returning to our warm bed for the remainder of the night. If only we'd either stayed home, or been able to leave earlier today, we wouldn't be worried all night, I thought.

Since finding the perfect stationary position for the boat was such an issue, much of our conversation was about how we might remedy the problem for the next trip we planned to make in August. Of course a dock would have been ideal, but a solution such as that required much more expense than we could afford. For some time, Tom had been thinking about a pulley system in order to move the boat in and out. It would consist of a large loop of rope, which would be attached to two anchor points. A tree on the beach would serve as one anchor while the other anchor would be installed deep into the mud as far out as possible during a very low tide. According to the tide book, there was one such tide available in August. We were looking forward to that as a future improvement. We knew if that system were to work, we would have a lot more freedom to come and go because our boat could spend more time floating as opposed to being beached the majority of the day. Whenever we needed it to go somewhere—we could just pull it in toward the beach, jump in, and motor away.

Day 10

Inside the cozy bathroom cubbyhole, we slept toasty warm once again. And while we were fast asleep, we'd been unaware of all the new snow which had fallen all night long. Even after we were up in the morning, it continued to snow huge flakes most of the day. In spite of some materials getting buried, we were still able to get the entry door installed and the windows put in, which helped with some of the drafty openings, but not all of them; the ceiling was still wide open.

Since crab was always on our mind, we'd picked up some more bait in town yesterday. One of these days we'll have time to fish for our own bait, Tom kept reminding me. We didn't have time for leisure activities just yet. Around noon when the water reached the boat, Tom was able to go out to put the herring to work. By dinner, the pot had caught nine beautiful Dungeness crab! Needless to say, we stuffed ourselves at the evening meal. Before bedtime, Tom got some of the wiring hooked up to the breaker panel. From this point on, we had good lighting available whenever the generator was running. With any luck, we'd have additional electrical outlets to use by the next day. After dark that evening, Tom and I insulated the rest of the cabin. It felt like heaven to be inside, out of the wind, rain, and all the new snow.

Earlier in the day we'd celebrated with a ceremonial "taking down of the tent." It was sagging with rain and snow, but it had served its purpose in

Alaska. On another note, the dreary weather combined with the complete isolation was making me miss my family a lot. I really wished the phone would've worked. But all things considered, we were doing well.

That afternoon Tom hooked up the propane wall-heater, but we could still see our breath inside the cabin for the next several hours. We commented that it wouldn't be long before we were warm and the floor would start to dry out. The only drawback was that the food would have to be moved outside. I was ready for that trade off!

Day 11

I must have slept great all night, because I don't recall being disturbed for any reason. I awoke in a complete sweat this morning due to the large propane wall-heater which was still going full blast. In order to cool down, I peeled back the heavy layers of bedding which had held me hostage all night. I swear, I could practically see the steam rising! Pup rolled over onto his back for his morning belly rub—he hadn't moved a muscle all night either. A quick glance at the floor revealed that the cabin floor was starting to dry out just like we had anticipated. I vaguely recall hearing the rain which poured down all night. As a result, everything except for the water tank, that is, was filled with puddles of water. Unfortunately, the gutters we picked up in town the day before hadn't started collecting water for us; they were still lying on the ground. Tom put them up first thing in the morning to start the collection process. From then on, we noted there was not one drop of moisture, except condensation. Nevertheless, we kept moving forward. Tom got the instant hot water heater mounted to the back of the cabin, just in case something magical happened in the rain department.

By nightfall, there hadn't been an ounce of precipitation, so we began conversations about getting water from the creek. Believe me, there was no shortage of fresh water in Alaska; it was just a matter of getting it to the tank somehow. On our property there was a small stream which ran a little more than a garden hose all the time. It increased with rain, of course, but either way there was sufficient water for all of our needs. If we were to walk in a direct line out the front door, the water source was about thirty feet away. But at that elevation, the system would require a pump to get the water to the storage tank, which would in turn involve power in order to function. Although it would've been fairly simple to set up, it wasn't a practical solution. In the wilderness, our theory was always the simpler, the better. We knew from previous experiences that the fewer hoops to jump through, the more enjoyable life could be. We planned to eventually get water from that very same stream, but we'd tap in from up the hill a little further.

Months earlier, during the planning stages at home in Oregon, we'd schemed that we would run a water transfer pipe from up the hill a little ways, allowing gravity to take care of the water flow from the creek to the tank. But we would need a substantial length of pipe to reach from that upper source all the way to the cabin. The distance was well over a hundred feet, and we couldn't decide whether to spend the money or not.

Camp was becoming more civilized by the day. After days of crawling into the cabin due to lack of stairs, I finally decided to take half an hour to "shank" together a makeshift porch. Tom wasn't too thrilled with my idea and tried to talk me out of wasting my precious time on something which would be dismantled in just a few days. But I was the camper who suffered most from that arrangement, so I was determined to remedy this problem. For one thing, the cooler of food I had to access regularly was outside on the ground, and the generator I needed to start to cook meals was under the cabin. But the main reason was actually so our soaking wet Pup could get inside without me having to lift the sixty-five pound, graham-cracker-eating carcass every time. Those were three good reasons to go ahead with my plan.

Against Tom's wishes, I pressed onward! Without cutting up any of our good lumber, I was able to round up enough scraps to get the porch's framework assembled. It wasn't pretty, but it was perfectly functional. Once the small platform was built, I attached a ramp to it using a piece of planking we had found on the beach our first day there. Attaching a ramp was certainly much faster than building steps, for which neither of us wanted to waste the time nor the lumber. It spanned twelve feet from the porch to the ground at the rear of the cabin. Eventually we planned to build a deck across the whole end of the cabin, but before that transpired, we would need to pick up some more lumber on the next trip to town. Whatever the case, the temporary porch served me very well for a few days.

Tom and I felt we were making great progress on our adventure. It had been six days since we'd hired the men to deliver our materials to the property, and it felt good to have the big push out of the way. We'd survived the biggest part of the Alaska project and were extremely happy that it had taken less time than planned to get settled inside our new shelter. We commented on the fact that if we'd stayed on schedule, the three extra days in the pouring rain and snow might have done us in. As it was, I felt I was at my limit.

Finding a couple hours of spare time to clean and organize today was a real treat in comparison to the grueling schedule we had been keeping. The dresser we'd brought from the car on the previous trip was providing a convenient place to store food, utensils, and dishes. That luxury was a huge improvement from having to dig through stacks of identical gray totes like I had been doing up to this point. Life just kept getting easier from there.

Inside the cabin we were really starting to live in style. We had lights, lots of food, dry clothes, and warmth. Tom kept drilling more holes for wiring and plumbing. It created a lot of sawdust, but the wood shavings actually helped to absorb the moisture from the floor, so I didn't mind. Today the crab pot only brought in one crab that was legal-sized. When Tom pulled the crab pot, there was one eighteen-legged starfish, orange in color, which had every last one of its long legs wrapped around the bait. I'd never seen a starfish like that before. It wasn't any wonder that the fully encompassed bait hadn't attracted any more crab. While Tom was out in the boat, he noticed that the ravens had punctured a gallon jug of engine oil. It had leaked all over our belongings under the bow and also down underneath the boat deck. Luckily, we had a fresh supply of paper towels on hand to clean up the worst of it. We weren't sure why the ravens thought a jug of oil looked so intriguing, but we knew we needed to write down two more items on our list for town: engine oil and paper towels.

As the day came to a close, the shower was installed and most of the plumbing was done. It was a bit aggravating to know that we could have taken a shower if only we'd had water. By then, the kitchen sink was also in place but missing one short piece of drain pipe. That small detail was on the list for our next trip to town.

Since the heater was keeping the cabin at a decent temperature, before bed, we moved our mattress from the cramped bathroom to the wide open space of the warm dry cabin where we thoroughly enjoyed being able stretch out. Of course, it felt good to be away from the insulation, but Pup still wanted to be in the bed. At last we were getting into somewhat of a comfortable rhythm.

The wall heater in the cabin is on full-time duty trying to dry our wet clothes.

23

Treasure Hunting

Day 12

High tide was early. In order to have the opportunity to head into town today, we got up at 5:30 a.m. after a wonderful night's sleep. Down on the beach, the boat was floating perfectly by 6:15 a.m. "Floating perfectly" meant that we didn't have to wait in order to leave. If we had slept in, we would have missed our opportunity. The weather was agreeable, so we headed out right away. While in town, we purchased supplies for Tom to finish wiring and plumbing the cabin. Also, we stocked up on frosting and graham crackers as well as boat fuel and nails. In between errands, we called the family to keep them abreast of our progress. Later in the day our phone even worked when we returned to our beach. The improved phone's reception was most likely due to the nicer weather we were experiencing. Back at the cabin, Tom baited the crab pot with the new bait we'd bought in town, which to our delight had quickly lured seven crabs into the pot by high tide that evening. Tom cooked them for dinner, and we cheerfully gorged ourselves on seafood again.

After dinner, for first time since we had been in Alaska, we took some time off work to try a little fishing. I had never fished before. Unfortunately, this time we caught nothing, but it was nice to take a short break. As we conversed about our unsuccessful outing, we weren't sure whether we had used the wrong bait, wrong hooks, wrong fishing hole or all three, but Pup had enjoyed himself immensely and was very tired from the excursion. It took a lot of energy for him to be so concentrated on his newly acquired skill.

By evening, the entire floor in the cabin was finally dry, so we unrolled some plush carpet remnants which made the cabin feel warm and cozy. At day's end, only a few puff balls of snow had come down which hadn't added anything to our parched water tank. We acknowledged that the beautiful, blue, sunshiny skies we experienced all day would have been extremely enjoyable if we weren't desperately waiting for moisture at this point. Tom had picked up the necessary supplies in town, so he could get the sink drain plumbed in. With that detail completed, all we'd need to have running water at the cabin.... was the blasted water itself!

Day 13

Life was good! Pup loved the plush carpeting, so he'd slept most of the night against the edge of the bed, not in it! Tom and I dined on delicious fresh crab for breakfast. I never would have dreamed of cold crab meat making such a superb meal that early in the day, but it did! Our trusty crab pot had caught twenty "keeper" crabs so far. Keeper crabs are males of a certain size and larger. The requirements vary by state, but in Alaska, the measurement is taken at a specific point on the crab's back where it must measure at least six and a half inches across. Females are always released as are all undersized crabs.

Later in the morning, we went beach combing and within a half an hour had come across a large assortment of tangled rope. Our "find of the day" was wound around various debris and stretched clear across the beach in a zigzagged disaster. At first, it was unclear how much of the rope there was because sections of it were buried in the tidal mud. It was crisscrossed over itself half a dozen times, twisted and knotted into quite a magnificent mess. Like an obstacle course, Tom followed one strand while I was on another, winding our way around the sea shore. We spent an hour or more pulling the barnacle-coated mess free, often becoming distracted by all the other marine life that was moving about at low tide. There were groupings of prickly sea urchins, hermit crabs, thousands of rock crabs and ongoing evidence of mud clams whose hiding spots were given away by squirts of water coming from the sand as we passed by. Hundreds of starfish, who were now exposed due to the lower-than-normal tide levels, were desperately awaiting the water's return. With all the life forms present, I was starting to feel guilty just walking on the beach. By then, I'd realized that even a crusty barnacle has moving parts. I doubted it had much personality, but now even they were receiving my careful attention. Because of their overwhelming presence I found them impossible to avoid. During our endeavors we discovered an even larger supply of steamer clams than what we had access to on our own beach, so we packed our pockets full of them for our dinner.

Every day I would get educated about something; sometimes Tom would feel the need to fill me in on the subject of fishing or boat styles. Mother Nature herself often tested me on tides. That afternoon as we untangled our find, my lesson was about the difference between "rope" and "line."

Tom told me that if it has to do with fishing, "It's never a rope; it's a line. Rope is for cowboys, and line is for fisherman!" he said with a bit of impatience in his voice. And what we actually found on the beach was not only "line" I learned, but "it was probably somebody's long line," Tom said. After that lecture, I didn't ask any more questions about it. I was just glad to have the rope! Once we scraped the snarled line clean from the years of barnacle accumulation, we coiled it neatly, and then with great satisfaction, we hauled several large bundles back to the cabin. Now we had a huge stash to use for something, but we weren't sure for what just yet.

After a quick snack, we left for another walk, heading down the beach in the other direction from the cabin. Before long, we discovered a nice cedar tree that had come to rest at high tide some time ago. Much to our delight, after further examination, the log appeared to be sound and very usable for lumber at the cabin. This was exciting news. We had taken a portable saw mill with us to Alaska for just such an occasion. We knew that without a doubt we'd be back at high tide in the morning in order to collect some hunks to cut up for our siding. Continuing on with our excursion, we also found a long, sparkly piece of braided, stainless steel cable. Tom quickly regarded it as garbage, but my imagination went wild with all the things I could make with such functional material. My creative streaks tend to help me see potential in much of the world's trash; Tom, on the other hand, usually steers away from the lackluster subject. In Tom's defense, I have been known to embrace the same ideals as a pack rat. But this time, it really was a true find!

My mind began to churn out one creative thought after another. To design some kind of a fantastic Alaskan masterpiece, I was convinced that all I needed was some spare time. Images of a hanging pot rack began to develop in my brain. First, I would have to untwist and then separate the numerous strands. Then for the framework, I could peel bark from some cedar limbs, drill some holes and weave the wire to form a loose grid from which I'd hang my pots and pans I didn't have available at the cabin yet. Nevertheless, the sprawling treasure was an inch in diameter and stretched about twenty-five feet in length. Judging by the harsh kink and the occasional frayed areas, it quite possibly had been under severe strain at one time in its life, but otherwise it seemed very usable. As we continued to walk farther down the beach, we argued for some time about how valuable it was or wasn't. We found nothing else worth dragging home and eventually turned back toward the cabin. When we got back to the stainless cable again, it became "my baby" if I wanted it. And I did! Even though I knew that there would most likely be no time for creative play in the coming weeks, I dreamed of having some spare time on the next trip to Alaska.

Like a ball and chain, with great difficulty I lugged the sparkling cable back toward home. Pup was no help at all. He attacked the end of the lurching cable like he was a kitten. Tom provided no assistance either. With two loops over my shoulder, I struggled to drag the remainder of loose cable over the boulders and occasional driftwood while empty-handed Tom lollygagged a good distance ahead of me. The free end of the cable sprung forward after every few steps, turning the back of my leg into what felt like a pin cushion. The closer we got to the cabin, the more determined I became, and the madder I was getting about Tom's refusal to help.

After hiking over acres of slimy boulders, my oversized rubber boots had not only twisted my ankles numerous times, but had also transformed my feet into throbbing stumps. We were almost back to camp when all of a sudden,

Tom spotted something intriguing. And no, it wasn't gold. From a distance, it looked like several huge loops of black plastic pipe, and since he was so far ahead of me, he was inspecting it already. For the record, I was still angry, which made it easy for me to refrain from showing any excitement. As I approached, I could see that mildew had caused a thin green layer of color to form on the outside of the pipe. I knew it would still be ideal for transferring the water from the creek to our thirsty water tank which hadn't even collected one inch in five days. We hadn't planned on being able to drink the water anyway. Green or not, it would allow for showers, cooking crab, and doing dishes.

As we stood there determining how we were going to handle the project, it was obvious that it was going to have to be a joint effort to get the mess wrestled out of the brush and hauled back to the cabin. We bickered momentarily about how much he hadn't helped me with the cable for the last half an hour, as together we began to untangle the pipe from the vines which had grown all through it over the years. Once the six-foot high rings of spring-loaded pipe were free of brush and weeds, we stretched it out onto the beach. It appeared to be around 175 feet in length which was very possibly plenty long enough to reach from the water tank to the water source up the hill from the cabin.

Tom began to haul the sprawling pipe toward home. I could see that the monstrosity was too much for one person to drag, but after the recent episode with the cable, I wasn't feeling overly helpful. Up to this point in our trip, Tom may have been the one giving the tutorials, but at the moment, I was in charge of the lesson of the day! Just have at 'er, I thought to myself. Soon enough, Tom was promising that later he would make sure to help me get the cable over to our beach. At that point, I reluctantly abandoned my cable, stashing it in the brush as I made a mental note to come back for it at a later date.

Once we got the pipe back to the cabin, we got busy with the subject of water collection right away. The creek had a natural pooling area up the hill through the trees a short jaunt from the cabin. As we dragged it up the hill, Tom and I struggled to straighten the stiff, twisted pipe the best we could. We wove in and out of trees, attempting to make its route as straight as possible. Still, it insisted on displaying alternate dips and humps. Its curvy demeanor was fighting us like a giant Anaconda. Pushing one hump down forced two to pop up, I swear. At the top end, we ran the tubing under a tree root to keep it from launching back into the air. I stationed myself at the water source while Tom went down the hill to wait at the tank. We wondered if we could get the water to siphon out of the glorified puddle. The natural collection area offered beautiful, flowing water on the top four inches while the bottom of the puddle, of course, consisted of gritty Alaskan muck! Next, I held my end of our new found plumbing just under the surface of pooling water.

After thirty seconds or so, I lifted it out and listened for any noise inside the pipe. Nothing! We hollered back and forth through the woods in order to communicate what was happening, but no water seemed to be moving. After a few more attempts, I could hear the joyful noise of water surging over one hump, and then the next, gaining momentum as it went.

"Here it comes," I shouted. The water started to pull into the pipe and began gushing down the hill, snaking its way toward the tank.

Down at the cabin, the water supply had officially arrived! At first, we let the water run past the tank onto the ground for a short time to see if it would be clean enough to use. To our delight, it was. Next, we wondered if it was going to increase its flow. We thought it might start pulling too much water at once, ultimately sucking a bunch of mud into the pipe. But it didn't. If it had, that would've tainted the whole batch of clean water we collected in the tank.

Over the next two hours the water flow seemed to control itself pretty well. We started getting really excited about having running water inside the cabin. I couldn't help but think that I would no longer be washing dishes in a pan full of freezing water at the creek. What am I going to do with all my spare time? Needless to say, we enjoyed hot showers that night. Well, I did anyway. While I was enjoying our new water service, Tom came in to check if the shower was working.

"It is wonderful," I reported.

The bathroom was steaming up in no time because I like my showers HOT. I expressed my appreciation for how good it felt to be standing under a steady stream of cascading hot water. Soon there was a buildup of steam billowing from the shower stall. Without a door to close, the heavy fog gradually made its way out of the bathroom until it hovered just below the entire ceiling of the cabin. Meanwhile, Tom waited patiently for me to get done with my shower so he could also relish the experience.

Soon enough, it was his turn. Tom started the shower, and then stepped in. "It is freezing!" he griped, as he jumped right back out.

We were dumbfounded since just five minutes earlier it had worked perfectly for me. For reasons we didn't understand at the moment, he couldn't get the water to stay warm. I didn't say anything, but it crossed my mind that just maybe it was the sparkly cable gods getting even!

Wet, frozen, and disgusted, he wrapped himself up in a towel in order to step into the frosty outdoors for the troubleshooting session. Hesitantly, he headed down the slick, bouncy ramp leading to the back of the cabin so he could determine if something obvious had gone awry. First, Tom rattled the propane tank. There was plenty of propane, so the issue wasn't that we were out of fuel to heat the water. Covered with goose bumps, he adjusted the dials on the tank-less hot water heater, and then came back inside. When he tried the shower again, the water was finally warm….until he got in, that is. Cold again!

I snickered to myself as I heard Tom ranting and raving in the bathroom. He was as mad as a wet hen. We discussed that the water pump ran continuously while I was in, but while he was showering the water pump would repeatedly surge off, and then on again. Finally, I ran water from the kitchen faucet at the same time he ran the shower. Only then, would the water stay warm enough for him to take his shower. Whatever the glitch was with the hot water situation, the big news of the day was that we had 275 gallons available with plenty more available. That felt great! When the tank filled back up after our showers, we tied the pipe up in the tree so it would quit overflowing the tank.

Even though our stay in the wilderness had plenty of kinks to iron out, we felt satisfied that all of our plans were coming together.

24

Milling around Camp

Day 14

The beautiful morning sun highlighted everything within its reach, and the water was flat calm when we awoke early on a picture perfect morning. Maybe Spring was on its way after all, I thought. We were so excited about the cedar tree we'd found on the beach yesterday, we could hardly sleep last night. A look at the tide book informed us that it was a little over an hour before high tide, so we immediately made plans to retrieve some logs to cut up for lumber.

On our route to the boat we passed by our bundles of newly collected long line. Tom threw a couple over his shoulder to assist us on the outing, and off we went to collect our first logs. We were delighted that we only needed to travel a short distance down the beach for the project. Once on site, we sized up the treasure, checking it over from root wad to treetop. Customarily, whenever we found trees to cut up for lumber, we chose the prime logs which generally came from the middle of the trunk where the taper is minimal, and the wood is not too oversized for us to handle. Once we determined which pieces we wanted, using the chainsaw, Tom cut two sections, each of them measuring eleven feet, the length of boards needed for our vertical board and batten siding.

Even though we always made a point to arrive on an incoming tide, while Tom was busy preparing the logs, my responsibility was to make sure the boat not only kept floating, but also didn't get away. It was a simple but very important task. Following the removal of limbs, he rolled one log, then the other to the water where I wrapped a line around each of them so we could tow them back to the cabin. It was fascinating to see that the enormous cedar had the buoyancy of a cork and always floated beautifully.

With each log tethered to a cleat, we were ready for the trip. It was not our choice that we traveled slowly, due to not only the logs' substantial weight, but also their uneven resistance in the water. There was a cleat on each corner of the boat and the towing process worked most efficiently if we could haul a balanced load like we were doing today, one on each side. No matter what the size, the logs always seemed to be exactly halfway submerged. Tom was forever impatient because our tiny boat wouldn't make the perfect beeline with the heavy cargo. But as always, if we took our time, we would make it back just fine. As we approached our beach, I positioned myself at the stern to ensure that once the boat came ashore, the momentum of the logs wouldn't cause them to ram into the engine. It was fairly easy to guide them to either side of the boat.

On this morning it hadn't take long before we'd returned with two nice hunks of cedar, and we were eager to cut up some siding. But before the boat went dry on the beach for the day, Tom decided we should check the crab pot which had captured three keepers. Upon our return to shore, we feasted on a breakfast of eggs, bagels and crab and then went straight to work sawing boards until high tide around seven o'clock that evening. It was a long but productive day.

High tide always worked the best for the cedar collection process not only because it was less of a distance to roll the mammoth log to the water, but it also kept our vessel from getting stuck. Even after all of the trimming and maneuvering, it usually took less than an hour to retrieve the wood. We purposely timed it so when we got back to our cabin it was still high tide, and the logs could be deposited as close to the cabin as possible.

First we focused on cutting large beams. But when the log was enormous, it seemed fitting to take a moment to appreciate what nature had given us. I would not only take pictures, but I'd also make sure to count growth rings before we began slicing it up. The oldest tree we found was 227 years old, by my count.

In order to begin the milling process, the bar of the saw was inserted into our portable mill, a wonderful device which allowed us to cut through a log somewhat evenly. The mill itself was a relatively small aluminum frame, and without the saw attached, it was lightweight enough to be easily carried by one person. The manner in which a chainsaw mill works is somewhat primitive and very labor intensive as was most everything at camp Alaska. For the setup, the bar of the chain saw slides into the mill where it is clamped in place. The mill can be adjusted to cut thicknesses from less than half an inch to over a foot. The width, however, only cuts up to twenty-seven inches, which was not nearly wide enough to accommodate the age-old logs we had found. So, the first stage of the process always began with Tom flattening one or sometimes two sides of the log with a plain ol' chainsaw until it measured just less than twenty-seven inches wide. Then for the rest of the cuts we would use the mill.

As always, Tom was stationed on the trigger end, and I was on the opposite end of the saw. In order to cut through the log, he and I would apply steady pressure to the mill. In that manner, we could move down the log to cut one board after another. If the chain was sharp, as we made each cut the wood shavings spewed like a fountain from Tom's side of the log. The bigger the shavings, the better the saw was cutting. On my side of the mill I kept a close eye on the exposed swirling chain so it wouldn't cut into my knee cap, for instance.

Cutting lumber with a chainsaw mill was noisy business, and the continual blaring racket took over our camp. And although it took an extensive amount of time, besides the cost of occasional saw repair and fuel, the beautiful lumber was free. When the chain was sharp, the cutting went much faster, of course. It might have taken two minutes for the first board, but the longer we continued, the slower the process became. After fifteen boards the chain was dull, and Tom would take the time to sharpen the chain.

In most cases, the free cedar made the most amazing, clear, knot-free lumber I've ever seen. At the end of the day we still had our eye on one more hunk of cedar tree to cut up for siding. We were hopeful we could grab the log during the next morning's high tide. For dinner we dined on crab once again while discussing that we'd need to get to town the next day to get saw parts and groceries. It was nice not to have to worry about taking our showers in town anymore, but the hot water on the shower still wasn't working properly. We'd narrowed the problem down to the water-saver in the shower head which seemed to be restricting the necessary water flow for the pump to function properly. That evening, we dismantled the shower head. With a screwdriver I dug out the water-saver component. Finally, the water flowed more efficiently, so our "fine-tuning" must have done the trick. The adjustment allowed Tom and me take a shower, each at our desired temperature.

Day 15

Whenever we planned for a trip to town, it became an all-consuming task. Scheduling for the excursion would always start the day before. First, we would try to predict the weather for the following day to help us decide if the journey was even possible. With the tide book in hand we engaged in ongoing discussions about how far out we should leave the boat to go dry. The timing was crucial because if it was anchored too far up on the beach, then it was too long of a wait, depending, of course, on what time high tide occurred. If it was left too far out, we were forced to wait for the tide to recede because we had no way to get out the boat in deep water. Sometimes the location made a difference of hours, not minutes, so there was a lot of strategy involved. But once we had decided, then we would determine what we needed to pick up in town and whether we could haul it home safely. Large items like lumber were bought in small increments in order to not overload the boat.

Since we didn't leave the cabin very often, it was always a big deal to get to town. Due to the anticipation, we would usually sleep poorly the night before. If the weather still looked agreeable in the morning when it came time to leave, then we'd get serious about organizing for the actual trip. On this particular day, because of all the anxiety about getting to town, we opted out on collecting another cedar log this morning like we had planned. Since our travel opportunities were limited, getting supplies was far more important; consequently, it was hard to concentrate on anything else.

Each trip was a bit unnerving for me, because so much could go wrong along the way. There was engine failure, sinking, rough water, and whales, for starters. Once we were back to the cabin each time, I was always very relieved to be safe and sound again. As usual, I packed my survival bag, which was always extremely heavy. But up until today, I'd purposely carried the bag myself, specifically so Tom wouldn't make me take anything out of it. He was always overly conscious of any unnecessary weight in the boat. Honestly, I think he looked at the situation like it was more of a packrat problem. But the way I saw it, I was never going to be unprepared in a boat…ever again!

With that behind us, we gathered up our crab shells and food leftovers so we could recycle them into the water on the way in to town. We picked up all the smaller items around camp, specifically so the ravens wouldn't be allowed such an easy opportunity to wreak havoc while we were away. Invariably, they would find something and make certain to have it scattered about by the time we returned. Even an innocent pile of crab shells made a terrible mess if the ravens were involved. As we prepared to leave, we took one last glance around. We grabbed all of the dirty laundry, and finally, with great anticipation we were finally underway.

It was beautiful weather this morning, so our chances of reaching our intended destination looked quite promising. Tom had let the boat go dry at the most opportune location, so by 8 a.m. the boat was floating and we were able to leave. The boat traveled effortlessly across the smooth water as we headed into town to wash clothes, run errands, and pay bills from the library's computer. We also needed to get the chainsaw repaired. Hour after hour of constant abuse due to milling lumber caused the saw to require more maintenance than normal.

On our return trip from town, we stopped to do a little fishing. Generally, whenever we fished, we stayed close to home, primarily so we didn't use up our limited supply of fuel. But since we were already out, we tried a couple of areas which were farther away from the cabin. It was fascinating to learn about different parts of the vast inlet. Traveling quickly through the middle of the waterway certainly didn't showcase all of the many highlights which existed along the shore. As we paused from time to time for a look around, we noticed that each area had its own unique display. We learned that many small creeks emptied into the inlet but weren't visible until we slowed for a closer look. On the different beaches, various types of rocks were available depending on where we stopped. They ranged from gigantic mossy boulders to colorful pea gravel to acres of black and white speckled granite-type stones the size of bowling balls.

Add to that, after a storm, there was always recognizable debris which had moved from one beach to another. We also kept watch for anything intriguing, whether it was floating or beached. Once in a while we'd discover a loose buoy, and more than once we came across huge trees. Whatever we found, we investigated fully and then usually let float away. I thought back to our night on the water and how dangerous it would've been if we'd run into some of the larger objects, especially traveling at normal speed. I was so grateful we'd gone back to the beach that fretful night.

Since our last cedar find, we continually had our eyes peeled for beached cedar trees. On today's outing, we sighted another possible specimen to cut up which was even closer to home than the last one. The bark-free, weather-beaten limbs reaching out from the stranded giant resembled an angry octopus. Dried weeds and miscellaneous crisp, sun-dried debris were often tangled and drooping from the outstretched arms. We were never sure how long each tree had been sitting on the beach before we came along, but most of the treasures were a silvery gray on the outside by the time we found them. If the trunk wasn't already missing its bark, the large soggy hunks would usually peel off without much effort. Prying the gritty, dirt-filled bark from the log always extended the life of a sharp chain on the saw.

Back at camp we already had fifteen cedar boards milled from our cutting expedition the previous day. Once we arrived home, we decided to start installing the first pieces of siding on the outside of the cabin. In no time, we'd covered almost the whole side facing the beach. Of course, having all the windows helped our short stack of boards cover more area. We were both extremely happy with the way it looked, and the beautiful results motivated us to continue with the time consuming task of sawing more lumber. The cabin was beginning to have some awesome character. As we drifted off to sleep, we had cedar on our minds.

Day 16

We got up at daylight as the tide was coming in and decided we should leave to fetch the log before breakfast. The weather was a little windy with a lot of rain. We were glad we had made it to town for supplies the day before because we wouldn't have been able to reach our destination due to the bad weather rolling in. Fortunately, we only needed to go a short distance for the log, so in no time, we quickly arrived at the location of the beached tree. After a brief investigation, we chose the section we wanted. Pup and I stood near the boat while Tom cut the log and then limbed it in preparation for the rolling procedure. As usual, we had our log peavey, which is a leverage type tool with a long wooden handle similar to a shovel's handle. The functional part of the tool consists of a metal hook which bites into the log once pressure is applied.

After Tom and I removed the large rocks which were in the log's path to the water, Tom used the log peavey to roll the log bit by bit until it was floating. The weather quickly worsened! By noon, the Alaskan water, which was usually a pristine turquoise color, had since turned mocha brown. Waves the size of those normally visible in areas of deeper ocean water kept rolling in with unrelenting persistence, even on our protected beach.

Meanwhile, our logs were on the beach, waiting to be cut up. To prevent all of our hard work from getting away, we tethered the cedar logs to the trees on the shoreline using more of the long line we'd found on the beach. Due to the storm we also had to keep an eye on the boat, making sure that the anchor wouldn't come loose while it was bucking due to the monstrous waves. Around high tide, we made sure that it didn't float in too far, either. We learned that during stormy weather, the water level always comes in closer than the tide book indicates. Under those circumstances there was the potential that our boat could be beached for days. But today, we were down on the beach cutting lumber all day, so keeping an eye on the boat was no problem.

As we milled the logs all day, the rain made for miserable working conditions, but on the bright side, we noted that it was the first rain that had fallen since the gutters had been installed. We were really glad we hadn't been forced to wait that long for running water.

Following a lengthy cutting spell, we'd shut the saw off for a brief period, not only to sharpen the chain, but also so we could refuel. Since the exhaust was usually piping hot, it was good to let it cool down anyway. Customarily, while Tom was adjusting or sharpening the saw's chain, it was my duty to pack the finished boards up the hill to the cabin. As I threw each load onto my shoulder, I couldn't help but notice the strong fragrance they emitted. Up the hill, I'd already picked a spot underneath the tall Sitka Spruce trees where I proudly stacked all the new lumber. I carefully sorted the best ones off to one side to use for cabinets later on. As I stood back to look at my growing stash, I envisioned all of the character it would bring to the cabin. From time to time I wondered how many trees I had carted off the beach already, and I tried to estimate all the lumber for the walls in the cabin plus all of the cedar we'd cut. I just knew it was a lot!

As the day wore on, the rain and wind dramatically increased. It was reminiscent of the first horrible night on our property when we had been stranded. But unlike our first terrifying night on the beach, during this stormy day, we were able to enjoy daylight and a cabin in which to warm up periodically. Those features clearly made a huge difference in weathering a storm. During the cold weather, in order to keep the cabin comfortable, the propane heater ran day and night. After running full blast for a week straight, the tank had finally run out that evening. We were pleased with how efficiently it had worked thus far.

Day 17

The heavy moisture that came down in the form of rain yesterday had since turned into heavy snow. It either rained or snowed all morning, which pretty much gave us the license to lie around and eat. Our break was justified because we'd pushed ourselves pretty hard while cutting lumber in the wet, freezing cold temperatures the previous day. Thankfully, the wind had died down, so the boat was not in danger.

Later in the afternoon, the sun was peeking out, so we decided to hike up the hill to locate the upper property corner markers. Overall, the terrain wasn't as steep as our canyon property in Oregon, but it still had some climb to it. The drastic change in elevation definitely affected the snow accumulation. Even though there was snow everywhere, the snow level on the beach was only six inches which was quite a contrast to what it was just 450 feet up the hill where the snow was close to waist high. We'd taken the metal detector with us to eliminate a lot of unnecessary digging in our search for our surveyed corner markers which were now buried deep below the surface farther up in the woods. Our property was only an acre and a half. Even though that seemed small at first, we found that after living there, we only used the area directly in front of the cabin. The rest of our activities took place either on the beach or in the boat.

When we left the cabin in search of our property markers, the brush was dense; consequently, for the first stint of the hike we fought our way through thicket which was well over our heads in places. One hundred feet up the hill the property leveled out and the underbrush didn't even exist, so we easily wound our way through a packed section of uniformly tall, straight trees.

Tom shuttling a load of supplies from the other beach to our camp.

There were no limbs on the first twenty feet of each trunk because of how closely they all grew in relation to each other. Due to the canopy of branches overhead, the snow was only a couple of inches deep in that area. The frozen wilderness was just beautiful at the higher elevations. It was a shame we didn't visit more, but for us, all the necessary life-sustaining action seemed to be on the waterfront.

Later in the day, while I straightened up in camp, Tom dug clams for dinner just to say we had. On the Washington coast we occasionally got the chance to 'rake for steamer clams,' as they call it. It amounted to using a general purpose rake in order to comb the beach in search of clams living just under the surface of the mud flats. They were such a treat! Tom and I always loved it when we were lucky enough to have them for dinner. But in Alaska, we enjoyed the fresh crab so much that we couldn't get enough of it; steamer clams had become a distant second. That evening, we started in on some crossword puzzles, then cribbage, and then eventually did some reading. We acknowledged that we were finished with a good portion of what had been planned for the first segment of our Alaska adventure, so the evening hours were becoming more of a hangout session. Today at low tide we called home to get the weather report for Ketchikan. According to the computer forecast, there were ten days of rain ahead, which didn't sound very appealing.

25

Jigging for Rock Fish

Day 18

Just like the computer forecast had predicted, it rained most of the night but the bad weather didn't take hold, and the day started out with pretty nice weather. Regardless, our goal for the day was to put up the rest of our siding which we had already milled. But before that could be accomplished, we needed to take down my makeshift porch which was temporarily affixed to the end of the cabin. However, we couldn't justify removing the porch and ramp until we were fully prepared to do the deck because we didn't want to digress back to crawling on our bellies in order to get inside. Before starting the new deck we still had a fair amount of prep work to do. One thing waited on another; that was for sure. Due to all the work it was going to require to do the siding, we decided "To heck with it!" After all, the weather was beautiful, and we noticed that the boat was floating out front. Since we'd thoroughly enjoyed our break the day before, we loaded up to try our luck at fishing again.

Since we only had to buzz out to the island in front of the property, it took us only five minutes to be fishing. With our electronic device we located a rock pile in the vicinity, maybe fifty feet down. We each threw our hooks out and hoped for the best. I wondered how long we might have to wait. "Got one," we both said at about the same time. Our hooks had barely reached the rock pile.

Just as we'd hoped, the fishing was very profitable, and on this particular outing we caught twelve rock fish without any difficulty. The fish were generally only a foot long, so once they reached the surface, I was able to easily swing them over the edge of the boat without a problem. Since I hadn't caught a fish before, I felt obligated to apologize to each helpless, gasping fish while I was removing my hook from their flesh. I couldn't imagine that a fish doesn't feel pain, especially when there's a hook through their eyeball or even caught on their lip. The longer I fished, though, the better I felt about the subject. After a week of careful observation, my assumption was that they don't feel pain. I gradually let go of the guilt and began to enjoy fishing a lot more.

With our healthy catch on board, we headed for shore. For dinner, we stuffed ourselves on delicious griddle-fried rock fish and fried potatoes— shoestring style. Yummy! After dinner, Tom went out to bait the crab pots with the fresh rock fish carcasses. Since the crabs are more easily lured with fresh bait, we were anxious to see what would happen by morning.

During the evening hours, we decided to get our materials assembled in order to build the new deck. Just like in Oregon, we located some trees to cut down for deck support poles. The difference was this time the trees were cedar, not fir. They were also much smaller and, best of all, we didn't plan on peeling them at any point in the future. I flashed back to the building project in Oregon. Even though we'd planned on removing all the bark eventually, we hadn't peeled them at first. That was a big mistake! We found that when a log is peeled right away, the sap allows the bark to release from the log, similar to a banana peel from the banana. Almost without effort the bark can be removed in long stringy sections, leaving a glossy, smooth trunk. Back then I didn't know about such important details, and since we had been in such a rush to get out of the rat-infested barn, I had decided that I would do the all of the bark removal at a later date. By fall of the next year, the project of bark removal was long past the point of being a simple task. The bark was stuck tight to the pole, much like my summer clothes hug my body in the dead of winter after two months of holiday celebrations! In the meantime, the sap that was once slimy had turned into glue. Subsequently, that costly error took more than a hundred hours of chiseling to remove the dried bark from all four of the twenty-foot poles.

Although it had taken an enormous amount of patience, peeling the dried logs on our Oregon home had become an interesting task in itself. While I had worked with a hammer and chisel, I had been continually pestered by yellow jackets, hovering closely and sometimes even landing on my skin. At first I had been nervous, taking great care to shake them off of me before I bent down, for instance. I hadn't wanted one to get trapped behind my knee to send me tumbling fifteen feet from the deck to the ground. Eventually, I had realized why they had been so interested in my progress. Since they are meat eaters, they had been waiting for me to expose the tree destroying beetle larvae which were alive and well, burrowing just under the layer of dried bark. They had been able to detect them somehow! I had come across hundreds of the delicate cream-colored worms which were carving trails in the surface layer of the wood, ambitiously eating their way to adulthood. By the mannerisms of the yellow jackets I had discerned that the larvae were a delicacy coveted by the entire army surrounding me and my ladder.

I had worked on stripping bark only in my spare time, so it had taken months to get done with the project. Over time, the bugs ended up being interesting company. Swarming all around me, they each had fought for the privilege to fly off with a hunk of worm which had just been uncovered by my chisel. As time went on, the hungry insects eventually had the courage to land on the tip of my chisel to off load their snack. Bravely, some even removed food from my fingertip once we'd formed a "relationship."

Packing off a full-sized worm would almost ground the most experienced gatherers. From high on the deck I would watch them motor off, usually swooping very low, barely clearing the ground before they were up to full speed and able to fly away. From time to time, I had caught myself having conversations with my winged friends. "Just a minute," I would tell them. They were so impatient and I could only go so fast. We had seemed to have a mutual respect and amazingly enough, I never got stung.

With that experience behind me I was glad that I wasn't planning on peeling any bark at the cabin. While Tom easily cut the small trees down, I piled the remaining brush. Then he cut some three foot rounds of a cedar log in half, so they each had a flat spot on one side. The half-rounds would provide a solid base for the deck poles to sit on when we started building the deck's framework. The next obstacle was clearing the area where we needed to stand the poles up. The sloping terrain was laced with roots and rotten trees. Tom's hand-digging and chopping made very little progress, so to speed up the process, he used his chainsaw with an old chain to cut into the "muskeg," or spongy Alaskan earth, which enabled him to prepare a level area where the cedar pads would be set.

While he was busy with that, I began work on cutting all of the batten strips to cover the seams in our siding. As I have mentioned before, we sent all of our "second bests" to Alaska. Boots with holes were one thing; nearly worthless tools which needed to be tossed in the trash were another. Those fine tools made it even that much harder to do the simplest of tasks in the wilderness. Since day one, we'd been struggling with rusty tape measures, rounded screw drivers and ladders reinforced with duct tape. But the electric skill saw we sent couldn't have cut a straight line if its life depended on it. I knew from experience that cutting all the thin batten strips would have been a very disappointing project with the worthless saw we had at the cabin; they would've turned out like wavy egg noodles. What I needed was a table saw.

So to create a makeshift table saw, first I taped the trigger of my cheapo skill saw to guarantee that it would stay in the "on" position. Next, with screws I attached the saw to a scrap of plywood in which I had cut a slot in order to receive the blade. Then, I flipped that board upside down on a couple stumps, started the generator and plugged in the saw. On this day, the ugliest table saw in the world was created. The main service it provided saved me a lot of time measuring and marking the boards, not to mention the struggle I would've had trying to cut a straight line. I could shove the boards into the blade, one after another, forcing the miserable saw to cut whether it wanted to or not. Usually not! The flimsy blade would bind up, causing the generator to regularly overload and shut off. It wasn't the ideal set-up, but it was better than not having one at all! In that manner, I ambitiously cut several dozen strips for the siding and window trim.

We certainly had plenty of daylight while we were there in Alaska. Sunrise was around five o'clock in the morning and sundown wasn't until around eight o'clock this evening, so after a long eventful day, we still had enough daylight to go clam digging for steamers. That night we fixed them for a late dinner. At day's end, it turned out it was sunny most of the day with just a couple sprinkles. We were grateful for only a light drizzle after hearing the weather report a couple days ago. We cleaned up camp, so we would be organized as we anxiously planned another trip to town the next morning.

In times of desperation, this was our table saw!

26

Water Rodeo

Day 19

As usual, the night seemed extremely long due to the anticipation of our trip to town. As we stirred around camp the next morning, it was sprinkling again, and a glance overhead revealed the skies to be a bit unsettled; there was no way to be certain if the weather was actually going to hold. Since the tide was out, it meant our boat was on dry land, so we knew that it would be a couple hours before we could head for town, anyway. All in all, we were really hopeful to be able to make it in for the supplies we needed to finish our next important project, the deck.

We were quite anxious to get the deck constructed because of the additional clean, flat living space we'd have available. For a few moments we debated on cutting our own framing lumber but calculated we probably would've spent more in saw gas than it would have cost to buy the lumber, not to mention our time to cut it all up. Besides, we still needed the nails.

It was 9:30 a.m. by the time the water got to the boat, and Tom buzzed out to check the crab pot. Just as always, Tom pulled alongside the crab pot buoy and he took the boat out of gear, allowing the engine to idle. He'd reach over the side, first tossing the buoy into the boat before yarding the seventy feet of line up over the rail in a "fist over fist" method, coiling it as he went. Eventually the pot would surface and he'd hoist the steel cage over the rail and let the heavy metal frame flop into the boat with a crash so loud that I could easily hear it from the cabin. Today the pot captured six keeper crabs among other things. Starfish were generally the main side-catch, but on occasion there would be an odd-ball crab, or sometimes a small rock fish. After Tom emptied the pot and released the unwanted catch, he'd bait it again and then throw the pot back overboard. Once the pot was on its way back to the bottom, in one swift motion he would hurl the bundle of coiled line into the water before finally tossing the buoy overboard. To avoid chance of getting jerked overboard and dragged to the bottom, he took great care not to get his feet tangled in the loose coils of line.

It always made me nervous when he left to pull the pot, but for Tom, the activity was second nature due to all the crab fishing he'd done in his life. However, at the cabin, the act of pulling a pot differed quite a bit from the commercial boats on which he'd previously worked. On the catcher/processor vessel, he'd always had the aid of hydraulic machinery to do the hoisting of a much larger commercial-sized pots. On our small boat, of course, he didn't have that luxury, but in contrast we only had one small pot in seventy feet of water, not six hundred pots in four-hundred fifty feet of the rough Bering Sea.

Once the crabs were collected and the pot was baited, we prepared for our trip in. We determined that the weather hadn't worsened over the course of the morning, so we mucked our stuff to the boat and then left for town. We weren't five minutes into the trip just around the corner from the property when we began having serious engine trouble. After the engine coughed for a short stint, it died. Since the water was calm and I could still see our beach, I wasn't too scared. Very disappointed, but not scared. We were really counting on getting to town today. But there we were, dead in the water, drifting in devastating silence. I didn't want peaceful quiet right then. I desperately wanted to hear the motor running. Tom was understandably frustrated as he repeatedly tried to start the engine. It sputtered and coughed off and on but would never actually start. The bright side was that we owned one oar and it was onboard, so I decided that I'd better start paddling for the closest dry land. It was too far to paddle back to the cabin, but the nearby beach was only three hundred feet away. As I surveyed the situation, I knew we could at least get back home, even if we'd had to walk the boat back along the shoreline, and I was relieved knowing we had that as an option.

Regardless of what was causing the engine trouble, it was urgent that we get to town; we were running low on fuel for both the saw and the generator. In my mind, that quickly translated into no cooking, no electric tools and no visibility after dark. Undoubtedly, fuel was our life line; if the boat ever ran out of fuel, we would be stranded at the property indefinitely.

At the moment, we were certain that our boat had plenty of gas. And after a few minutes of troubleshooting, Tom was pretty sure that there must be water in the fuel, judging by the way it was coughing. So while I paddled, he removed, drained and replaced the fuel hose to the engine. Once it was re-assembled, he turned the key and the engine started right up! A huge relief!

We were puzzled, but it was running, so Tom took the boat for a quick run back toward home and we ripped right along. Once we were back in front of the property, we shrugged our shoulders in confusion, wondering what had been the cause of the recent hiccup. We turned the boat around, and then sped off toward town again. Everything went fine until we got just past where we had initially been stalled, and then the engine sputtered, eventually shutting off again. Without a word between us, just like some crazy routine, I bounced up to begin paddling. He repeated the previous procedure with the fuel hose, but this time he could not get the engine started for at least ten minutes.

While he fiddled with the fuel again, I rowed our boat to shore, which brought to mind another famous childhood song. After completing several verses, I had almost "rowed the boat ashore, hallelujah," when the engine started up. The boat took off for a short bit, only to stall again three minutes later. Oh, what could possibly be wrong? This was a new engine. During this particular problem solving session, a more thorough inspection revealed cedar shavings in the fuel. We were puzzled. How could saw dust be in the fuel tank? The gas cap was tight. We checked the eight-inch clean-out hatch on the gas tank; it was closed, too. After poking around some more, we found that the saucer-sized hatch had a gap around the edge where it was mounted to the tank. The tank wasn't sealed after all! The large crack had apparently been caused from too much suction and not enough venting to the fuel tank. Tom concluded that the cause of the problem was probably our powerful new engine; it required more venting than the weaker engine we'd had previously! Whatever the case, we recognized the shavings to be those from our chainsaw mill, and we remembered seeing them showering onto the boat during some of our cutting sessions in the pouring down rain. Obviously, both rain water and shavings had been draining into the fuel tank during the last couple of days of torrential downpours, therefore causing our dilemma. After this discovery, we came to the conclusion that all the fuel in the boat was unusable, and at this point, we decided that we better get home and stay home if the engine wasn't going to run better than that. We absolutely did not want to get stuck in the wide open water without a functioning motor. Been there, done that!

Staying home sounded good for a moment, but after further thinking, we concluded that "option stay-home-and-wait" would not be a long-term solution to our problem. Putting our heads together, we came up with one other scenario, which was to go back home to grab our remaining generator fuel. There wasn't much left, but we schemed that if we dumped the clean fuel into the portable gas can which had come with the new engine, we might have enough fuel to make it to town.

Within a minute of getting the engine started, we chose to go back home to get our spare fuel. Pup's airplane ears were out again, and I could tell that he was certain we had lost our minds after our third trip home in thirty minutes. When we pulled up to the property, Pup and I waited in the boat while Tom ran up the hill to get the remaining fuel that was stored under the cabin. After retrieving the gas can, we estimated that we had less than three gallons of good fuel to get to town. Doubtful it would be enough to take us all the way there; we chose to try the contaminated fuel one more time to see how far we could get. Unfortunately, we went only a short distance before we began experiencing the same problems. At this point, Tom began switching over to the portable fuel tank. As we floated in the flat calm water, we went over the pros and cons once more. We knew that the longer we waited to get to town, the less fuel we'd have to get there. But we knew that we might not make it to town, either; and then what? Paddle to shore with one paddle in the open water? We talked about which sounded worse. We acknowledged the gamble we'd be taking, both agreeing we needed to go for it. As soon as the fuel hose was switched over, we nervously departed.

Naturally, for the trip in we were both on high alert. It wasn't a "do or die" experience necessarily, but it rated up near there. As we traveled along, Tom was in full concentration while Pup and I sat quietly on the deck of the boat; I had my fingers crossed. The stress in the air was palpable. As we neared the mouth of the inlet, Tom yelled up front to inform me that the bad fuel was spewing out of the disconnected hose on the large fuel tank. It was in the process of siphoning all of the remaining fuel and was now draining into the back of the boat. As he spoke, my immediate concern was that the extra weight of spilling fuel would sink the boat. But we couldn't turn back; we had no choice but to continue, and he couldn't get the leaking fuel stopped while his full attention was on driving. We were still traveling at a good clip, so it was urgent that Tom stay focused. But after thinking it through for a second, I was somewhat relieved. I realized that the fuel's weight had already been on board, so weight wouldn't be the issue; catching fire and sinking maybe, but not sinking from too much weight. That was the good news!

Not much farther into the ride, without warning the engine was instantly silenced. Were we out of fuel? We weren't even halfway to town yet. I panicked. I knew that heading into the open water was no place to be without a working engine.

In no time, I was on my feet, demanding to know, "What happened?"

"It's just a kelp bed. Just calm down," Tom said impatiently.

We coasted to a halt and were once again adrift in the water which was, of course, a lot rougher out there. It was a helpless feeling to be in hundreds of feet of cold water in a small boat that wasn't running. The weather was gray, and the dark water was getting more turbulent by the minute, or so it seemed. Was this a mistake? But then again, I was especially on edge; maybe the situation wasn't that bleak!

So, we had run over a huge wad of kelp which instantly killed the engine—that sounded reasonable enough. With the engine stalled, Tom asked if I would move to the stern to pinch the fuel hose in order to get it to stop siphoning. I did so immediately, but very quickly we determined that I couldn't stay there; it made the bow come out of the water too far during travel, which would have only created more problems. For one thing, it wasn't just me that moved, it was Pup, too. Our combined weight was more helpful in the bow of the boat for ballast. There was nothing we could do at that point but continue to let the fuel drain. I returned to my designated spot in front of the cabin, and then we took off again at full speed.

The water was very choppy once we left the protection of the inlet, and the further we got to town the worse the windy weather got. With each bounce of the boat, the water would burst over the bow. For me, the ride became a tooth-loosening, disc-rupturing, and butt-flattening experience, and I'm not joking. At that point, if I had sat up straight, my tail bone would have been immediately crushed like a soda cracker. The least painful way I found to sit or lie, whatever it was called, was half-reclined, like I was on some type of classy motorcycle. I was leaned way back, knees slightly bent, with my feet flat on the floor. The only thing missing in my imaginary bubble were the make-believe handle bars to wrap my nervous hands around. Unfortunately, there was nothing to hold onto but myself.

It was the roughest ride I could have ever imagined. It was as if I was being flipped like a hotcake from the skillet. Perhaps, if I had been standing like Tom was, at least my knees would have been absorbing some of the shock. As we forged ahead I tried not to complain. I knew the ride would eventually come to an end. Tom couldn't hear me anyway. We'd been in full agreement on our line of travel: a "beeline" to town, as in a direct, straight shot. I fully understood the concept of getting there as quickly as possible. That plan differed greatly from our usual line of travel when we typically traveled a lot slower in more of a zigzag pattern where the boat would best handle the waves.

As we continued on toward town, at last I could see a house here and there on the hillside, so I knew we were making progress. I realized that there was still a fuel issue, and we were still in the "bee-line" mode, but I was involuntarily hollering as I tried to tolerate the last ten miserable minutes of the ride. It was only getting worse.

At one point, I didn't think I could endure the beating for one more minute! I raised my arm to violently point toward the right. My angry hand came into view at the lower part of Tom's window. Even though he couldn't see my face, I was still able to send a clear message. We both knew that "to the right" meant not only a closer paddling distance to shore, but it also suggested a less abusive path. Instead of turning though, he shouted something like, "My cat will find my shoe." What did he say, I wondered? There was no way I could stand up to clarify; I'd be ejected. I couldn't decipher what he'd said, but I could hear the stress in his voice and I knew he had no intentions of changing our route.

So I suffered. The remainder of the ride I continually apologized to Pup, who has always been very protective of me and was now very concerned for my well-being. It's because of his constant concern that I am escorted everywhere I go throughout the day. It doesn't matter if it's to the laundry room, or the bathroom, he makes me his priority. He guards me so well that my own family can't hug me without Pup's chattering teeth on their leg or high-pitched barking in their ear. If a circumstance arises which causes me to blurt out the words "Ouch!" or "Don't!" then the person I happen to be closest to usually gets nipped, unintentionally, of course. He later apologizes.

Sometimes it's a good thing he is my personal body guard! When we had been working in the woods, Pup had saved me from great harm. Once he alerted me when I had been in the direct path of a huge boulder tumbling down the steep hillside. After spotting the imminent danger, he had run over and had slammed into my leg. When I had looked at him, his airplane ears were out and he was staring up the hill. It was because of him that I had looked up and had been able to get safely out of the way. Since his intentions are to look after my happiness at all times, I knew that the current, brutal boat ride was greatly upsetting for him to witness. For his sake, I desperately tried to muffle my outbursts, but no matter what, I couldn't.

Once we'd almost made our way to the jetty, Tom decreased our speed to a more comfortable pace. By the time we reached the dock, I realized that sometime between home and town I had developed a sore throat. It was from involuntary moans and screams, I was pretty certain. My throbbing teeth felt like they were hanging by a thread. Pup and I had gotten tossed all over the deck of the boat but somehow still remained passengers on the vessel. Tom apologized as we arrived at the boat launch. He had been as nervous as I was about getting stuck in the deep open water with no fuel, and Tom surely didn't want to live through another sermon from me about boater's safety.

One thing about being up in Alaska—we either had really good days, or really horrible ones. That day was definitely the latter of the two. Nevertheless, as quickly as possible, we ran errands and picked up the framing lumber for the deck. I felt like I'd just climbed off either an elevator or a roller coaster; I was dizzy but relieved I wasn't in worse condition. As we gathered our supplies, we noticed that the weather had drastically deteriorated. First the wind had arrived, which had caused the water to be rough on our way in, but once we were in town, a heavy rain began to fall. We kept our eyes on the water's temperament. The longer we stayed, the rougher the water continued to get. Over an hour had passed while we were doing our errands and then it was time to head back to the cabin. As we drove our car back toward the boat launch, whitecaps were visible everywhere, even in the usually-calm water along the bank. Right then, the water was too rough for me to even partially consider trying that bronco ride again. Tom had witnessed how shook up I had been after the boat ride in, so we had no choice as we sat impatiently in the car alongside the road. While he complained, I spent my time on crossword puzzles. That was no party, let me tell you. But quite frankly, at the moment, Tom's happiness was on the tail end of my "things I care about" list.

Over time, the rain finally began to lighten up, and the water eventually showed signs of settling down. A couple hours would pass before I would nervously agree to attempt our trip home. At this point, we had plenty of fuel, so we could afford to take a less aggressive return route which should certainly help.

Luckily, the longer we waited, the more the weather continued to improve, but the open water we had to cross was still worrisome. As I expected, the ride was a little rough, but we were able to travel at a reasonable speed unconcerned about the boat's fuel supply, which was now full to the brim. It also helped to have the extra weight of both the fuel and the lumber onboard which allowed the boat to ride lower in the water and also kept me from bouncing so harshly off the deck. The stack of boards beside me also provided something for me to hold on to. I was very grateful once we'd made it across to the opening of the inlet where the ride was only slightly bumpy with a lot of salt water splash. After what I had been through earlier in the day, believe me, the splash was no problem; it felt like a spa treatment!

The kitchen sink and storage dresser and the last four paper plates we owned that were drying out after dinner.

27

All Hands on Deck

Due to our miserable, white-knuckle, time-consuming ride in to town which was followed by the inconvenient two-hour weather delay, we'd arrived back on our beach much later than planned. By the time we'd returned, the tide was out; as a result, we were required to pack our deck lumber, propane tanks, and groceries a long way across the sloppy tide flats and barnacle field all the way to the cabin. Because of where the boat had to be left when we got back, we knew for sure we'd have a boat dilemma if another storm were to have come in that night. Much to our relief, it was looking as if the storm had already passed through this time around. However, we had been wrong before. It was 5 p.m. by the time we had finished unloading. We were quite exhausted from the day's drama, but we knew that if we hurried, we'd still have enough time to remove the makeshift porch and get the last couple of pieces of siding on the cabin. That should go quickly, we thought, so we felt that it was still highly possible to get our new deck's framework up before nightfall. The day would have a chance to end well anyway!

It took five minutes to tear off the porch and another ten minutes to put up our siding. Then, one by one, we stood up the six-inch diameter poles and braced them into position with our new lumber. Within the hour, the framework was all nailed together, and we were able to lay sheets of plywood down in order to have a safe place to walk for the evening. It was so exciting to have room on the deck to cook crab, change out of wet clothes, and keep the cooler within easy reach.

Day 20

We awoke around 5:30 a.m. and enjoyed a delicious crab breakfast. We were anxious to get started cutting our cedar decking out of the logs we had already floated ashore. The decking lumber was going to be cut a lot thicker than our siding, so to start with, Tom re-adjusted the guide on the saw mill. Once we finished milling the available logs, we spread the boards out on the deck. We determined that we needed five more short boards to finish, but it already looked awesome!

We headed out to fetch another chunk of log to cut up, deciding we'd go fishing as long as we were already out in the boat. Near the island in front of the cabin again, we quickly caught eleven rockfish. We found that one fish had ingested a shrimp. For us, it was proof that shrimp were in the area. We'd keep that in mind for future reference, because we really wanted to get some shrimp pots collected for the next trip to Alaska. After fishing, we motored back toward the cabin to collect the next log we would be retrieving. It was only a couple hundred yards on the other side of the creek by our property, making it a real quick mission. In no time, we were back and promptly finished cutting up the lumber necessary to complete our decking. After that, all we had left to do was to fasten down the boards. However, we couldn't actually finish because now we were out of both nails and deck screws.

Nails and screws were always on our list whenever we went to town. Then we would get to the hardware store only to choke on the price. As a result, we always returned home with a fraction of what we actually needed. It never failed; the instant we got back home, we'd regret not buying more, knowing full well we had to have them to continue working on the cabin. Because of our ongoing nail and screw shortage, I had been using every nail I could find, even the bent ones I had straightened from off the ground. Tom and I went around and around, promising ourselves that when we visited Alaska on the next trip we would bring all kinds of screws and nails with us to properly finish fastening everything together.

As far as the deck's roof, we had already compiled all of the necessary materials, so we began work on that next. It went quickly because of its small

size. With the decking completed, the generator could be stationed just outside the door as opposed to sitting clear down under the cabin in the dirt. It was extremely nice to have all the extra room just outside the door. We were really getting comfortable. In fact, it was sad to think we would have to head back to Oregon the following week already. But because we knew that our departure time was drawing near, we discussed that pretty soon we should probably buy our ferry tickets out of Ketchikan.

That night for dinner, we feasted on griddle-fried fish and hash browns with onions. We found ourselves stuffed again. Pup even gulped down three bowls of food. We noticed that in spite of over-eating every day, after just over two weeks of camping in Alaska, Tom and I had drastically trimmed down. No doubt it was because of the exercise, but we also couldn't discredit the constant supply of all-natural food at our fingertips.

By evening I was tired. It had been a beautiful sunny spring day all day, making it enjoyable to just keep working. Actually, it was so warm that I had to put snow in the cooler for the first time!

Day 21

When the tidewater returned to the boat that morning, we motored out to check the crab pot. Only one crab had been lured into the pot. Tom put some fresh rockfish carcasses in the pot, and then checked four hours later to find four more crabs in the pot. That brought our crab total to thirty-six. While we were out in the boat, we ran over to collect another section of log to cut up for siding. Upon our return, we cut eleven more boards which we'd use to complete the siding on the back of the cabin. We were done cutting boards on this trip. By then, our chains were dull beyond repair, and we were glad to be done milling lumber. That morning I installed all the batten strips on the front of the cabin, including trim around all the windows. While I was busy with that, Tom fastened the metal trim pieces along the porch roof.

Again, it was nice weather. We reduced our clothing to only two sweatshirts and two layers of pants today. Spring was on the way! The weather report we'd heard a few days earlier regarding the steady rain was obviously wrong. For that we were grateful.

That night, we inhaled piles of fish and potatoes for dinner, and of course, we felt like we'd overeaten once again. Then we both worked tirelessly on our crossword puzzles until bedtime.

28

Goose Egg on Easter

Day 22

"Stiff and sore" were the words that came to mind as I opened my eyes after a great night's sleep. After the treacherous job of nailing on the batten strips the day before, I vividly felt each painful movement as I awoke for the day. Since the front of the cabin was elevated, the sixteen foot ladder which we'd sent from home was much shorter than what I'd needed to properly do the job. And as a result, I was forced to reach precariously overhead to get the task completed. In order to get some of the higher batten strips nailed on, it required me to hang from the rafters like an ape. But before I went up the ladder, I pre-nailed the board I was attempting to put up. Then I made my way to the tiptop of the ladder. While I made sure to have one hand hanging on for dear life, in my other hand I carried both my hammer and my small board. Next, I propped the nail-started board over the window. Before it had a chance to lean away from the wall, I'd quickly strike the nail. A perfect hit would attach the board. A less than perfect attempt sent the board tumbling to the ground. Let's just say, I'm not perfect. No wonder I was feeling so sore and tired!

That morning, we'd installed the last of the siding and then contemplated running to town for nails and supplies. The weather looked a little challenging with gray skies and briskly moving clouds, and as a result, we opted out in order to avoid potential disaster. It was a painful decision, however, because we were in desperate need of eight-penny nails which were necessary to finish putting up the batten strips. I'd already dug around in the dirt but couldn't find any more bent nails under the cabin; consequently, the siding project was at a standstill.

Without nails, the rest of the work on the cabin would have to wait. For the time being, we were forced to focus our efforts on other projects. During the late afternoon, we rested and worked on crossword puzzles again. Fortunately, we didn't end up going to town, because as the day progressed, it became apparent that the bad weather which had rolled in would have held us hostage there. That day was the breaking point for me. It was official: the adventure part of Alaska was beginning to wear me out. I was starting to get real tired of feeling trapped, whether it was at the cabin or in town, and the continual decisions about it all were very time-consuming.

Day 23

We slept uneasily due to the storm that raged throughout the night, but by the time we got up it was only raining, and the water was calm. Our main focus was getting to town for supplies in order to finish the projects before we left for Oregon. Briefly, we waited around in order to judge the weather's mood. As usual, I had packed my typical emergency bag and then lugged it to the boat. Tom had carried the neatly folded tent out to the boat as well. Our desire was to leave it in the car, so it was ready for the trip back home to Oregon.

The skies were gray, but the water was cooperative, so before long, we left for town, stopping to check the crab pot along the way. It had captured six crabs. We took them back to the cabin before we headed out again. We made it about half way to town just past the dog's leg where the weather turned much worse. The unfriendly wind that greeted us at the corner took us by complete surprise. The rain wasn't just falling either; it was coming down with a vengeance. The sleet began peppering my face, forcing me to shield both Pup and myself using the tarp, which we always made use of, but on the average day it was only up to our chins. The closer we got to town, the more the weather worsened. Once we neared the open water, we determined that the conditions were far too rough. Due to the heavy sleet, we couldn't decipher anything up ahead and above all, we knew that there was no way we could safely continue. Very discouraged, we immediately turned back and headed for home.

Did somebody say "dog's leg?" A couple of times, while in Alaska, I'd heard people describing where the fishing hotspots were located. What was said was, "Just past the dog's leg on the north side," or something to that effect. There was one such "dog's leg" up to the point where we were located, so I'd heard. With that said, when I looked on the map I could see why it is referred to as a dog's leg. The bend in the inlet looked just like a dog's hind leg. It could also be called a "zigzag" or "the corner" but a dog's leg, really, said it all.

Today, after having been denied our trip to town due to the unruly weather, we decided to do some fishing on our return trip. During our explorations, we actually found a new hot spot where we caught the biggest rock fish yet. So far, we'd caught fifty crabs on the trip and who knows how many rockfish. Since landing a mess of rock fish never took very long, we were back to the cabin in no time. It was a good thing because not only had I forgotten to load the garbage bag, but the bag of recycling had been left on shore, too. The tide had come in, but luckily, both bags were still intact and floating just barely off the beach. It was our good fortune that the ravens were out to lunch somewhere else that day!

Once we were on the beach, Tom filleted the rock fish while I got the rest of our lunch prepared. After lunch, we went outside to work. In an effort to clean up the property before we headed back to Oregon, we decided that it was time to cut up the large collection of cedar saw mill remnants which had been piling up on the beach in recent weeks. Each log we cut up created four attractive leftovers. Since the first cuts from a log are always flat on one side and round on the other, they weren't really suitable to be used for the framing of the cabin. But they could be used for creative trim and custom finish work; therefore, I had plans for them.

Since I had accumulated quite a large pile, Tom would occasionally make me weed through them to see what I would be willing to part with. Usually none; they were all too beautiful. Now at the end of our stay, he beckoned me down to the beach, and I could tell by his demeanor, he meant business. While

I supervised, he flipped through each remnant like they were on death row; I stood aside, carefully judging each one on their individual worthiness. With a satisfied smirk, Tom promptly removed my selections and irreverently hurled them into the firewood pile; it felt like an execution to me. Little by little my treasure trove dwindled away. I packed the chosen few up the hill while Tom used his chainsaw to cut up the remaining wood which all got stacked under the deck for firewood.

Out on the new deck, Tom cooked crab for dinner while I griddle fried the last of our potatoes. Our eyes were continually evaluating the uncertain skies while we dined. With any luck, we were hopeful of getting to town in the morning because we were out of several supplies. We had only a few days before we had to head home, but we could get a lot done in that amount of time if only we'd had the materials we needed. By evening, the weather had cleared up and was absolutely beautiful. The pinkish-colored sky glistened off the glass-like surface of the water. The distant airplanes were providing the only noises we could hear besides the hum of an occasional insect traveling by. Right then, a trip to town would've been simple, but if we would have left for town at that time of day, the hardware store would have been closed. That was for sure our most important stop. It was our ultimate goal to be able to pick up our supplies in the morning, weather permitting.

Day 24

We anxiously awoke around 5 a.m. to see about getting the boat ready for town again. The tide was in, so we anxiously departed around 6:30 a.m. It was a beautiful spring day, which offered flat calm water as we motored off. It was going to be a relief to finally get to town! The ride in was very chilly but smooth. In no time we were there. What a relief! The parking lot at the boat launch was empty, but it was pretty early still. There wasn't much traffic buzzing about either as we made our way through to the other end of town where we pulled into the parking lot at the hardware store. Of course it was vacant; it was only 7:15 a.m. We were early, but we were there, at last. We were so excited to finally make it into town after our failed attempts. The store was dark, so I got out of the car to clarify what time the business would open. To our dismay, the sign on the door read: "Easter Sunday—Sorry, We're Closed!"

What a letdown! That blunder would shed light on the fact that we were a bit out of touch, living in our remote world of adventures. There was nothing we could do about it at this point. We called a couple of other stores; no nails! Disappointed, we stopped for groceries and returned home without the intended purchase. For sure, it would be too far for us to hit town the next day just for nails, so sadly enough, we knew we would not be able to get our project done before we headed back home to Oregon. Even though we were extremely full of regret, we tried to convince ourselves that it wasn't the end of the world. We frequently made a point to say, "It's just a cabin," which enabled us to thoroughly enjoy our time in Alaska. After all, nothing had to be finished!

When we got back to the cabin, we spent some more time cleaning up outside. There was a feeling of quiet sadness in the air because we would be leaving soon. Now that our first trip to Alaska was coming to a close, during our rockfish feast at dinner, we discussed our trip back to Oregon. It was Sunday—Easter Sunday, to boot! Our ferry tickets were for Thursday at 1:45 a.m., which meant we only had three days left in remote Alaska. Very soon, it would be necessary to get our belongings organized; we'd have to decide which ones to leave and which ones to take home with us. For two days we'd been talking and planning for the last boat ride in, making sure we wouldn't have to transport more than a safe load. Every day, Tom carefully studied the tide book, calculating where the high tide would reach on Wednesday, the day we needed to leave. The tides were on a cycle that was resulting in a lower tide each day, so we knew we'd have to be very careful. That meant no mistakes allowed. The last drama we needed to top off the adventure was to get beached and then miss the ferry.

29

Homeward Bound

Day 25

Morning arrived and our conversation went straight to the subject of Tom heading back to work. He was scheduled to leave for Togiak, Alaska, for the herring fishing season, which was the sole reason we planned to leave Alaska when we did. Even though we'd been through some difficult times, thinking about leaving our remote wonderland already was causing me a great deal of sadness. Up until this point, I hadn't realized how Alaska had changed me for the better. During our isolation it had become somewhat refreshing only having to worry about our own difficult yet rewarding hardships of surviving camp. It was a love-hate thing. I disliked being isolated, but I loved the independence it required to survive; I enjoyed the challenge. As our visit came to a close, I felt I'd just started to form a friendship with the wild outdoors. I had come to realize that since all of our days were spent in survival mode, I had forgotten about most of the world's depressing problems. Just being out of the swirl of constant bad news it seemed almost therapeutic. Perhaps I hadn't truly appreciated having the "weight of the world" lifted from my shoulders. There was no doubt that my overall health had improved since I'd arrived. Could the stress of plain ol' survival be considered a healthier kind of stress, I wondered? The emotions I'd learned to rely on felt primal in some way. And facing my fears head-on had certainly encouraged me to find out exactly who I was.

The morning started off with more cleaning up around camp. It was a nice day, sunny and kind of warm again. So to begin the project, Tom de-limbed the trees which he'd cut down our first day here. They were still propped in the neighboring timber with nothing but the butt-end touching the ground. We burned the resulting brush, which created a raging inferno in the frozen wilderness. The fire was so hot, in fact, that the flames eventually erupted on the side of the ice-covered tree nearby. I was grateful we were going to be there another full day to make sure that the fire was fully extinguished. As we continued, not only did we burn up the loose limbs lying around, but in addition, all of the cedar lumber scraps I'd been pawing through which were ready for incineration as well. In recent weeks I'd been in constant disagreement with Tom over their potential worth.

During the cleanup process, we realized that unbeknownst to us, the ravens had managed to take off with a couple more of our possessions after all. Tom came across my stocking hat tucked away deep in the brush. The mystery of where the pudding had gone was partially solved; two empty containers surfaced just uphill from the beach. At the close of the day, we were still looking for the elusive tub of butter, among other things.

As for the cabin, there were certain belongings, like shovels and gas cans which needed to be locked up before we left for home, so we began moving them inside. We were hopeful that when we returned in August, the cabin would be just how we left it: no bears, no falling trees, and no human intruders. Making our way around the perimeter, we came to our water storage tank—it was located just outside the kitchen window at the rear of the cabin. Thinking ahead to our summer visit, we weren't sure how much water would be available when we returned. For that reason we decided to leave the water tank full; there would be no chance of it freezing between now and August. Next we assessed the kitchen window. Since it was the only window in the cabin which could have been reached from the ground by either bears or humans, we protected it with plywood. We placed a sheet of plywood over the water tank as well in case a heavy moss covered limb was to break loose from one of the trees above. We definitely didn't want to find a punctured tank upon our return.

Soon enough, we became fixated on thoughts of missing the ferry. At low tide, when I was finally able to establish phone service, I checked on the ferry tickets. By then, Tom was in a huge hurry to get home because he had just found out he was supposed to fly out to Togiak in eight days. It was his strong desire to get back to Oregon before he left for work. For sure, he didn't want me driving all day and night, towing the boat through Canada by myself. Following our discussion, I placed a call to my sister. In the course of conversation I voiced my concerns of missing the ferry. Her brainstorm was that we should stay in a motel to alleviate the worry of being stranded at the property due to a boat parking mistake. At first it sounded like a waste of money; an extra night in a motel? They aren't cheap in Alaska—especially with a pet in tow. But after a few minutes of serious consideration, that idea was bringing me much relief. We should stay in town, I reasoned. When I came up off the beach from talking to her on the phone, I mentioned the idea to Tom. It would mean we'd be departing from the property the next day, instead of the day after when we'd originally planned. Tom was undecided.

After dinner, we tidied up a few more things and went to bed. The discussion about our departure continued. Maybe we should depart tomorrow, we decided. But even though we didn't need to leave until the evening tide, we figured that as long as we were paying for the motel, we might as well be there all day. With most everything put away now, there was nothing left to do at the property except worry about getting stuck. We were out of supplies for our projects, and the majority of our camp was already secured, so all things considered, it made perfect sense to leave a day earlier than we'd originally planned.

In order to weigh our options, we would need to check the tides again. We decided to get back out of bed to see what we were up against. After consulting the trusty tide book, we determined that high tide would be at 4 a.m. the next morning. Once our brief discussion ended, our moods had shifted into high gear and we found ourselves scurrying around with flashlights while we got the rest of our camp in order. We filled the water tank using the water source up the hill and then tied the pipe up high in the tree again. We didn't need all that extra water flowing under the cabin while we were away.

Now that we knew a lot more about what living in Alaska was like, Tom had already made definite plans to restructure the boat before our next visit.

We had decided a few days earlier that before we left for our home in Oregon, we wanted to remove the boat's steering cabin; it was destined to be our future outhouse—our bathroom in the cabin had a shower and sink but wasn't equipped with restroom facilities. We concluded that removing the cabin would be even more difficult to do once the boat was floating in the morning. So, it was midnight when we began to dismantle the cabin from the boat.

As soon as the structure was disconnected, right away we began to maneuver the well-built wooden shelter over the side of the boat. Once it was on the beach, we each took one end and hoisted the heavy-duty cabin onto our shoulders. I had the lightest part of the load and was stationed in front with the flashlight; Tom was at the rear. We slowly transported the monstrosity through the tidal mud, taking great care not to stumble. Although we stopped to resituate more than once, our final stop was at the base of the hill where we set the heavy load down for another planning session. We quickly determined that it was going to be too dangerous to attempt a trip up the hill in the dark. We were out of breath, anyway. We knew we'd have to finish getting it yarded up the hill at first light. That would be the extent of our preparations for the time being.

Back in bed again, we ironed out exactly what had to be done before we could leave in the morning; we would each have several things to accomplish. Since our boat would be floating at daybreak, and our anchor would be put away first thing, that meant at all times, one of us would need to stay standing guard in the water alongside the boat until we headed out for the last time. It would be extremely important to make sure our vessel was not only free to move, but also that it didn't float away. Tom and I would have to trade off. On that note, we tried to get to some sleep. We were understandably anxious about the morning's tasks, so it took a while before we finally dozed off.

Day 26

When our eyes sprang open from a sound sleep, it wasn't pitch dark anymore. This was it! It was barely daylight when we began the first order of business, which was getting the elephant-sized boat cabin maneuvered up the hill. Rolling, shoving, heaving, and slipping on large skunk cabbage leaves and mushy soil, we eventually made it up the steep slope. Our now wet knees, feet, hands and elbows were caked in loose fir needles, like sesame seeds on a helping of delicious Asian Chicken. After that exhausting event, we took turns moving the remainder of our belongings inside the cabin. At last, Tom unhooked the battery for the twelve-volt lighting system, while I rounded up the last of the garbage. After our camp was all buttoned up, I took some pictures and said our final farewells to our cozy refuge in the Alaskan wilderness. It had served us well.

There was no turning back. We energetically headed for town around 6:30 a.m. During our last ride in, I was able to sit up on the bench where the boat cabin had been mounted. From that vantage point I could experience the full beauty of the pristine water, which could not have been more spectacular. As we traveled along, the water in the inlet was mirror-like again, reflecting the mountains perfectly from every direction while the vibrant colors of the Alaskan sunrise glistened on the glassy surface.

Once in town, we checked into the motel and enjoyed the stress-free activity of lying around all day. We knew our check out time was noon the following day, so we purposely saved all of the errands for then, knowing our ferry didn't depart until well after midnight. We feasted on the crab we'd brought with us and noted that there would be plenty to snack on during the long drive home. Since we'd been without television for over a month, we were quickly brought back up to speed on the news, commercials and other programming as well. We hadn't missed anything.

Soon, it was time to retire for the evening. Before climbing into bed, I stood at the motel window to observe what I could. Both the sky and the water were pitch black in color. Our room was only a stone's throw from the Tongass Narrows. The darkness which blanketed everything was only slightly invaded by a distant porch light across the water. At some point my eyes were drawn to the occasional blinking beacon anchored off shore. And other than the water that I could hear lapping rhythmically and ever-so-gently against the rock wall just feet away, it was completely silent.

With my soul still in wilderness-mode, I drifted off to sleep. I was very aware of not only the water's quiet voice, but also the weather outside. I realized that over the course of the last month, my ears had been retrained to focus on different noises—sounds of survival. Because of our recent experiences, my idea of a good day had drastically changed. It used to revolve around stressful subjects like the news or money. But as I listened to the waves and their perfect rhythm, I felt so comforted to know that we were in town and could relax. I felt safe and at peace. I breathed deeply with great relief, knowing we didn't have to worry about Mother Nature pushing us to the limit. Our boat didn't have the opportunity to disappear on a windy day, or sink in a vicious storm; it was safely stowed in the parking lot behind our car. Now that we'd left the cabin, the tide was completely irrelative. I wondered how long it might be before my thinking changed; the tide had been so vital to our existence at the cabin. Back on the mainland, we once again had a little more control of our destiny. But then again, did we really?

Day 27

With mixed feelings, we spent our last day in Ketchikan. Even though I found it a relief to be back to civilization, I was sad to leave behind all that nature had to offer.

Tom's serious ferry-line anxiety issues hadn't disappeared, and I was only able to keep him pre-occupied with various menial tasks until 7:30 p.m. It was no surprise that we were the first car in line again, with just over six hours left on the clock until our departure! I'm not kidding. The ferry terminal itself didn't even open for four more hours. By then I knew it was a non-negotiable subject. To pass the time, Pup and I ventured on many dark walks around the parking area. We walked to the dock where I nostalgically inhaled the familiar odors of salt water and creosote while I listened to the slurping sounds of the water as it wrapped itself around the pilings on the pier. Pup and I took our sweet time knowing that I would have to leave him alone again during the ferry commute. Each time we circled back to the car we found Tom faithfully holding down his seat.

Day 28

It was around 1:00 a.m. when we boarded the ferry, and our departure took place on schedule. Shortly into our sailing the weather turned sour which resulted in a very rough ride. Instantly, I was concerned for Pup, who was alone in the car on the lower deck. More than once I did a mental inventory of our car, picturing what I'd stacked where. I wondered if anything might fall on him during the bumpy commute. Thank goodness I couldn't think of anything. Tom and I tried to nap on the carpeted floor of the somewhat sound-proof reading lounge, but it was difficult to rest. The ferry rolled from side to side, and I kept imagining how big the waves must have been. I was so relieved to be heading home. I was tiring of braving the intimidating waters of Alaska.

It was still pitch dark when we arrived to port in Prince Rupert, British Columbia. By the time we made it off of the ferry, there were multiple lanes of vehicles with headlights aglow, all of us trapped like cattle behind the Canadian border patrol. We were all herded past one manned booth, which was a less than efficient process considering all the commuters wishing to enter Canada that morning. An hour passed as we inched forward toward customs. We could see ahead that several cars had been pulled aside for further inspection. As we approached, Tom repeatedly vocalized his impatience. I didn't console him; this had been all his idea. It didn't help that we were both tired from traveling all night. When we finally pulled up to the inspection zone, Pup was on my lap but climbed into his seat behind Tom as the agent approached the car's window. The male officer quickly surveyed our car. Without a word the agent looked Pup over. He quizzed us on where we'd bought his food, and then asked to see it, making sure we weren't going to take tainted dog food into Canada, I supposed. I reached behind Tom's seat to flip Pup's food container open for an inspection. To my dismay, a white bag of powder was sitting in plain sight. I started laughing, and began to explain about Pup and his seizures, and the reason for the powder.

In a stern tone, the officer commanded, "Let me see the baggy."

"It's lamb starter," I continued. I hadn't thought of the fact that his powdered milk resembles cocaine.

"When he refuses to eat his food… this is what I use," I explained. I handed it through the window and the officer fondled it for a second. Thanks to the blessed ravens, the powdered milk sprinkled onto his hands through the numerous beak holes in the bag. He put the bag to his nose for a sniff while Pup curiously stared him down. Instantly, the guard tossed the bag back into the car, dusted off his hands, and sent us on our way. I glanced at Tom. We made eye contact and I smirked at him. He rolled his eyes in complete disgust. I was his worst enemy right then, almost getting us delayed with a dreadful time-consuming inspection.

Once we were in familiar territory, it was refreshing to know what to expect on the drive through Canada. We opted to motor straight through to Westport without a nap. We arrived at Vern and Nancy's on the Washington coast twenty-four hours later where we rested for a couple hours. Well, I couldn't rest; I had pictures in-hand to enhance my many stories as I told his mom about what really happened when we were stranded in Alaska. Two hours later we departed for our home in eastern Oregon, just eight hours away.

Over all it was an amazing trip. We had spent twenty-eight challenging but rewarding days in Tom Jones' fantasy land. It actually seemed like we'd been gone much longer due to the many challenges we faced, not to mention the countless setbacks. The wild outdoor experience had rigorously tested me physically, mentally and emotionally. Not only did I have a new opinion of myself, I had learned a great deal about my husband along the way. But I must admit that our personal differences have never been as apparent as they were during the hardships of my first visit to the great state of Alaska!

How would our summer trip be different, I wondered?

A SUMMER
WONDERLAND

30

A Whole New World

Just as we had anticipated, in mid-August we returned to Ketchikan for our summer visit. It had been less than four months since Tom and I'd left Alaska following our previous stay. He'd been home from Bristol Bay for only two and half weeks, and even though Tom had been working in Alaska since April, he was still very anxious to get back to the property at the first opportunity. Just since our time here last spring, Tom was now a resident of Alaska! And although I didn't yet have the same fever he did, after experiencing Alaska for myself, I was beginning to better understand where Tom's unstoppable drive was coming from.

A few days earlier, we'd left Oregon, and like before, we drove through Canada with our boat in tow. Once in Prince Rupert, we caught the ferry and with much less anxiety this time, we'd arrived in Ketchikan for our summer stay. It'd been several months since my initial Alaskan baptism-by-fire, and I'd had some time to come to grips with all the drama that had taken place during our previous adventure where my gut instinct and I had been reacquainted and had since become the best of friends.

It was a beautiful day in August as we prepared to make our way to the property; there was no doubt that I felt much more confident with such valuable experiences under my belt. Moments ago, we'd arrived at the boat launch where the available parking was scarce. Other than the large number of boaters who had beaten us out on the water this morning, the sights were very familiar which I found extremely reassuring. Once the boat was in the water, Tom tediously shoe horned our car and empty boat trailer into the only available space before we readied ourselves to embark on the boat ride out to our property. Pup and I donned our life jackets while Tom lowered the boat's propeller into the water and then warmed up the motor. On our newly revamped vessel, the boat's steering station had been relocated. It was now up front and to the right. Due to those revisions, Tom would be sitting instead of standing, and now he and I sat together on a full bench seat stationed more toward the bow. From that vantage point, Pup and I could easily see where we were going, a huge improvement from before where we used to sit, more like cargo on the deck in front of the steering cabin.

The dock was hopping with people who were cleaning fish and milling around as we sped away. I was delighted to discover that Alaska's summer weather certainly presented a much more inviting atmosphere. The breeze coming off the water was actually warm and boaters were everywhere as we headed out past the jetty. Pleasure boats, charter boats, and skiffs were all moving about in different directions, clearly each of them on its individual mission. During our ride out to the property, I consciously absorbed all of the beautiful scenery as we sailed along without so much as a ripple. It was more like what I had expected to encounter on my first expedition to Alaska. As our boat skimmed across the water's surface, I found my comfort level to be improving by the minute! I couldn't believe how pleasant it seemed in comparison to our previous visit. If the Alaska trip continues to go this well, maybe I can relax and enjoy myself this time, I thought, as we traveled along effortlessly.

It was early morning still when we motored into our familiar stomping grounds eight miles or so up Carroll Inlet. When we came ashore, except for the splashing noises of the fish which were jumping everywhere, it was absolutely silent on the beach. The fragile shoots of fresh spring grass stood tall and undisturbed, providing a burst of color which stretched around the curve of the neutral-colored beach in our small yet familiar cove. As we climbed out of the boat, we immediately became aware of fresh bear sign on the grassy shore, and judging by its appearance, the bear had been eating plenty of berries. I showed the purple-tinted pile to Pup. He sniffed it carefully and his eyes bulged just slightly as he made eye contact with me while I told him, "That's from a bear, baby. You have to be so careful, huh?" before he immediately led me away.

We quickly surveyed the area, knowing that our bear spray and guns were up inside the locked cabin, and we remained optimistic that there wouldn't be an encounter of any kind before we were able to retrieve them. With our arms heaped with supplies, we hiked up the hill, carefully surveying all of the changes which had taken place while we were away. The most obvious difference—the flourishing greenery had replaced the snow that had vanished since we left. As we neared the cabin, we took notice of the enormous leafy foliage which had sprung up both in and around our pathway; it made our cabin's surroundings appear more like an exotic island than a rustic Alaskan getaway.

We stood in awe for a moment, observing nature's lush, green carpeting that covered every available inch of the forest floor. In all directions, a thick moss blanketed not only the ground but also continued on up over logs and stumps, smoothing out everything in sight with a healthy cushion of lime green. The moist summer air exuded the rich fragrance of a magnificent rainforest as the overwhelming aromas of abundant moss, wet bark, and newly emerging plant life came together—all in a perfect blend. Varieties of mushrooms were abounding amidst the ideal climate provided by the tall timber. It was a completely new environment from what I remembered.

For our stay this summer, our intentions were to preserve a healthy batch of fresh seafood. And to make sure that our seafood preservation project would be successful, for this trip we'd brought along canning equipment, plenty of jars, and two new crab pots, along with a ring net and some additional fishing gear. With the cabin already built, we expected that we would have all kinds of spare time to play around. This was definitely a more inviting environment. Of course, at some point we planned to finish up on the cabin, but that wasn't going to stop us from living in the moment.

Once we were inside our cozy Alaskan hideaway, we noticed that everything had remained untouched in recent months, for which we were very grateful. We agreed that we should go fishing right away, so we went about getting organized for the activity. As we continued to unload the boat and pack our supplies up the hill to the cabin, Tom suggested to me that because there were so many fish nearby, we'd just fish from the shore instead of going out in the boat. That sounded good to me. Without delay, we unearthed our gear and carted it down to the beach where Tom spread the entire contents of the tackle box onto the bow of the boat and began preparing the poles for the upcoming fishing excursion.

"This will be the same pole you used before," he told me, "but the hook and bait will be different than jigging for rock fish." He continued to dig through the fishing gear, apparently in search of specific items he intended to tie on the end of the fishing line. As I looked on, the sun beating down overhead had me wishing I'd brought my sunglasses. Even though Tom had explained how different the summer weather would be, having some shades wasn't even a consideration when I'd left for my trip north to the cabin. Between the warm weather and the colorful scenery, it almost felt as if we had arrived on a new piece of property.

Just off shore, the constant commotion of the fish that were jumping and splashing in close proximity sent Pup into a barking frenzy. Clearly, salmon season was in full swing, which was a new development from our last trip. Pup and I had never seen such a sight. He began to tromp back and forth along the water's edge, conversing excitedly by way of his constant, high-pitched yelping.

I was busy taking in the familiar sights from our beach when something caught my eye. I noticed Tom curiously pulling something from his lips.

"My tooth just broke," he announced. I instantly slouched, overcome with serious disappointment.

"What did you do?" I asked, disgustedly, while placing both hands on my hips.

"Oh, just biting off this lead and it broke, I guess," he muttered.

"Oh, ya think?" I scolded. Biting into a fishing lead is like dining on gravel. Does every trip have to start off with a disaster, I wondered? My mind raced, trying to determine the true impact of what had just happened. Although not life-threatening, a full set of teeth are important, in my opinion, which wasn't good news for Tom right then.

"What a perfect way to start the trip," I said sarcastically. "Let me see," I asked, while at the same time searching for the courage to accept the sad truth.

He flashed a fake smile in my direction in order to show me the damage. Sure enough, a huge gap appeared where half of his front tooth had snapped off clear to his gum line. So now I'll be stuck looking at this wonderful sight for six weeks, I processed. It might not have bothered me as badly if Tom would have shown even a hint of sorrow. Perhaps some guilt, remorse, or even some healthy embarrassment would have helped…but instead I got zilch on the radar. He just continued on unaffected as he handed me the fishing pole I would be using for the day. After all, he'd had plenty of experience with broken teeth while working at sea, so for him, this unfortunate occurrence wasn't even a slight concern.

Completely uninterrupted by the broken tooth, he carried on with his instructions of how I was supposed to fish for salmon. Due to the giant passageway in his front row of teeth, I could hardly concentrate on what he was saying. His next few sentences were dotted with intermittent whistles, while he learned to pronounce his words differently with a wind tunnel now present where a full tooth used to be. Unable to avoid my judgmental mood, I zeroed in on his mouth from time to time. Did I know this strange man?

As the day wore on, I struggled to cope with Tom's hillbilly makeover. I slowly came to grips with the fact that his new appearance would most likely have to be this way for a while. Just knowing Tom like I do, I knew that the urgent detail of finding a dentist was completely out of the question; we were in Alaska now—where all else takes a back seat. I attempted to put it all in perspective, which wouldn't be something that happened right away!

31

Thief in the Night

Even though we'd barely arrived, it wasn't long before Tom had reeled in several beautiful salmon this morning. On the other hand, I struggled to hook let alone land even one fish. The salmon fishing experience was nothing like jigging for rock fish. After a suitable cast of my hook, which didn't happen at first, the hook had to get "set," or jerked into the fish at just the right time. I learned that when I was either too early or too late on the jerk, it would yank the hook clear out of the water, sometimes causing it to sail clear back over my head and into the rocks behind me. I could tell that it would be a while before I would get this system figured out. Tom's efforts were successful though, and we kept all of his catch which we would later use to bait the crab pots.

For this trip, we had two different kinds of crab pots. The pot we'd brought up and then left after our first trip to Alaska was a solid-framed pot, approximately three feet across with a flap opening designed specifically for easy access not only to hang the bait, but also to collect the catch. Now that we'd arrived, it would be joined by two other similar crab pots we'd brought along with us. They were the exact same design, just a little smaller in diameter.

The other slightly different style of pot we were going to employ was a ring net. A ring net is a collapsible pot which gets baited and then set into the water for just an hour or so. Once in the water, the top ring is designed to collapse directly onto the bottom ring. The bait then attracts the crabs which are allowed to come and go as they please, which is unlike the other pots which trap the crab. When the time comes to check it for visitors, the pot is simply pulled up out of the water, allowing the sides of the pot to lift up so the crab cannot escape on their way to the surface. After the pot is out of the water, the sides collapse again, providing easy access to the catch.

So with crab in mind, after dinner, Tom baited our three crab pots and put them out in the water to "soak" for the night. When a pot is soaking that means it is actively fishing. Next, he secured the remaining bait in the ring net, which he left in the boat with full intentions of also setting it out to soak for a short time the next morning. We reminisced about the luck we'd had during our first stay in Alaska when we'd caught fifty-two keepers just a few hundred feet from our own beach. For a five-week stay under those circumstances, fifty-two crabs were a good deal more than we had ever anticipated. And fishing wasn't a priority then; we'd been focused more on survival and getting the cabin built. We wondered how the future crab catching would go in comparison to our previous trip when we'd used only one pot.

We fished off and on all day until we were sunburned and tired. As we began to close up camp for the evening, the tide was in, at which point Tom pulled the boat up close to the trail for our first night back.

In recent months I'd learned so much about the tides. Sometimes the tide was our enemy as Mother Nature snuck up and secretly swiped our possessions sitting too close to the high tide mark. The next day, the tide could be our best friend as undeserving gifts would show up on the beachfront without notice.

Ironically, the tide boasted a predictable presence. It came twice each day, no matter what. But since its schedule was always changing, we could always depend on a different scenario than the day before. The part of the tide I had an aversion to, however, was the constant fear of boat associated dilemmas when we hadn't made the right decision about where to let it go dry. But for our first day back, somehow, we'd managed to have the most ideal tide schedule. If I could've chosen the most perfect tide to have all the time, I would've picked this one: high tide at 7 a.m. and 7 p.m. It allowed the boat to be stationed on dry land for the entire night. That scenario meant we would have no worries about our vessel either sinking or getting away while we slept;

consequently, we could count on a good night's sleep. Life at the cabin doesn't get much better than this, I thought!

The following morning, just as we had hoped, after a great night's sleep we awoke to find the boat sitting safe and sound with the tide water conveniently approaching. We were planning on having a look around the area this morning to see if any new cedar trees had washed up. As the day began, I was cooking our typical griddle-fried breakfast of hash browns and eggs while Tom went outside to do his daily survey. Before long, he came back in and proceeded to tell me a story about what he had come across while he'd been down on the beach.

"You know how I just let the boat sit on the beach all night?" he began.

"Yeah?" I answered.

"Well, when I went down this morning, I could see one of our buoys sitting clear up in the grass by the trees," he continued. "So when I went over to see what was going on, I could see our crab line stretched way up into the woods."

"Yeah?" I answered back. At this point, I put my spatula down to encourage him to finish his story.

"Then," he said, "I walked a little further and could see our ring net sitting in the brush with half the bait missing!"

"What happened?" I asked, with a crinkled forehead.

"It had to have been a bear," he said with full confidence. "Those crab pots weigh about twenty-five pounds plus bait, and besides, what else would've eaten the salmon and left the rock fish?"

We presumed it must have been a large animal to have had the wherewithal to lift such an awkward, heavy object out of the boat. Not only that, the ring net had been packed way up into the brush, dragging a crab line and buoy along with it. After discussing the situation, we both agreed that it probably was indeed a bear. We surmised that when the thief climbed into the boat, he must have attempted to grab the bait wad with his teeth. But because the bait was attached to the net, he was forced to lift the whole thing….ring net and all. We imagined that the heavy steel rings must have created quite a racket, and we couldn't believe that we hadn't heard a sound all night. We were positive that the bear sign we'd seen on the beach the day before was very fresh, since it had been deposited within twelve hours of our arrival, sometime after the previous high tide. The large numbers of salmon that had been jumping non-stop from the moment we'd arrived were most likely providing their regular meals.

We weren't too surprised about the presence of bears but we hadn't predicted that they would be so daring that early on during our stay. For that reason I was really glad we'd brought along a small fridge. Besides keeping our food cold during the warmer weather, the other purpose for toting the modern convenience all through Canada was so that all of our food at the cabin could be kept safely indoors away from the bears. Of course, the generator had to be employed to make it operational, but it didn't have to be plugged in all day. If the fridge could run for two hours in the evening, it would be plenty long enough to chill the food and keep it cold all night. It was a routine which would work well with our regular schedule where each evening consisted of games, reading, and snacking for at least a couple hours after dark. Then, the generator would also be on again in the morning while I fixed breakfast and got ready for the day.

It was nice to look forward to a more relaxed agenda on this trip, and it sure was easy to get back in the swing of things. We had many of the kinks worked out already, so in some aspects, it seemed almost as if we had never left. Without hesitation we resumed many of our old routines, such as playing cribbage, and my taste buds hadn't experienced the flavor of a frosted graham cracker since I'd left four months earlier. But now at the cabin, once again, all three of us were eating the calorie-packed treats like they were going out of style. We'd need the calories anyway; we had big plans in store for our summer stay.

Right away, we planned on cutting some lumber to finish the interior of the cabin. One morning, we headed up the inlet to retrieve a log we'd discovered earlier in the trip. On our way there, off in the distance my eyes honed in on something very peculiar. It was a pattern of blinking lights stationed against the hillside and couldn't have been in a more opposite direction from town. Hmm? I thought. Could those possibly the ones I saw the night we were stranded in the dark six months ago? It was only seconds after I spotted the array of intermittent flashing beacons when I'd shifted my squinting eyes in

Tom's direction. He looked back at me in such a way that I could tell that he was hopeful that I'd drop the subject about which I hadn't even opened my mouth to speak of yet. The look on my face was yelling, "See! I told you!"

The lights were coming from a Loran station, a nearly obsolete radio navigation system monitored by the Coast Guard. Due to the Coasties' frequent traffic past our place, we'd already suspected that they must be manning a post beyond us somewhere. As far as the mysterious lights I'd seen during our excursion on the dark water, I hadn't made the connection whatsoever, but knowing Tom, he'd long ago solved that puzzle and had wisely chosen to keep his thoughts to himself. But now I had solid proof that we were going the wrong way in the dark on the miserable night from hell. I revisited the wide range of emotions I had experienced during those terrifying events. I remembered that our fretful night had begun with complete trust as we'd pulled away from the beach with the help of the fading light of the setting winter sun. Once darkness had taken over, I quickly had transitioned from sincere hope, to hope laced with serious doubts once I realized Tom wouldn't admit that he couldn't properly operate the electronics. Soon I had become overwhelmed with pure terror after he had repeatedly ignored my concerns of crashing into the rocky island. Following a brief delay, my primal rage had surfaced in response to his apparent negligence before I finally had reached a level of determination like I've never felt before. Amazingly enough, now that the experience was behind me, I could appreciate all that I had learned. No doubt, I had come a long ways since my first visit.

A short time later, we came ashore where the cedar tree was resting on the beach. Pup and I looked on, as Tom ambitiously prepared another log for its trip to the water. Back in daydream mode, I remembered how frightened I was during that ordeal our first night here. While I wrestled the heavy stones that would soon be in the log's direct path to the water, my thoughts flashed back through many of our dangerous logging excursions and miserable living conditions before reminding me of my conversation with my inner self when Tom had begged me just to try Alaska. The question, "How much worse could it get?" echoed off the walls of my skull in a mocking tone. I'd naively fallen for that line and I wondered if I'd be so gullible to let something like that happen again in the future. On the other hand, I found myself once again asking the same question. Could it get much worse than the long miserable night in cold terrifying darkness in remote Alaska? We had been through an awful lot and we were still standing, after all. As Tom prepared the log to roll it toward the water, I mentally coached myself, swearing not to ever forget all that had happened here.

Before I knew it, we were back on our beach where we went to work sawing lumber. Sawing logs seemed like "old hat." We quickly produced a stack of 1 inch by 8 inch cedar boards, and by the following evening the beautiful, rustic ceiling was installed.

32

A Self-Sufficient Mentality

Due to the cabin's limited floor space, since our last trip we'd been deliberating about the ideal location for our bed. Building a loft seemed the logical choice, but Pup can't climb ladders—that was out! The next design we considered was for a bed we could crank to the ceiling once we awoke for the day. But that wasn't the best use of space either; the pole required to support the fourth corner of the bed would be inconveniently affixed in the middle of the floor. Plus our ceilings were too low to be able to raise the bed frame clear out of the way. Our least favorite idea was a bed that folded into either a couch or a table; ultimately we decided that it would be too much trouble to stow the entire ensemble each time.

We finally decided on a permanent platform that would occupy the space between the kitchen area and the bathroom. Once the location was determined, it was necessary to figure out how high to build it off of the floor. We already knew the space underneath the bed was destined for storage, but the water pump for the cabin was stationed under there as well. I knew it needed to easily accommodate Tom, or there would be no end to the complaining about him having to squeeze under the bed to fiddle with the water pump should the need arise. I've learned over the years that plumbing should always be easily accessible for the plumber, which wasn't me! To establish the correct height, I suggested that Tom get on his hands and knees, so I could take a measurement of him in the crawling position. As a result, the platform for the mattress was built about two feet high.

With the bed's location issue resolved, the exposed insulation was still a problem for me. Call me spoiled, but I had no desire to be cradled against the bothersome fiberglass while I was trying to sleep. That was fine for a night or two during our last trip, but that option had been an upgrade from the freezing tent. I wasn't quite that desperate anymore. Even though we eventually planned to cover all of the interior walls with cedar boards at some point, the logs still had to be found and lumber cut. If we waited for those time consuming tasks to be completed, the sleeping arrangements wouldn't be improved for days. So, to keep production moving along, we opted to install paneling where the bed would be stationed, thus covering the itchy insulation immediately.

Lucky for us, since the water was so docile in comparison to our first stay in Alaska, that on our second day there we didn't even have to think twice about making a quick run to town to pick up supplies. Not only did we grab the lumber for our bed's platform, but we also bought the paneling for the walls, and it wasn't long before the bed project was completed. We quickly filled the spacious storage area with miscellaneous cabin clutter such as lanterns, extra clothes and the large tool box, all the while, freeing up a tremendous amount of precious floor space.

Once we got the basics of the cabin in order, we spent the rest of the day outside enjoying the gorgeous weather and the beautiful sights. The water was so pristine that just glancing across the cove, we could see fish swimming everywhere. Many times they were so close to the surface that the tips of the fins were causing wrinkles in the water. Tom could somehow see them traveling deeper in the water as well. His eyes just work that way. I couldn't get my vision to see below the surface unless I was well above the water. For that reason, Pup and I moved to the small rock cliff around the corner where it was especially easy to spot the large schools of fish. Pup and I began our fishing escapades there.

Since I could barely see the fish to begin with, I wasn't having much luck. And being a newbie to the salmon fishing world, even in the deeper water, in no time I'd snagged my hook and it wasn't on a fish. My gentle coaxing couldn't tug it loose from its hold on the rock, no matter where I stood on the beach. The crystal clear water allowed me to see the fishing lure from the rocky platform on which I stood, but it was far too deep to rescue without a diving expedition. I wasn't up for that. After having a look at the tide book, we decided that we would attempt to retrieve the inaccessible lure at low tide in a couple of days. We still had one fishing lure left in the package, so in the meantime, Tom rigged my fishing pole up again, and soon I was back learning to cast my hook.

From then on I stayed closer to the cabin, where I spent hours practicing my cast. The large expanse of shallow water on our beach provided a more challenging learning arena. When I failed to reel in at the perfect steady pace, my hook was easily snagged on one of many barnacle encrusted rocks. I was quickly figuring out that a fisherman is instantly out of business without a working hook. Soon the second hook was stuck; I was at a standstill until I waded out to disengage it from the rock on which it was hung.

With Tom's patient coaching, I managed to snag a couple of salmon some-how, but during those first few days, because of my ongoing errors, the entire time I fished, I was usually soaked clear to my waistline with my boots full of water. The water was quite warm; therefore, it didn't matter that I was wet. Pup was by my side, of course, also learning a new hobby. But he doesn't swim, so he'd pace the water's edge waiting for me each time I waded out to retrieve my hook. He enjoyed the constant activity of that type of fishing, but with all the racing around, the barnacle-covered rocks had started to chew up the bottoms of his feet. After a couple of hours of ambitious romping, he was begging me to take a break and head back to the cabin.

* * *

During the first couple days, we were catching plenty of both fish and crab. And the property was also action-packed with wildlife activity, which was quite a contrast from our winter stay. In addition to the bear presence, during Tom's morning survey on our second day, he witnessed two whales passing by in the waterway in front of the cabin. Their powerful intermittent bursts of mist broke the perfect silence in our remote setting. It was exciting to see the animals in their natural habitat. Maybe this was how Alaska was supposed to be: fun, peaceful, entertaining, and full of amazing wildlife. Besides Tom's tooth, the only thing that had ruined my day since I'd been there thus far was losing my new fishing lure in the deeper water after getting it hooked on a rock. According to my drama-meter, that was a drastic improvement from the initial white-knuckle, labor intensive trip to Alaska during the bone-chilling temperatures in the month of March. Yet the thought crossed my mind that maybe I wouldn't have appreciated the summer visit as much if we had started out that fantastically on the winter trip. On the other hand, if we hadn't been there to build the cabin in the frigid temperatures while the bears were hibernating, then this summer we would have been living in a tent scared to death all night in the midst of bear country. I liked that idea even less.

* * *

In just the first couple of days, the crab pots had caught sixteen crabs, which was a good deal more than we could eat! At that rate we planned on getting the cabin set up to cook, pick and preserve a lot of crab during our stay over the course of the next several weeks. Since the salmon were so plentiful, Tom was generously baiting the crab pots with "humpies" which were getting ready to spawn in the creek nearby. Tom explained that pink salmon are casually referred to as "humpies," because of the large, unsightly humps which develop on their backs as they deteriorate during the spawning phase. When we arrived in mid-August, to my untrained eye, the humpies weren't really obvious humpies yet; the salmon's exterior still displayed a smooth, clean and healthy appearance. The drastic changes begin to occur once the salt-water fish returns to their stream of origin in order to spawn. Soon after, the fresh water in the stream induces the decaying process, and within a short period of time, the fish spawns and dies. But not without purpose, though, because those carcasses provide guaranteed food for the new hatchlings that will soon be fighting for survival.

During the first few days, we spent the majority of our daylight hours fishing. We agreed that working on the cabin during daylight hours would interrupt our precious fishing time; consequently, we remained focused on installing trim and other finish details after the sun went down. Since we needed the lights on after dark anyway, the generator would be running already; thus, we wouldn't be wasting fuel just to cut a board here and there.

* * *

It wasn't long before we arranged to meet up with a new acquaintance in town, but I was hesitant about making a public appearance due to Tom's tooth situation. To be honest, it was really bothering me. On the advice of his dad, we had picked up some superglue in an attempt to fix it ourselves. One morning, while the sun was shining in the front window, it seemed the optimal occasion to make the repair.

First, in order to see how I might get the broken shard back in its proper position, I dry-fitted the piece in Tom's mouth. Once in place, the complete row of teeth looked good as new! After I removed the broken tooth again, I opened the glue package and popped the seal on the tiny tube. Before I knew it, the glue wrapper was already stuck to my left hand, while my right hand had experienced an accident of its own. Instantaneously, my pointer and middle finger became joined as one, which wasn't looking too good for Tom right then. During a brief delay, I successfully separated my fingers with a razor blade and in no time we were back to square one. Despite my reckless behavior, Tom was still willing to continue with the procedure as long as it would make me happy.

In the midst of our constant laughing about the dentistry I was getting ready to perform, Pup was getting pretty wound up. He really enjoys participating in our sessions of laughter—it's as if he is laughing, too. He was marching around the cabin, barking happily, which made it impossible for Tom and I to communicate in flowing sentences.

Next, in an attempt to avoid putting my less than sterile fingers into Tom's mouth, I inserted my hand inside my makeshift glove—the common sandwich bag. Immediately, I realized that the more sanitary option wasn't going to work. I couldn't even hold on to the tiny, slippery chunk of his tooth. As

I fussed around with one idea after another, Tom was patiently waiting with his head tilted back, as he attempted to recline himself in the rigid metal folding chair.

Meanwhile, Pup was sharking around the edge of the table like he does when he's sniffing out frosted graham cracker leftovers and his tongue regularly makes an appearance. On one of his inquisitive passes, his pig-like snout snorted at the tooth for a quick assessment. With a quick glance toward each other, we acknowledged the potential mishap, but thankfully, the precious fragment still remained on the table.

In all seriousness, once again, I examined the gluing surface of the tooth, and then peered into Tom's mouth one more time. I could see that his lip was going to be in the way for the procedure; keeping in mind that with superglue involved….the results could be tragic. To keep his vulnerable flesh out of the work zone, I rolled up a paper towel and packed it between his top lip and gums. Tom's uncontrollable bursts of laughter wouldn't allow the temporary dental buffer to stay put for very long, forcing me to reinstall it more than once.

After several minutes of messing around, somehow, we were able to settle down and find a quiet moment.

"Now where is the tooth?" I asked, snickering again.

A short scan confirmed that it was still sitting on the cluttered table. Once again, I got myself in position to see into Tom's mouth for the renovation. I applied a sufficient amount of glue and without delay, I inserted the broken piece back into the empty slot. Using gentle pressure, I held it steady for a moment so the glue had a chance to dry. When I stood back to view my handiwork—voila! It looked like new. Both of us couldn't quit laughing at the absurdity of the situation. But at long last, the tooth was glued in place, and we were ready for town. It was nice to have my husband's complete set of teeth to look at again, and as I studied his renovated chops, I was very hopeful that his makeover would last.

As for our meeting in town, the tooth's first appearance went very well. However, returning home, we stopped for a stint to try out a new fishing hole. In between casts, we were snacking on chips and pepperoni sticks. Sadly, Tom felt his tooth come loose again right as a fish hit his line. With his hand to his mouth he fumbled for a second, but the fish soon became a priority and he began to reel in. In the heat of the moment, he spit the mess into my hand. Afraid of losing the tooth in the boat, I quickly dumped the assorted crumb pile into my carry-all bag, optimistic I would be able to retrieve it later that afternoon in preparation for its next public appearance. The important thing was that we landed his fish and even caught a few more while we were at it.

The more time we spent in Alaska that summer, the more we realized that our visit was sure a stark contrast to our first stay. The abundance of sun, fish, and daylight made our summer visit so much more enjoyable. About a week into the trip, I was working on breakfast again when Tom went out again for his morning survey, and his time he came in he tell me about a wolf he'd seen on the beach. In stealth mode, we snuck down the trail, and sure enough, there he was, a tall, dark gray-colored wolf strolling along the high tide line, most likely poking around for food. As time went by, even though we would continue to hear the wolves howling occasionally, that morning was the only time we ever saw one.

Following our breakfast we began getting organized to can some crab. After reading the directions included with my mother-in-law's forty-year-old canner, we felt we had a good understanding of what would have to take place. Of course, picking the crab was the obvious part of the project, and since Tom was the designated crab catcher, cleaner and cooker, I felt a bit obligated to fill the crab cracker vacancy. After some trial and error, I quickly found out it was easiest to pick the crab near the window in the morning sun; the stray shells were easier to spot under the bright light which was streaming onto the table. I remained extremely focused during the first days of picking but could only process three crabs an hour. With all of the crab we were catching, I would never be able to keep up at that pace. I vowed to improve.

After the crabs were processed and we had enough crab meat to justify running the canner, Tom and I would fill the clean jars first with crab meat, then salt, then sterile water, and of course, top them off with lids. From there, Tom took over the canning process using a propane burner which was stationed on the deck. He processed the crab according to the antique instruction booklet. Over the course of our stay, there were three occasions when we ended up with jars that didn't seal. We cheerfully took care of the problem during our evening snack session by feasting on crab dip made with cream cheese which we spread on various crackers. It was delicious!

*   *   *

After a long ten-day spell of dry weather, a generous summer thunderstorm had passed in the night. As frightening as the storm was, thanks to the gutters, something good had come from it; the water tank was overflowing again. With all the canning going on, we were using tremendous amounts of water. Not only were we washing and rinsing a lot of jars, but Tom was also doing some serious crab cooking. By the first week he had cooked seventy crabs already. Since he normally boiled the crab right after they were caught, it meant a couple of huge pots of water a day just for cooking.

By the end of week two, our pots had captured 134 keeper crabs. With all the salmon available for bait, sometimes Tom would check and then bait the pots twice a day, which kept us continually cooking, picking and canning crab. By then, we'd devised a pretty good system, so processing the crabmeat had become a simple routine. By then I could pick six crabs in an hour.

In between the crab activities, I began to landscape the muddy path in the area around the cabin. On my daily search for the perfect rocks, "the bigger the better" was my motto. The ones I almost couldn't lift were definitely the best because once they were transplanted in the pathway, they didn't wiggle at all. Smooth, flat rocks of all sizes were scattered all over our beach, but they were only available when the tide was out. Whenever I spotted a suitable candidate, I moved it to a pile at the base of our trail. Lifting each rock up from the ground always uncovered multiple purple-colored rock crabs which were no bigger than a fifty-cent piece. At first, the feisty crabs would raise their claws as if they were going to take me on; then they'd apparently realize that it might be safer to scurry to the nearest available rock for cover.

Over the course of a couple weeks, one by one, each stone that I'd selected eventually made it up the hill. The exposed tree roots that had been tripping us since the first day were now providing stationary dividers to hold the rocks in place. Soon enough, the main trail from our cabin to the beach was paved with flat rocks. The clean, wide, reflective path was especially nice for navigating in the dark. After years of just being rocks on the beach, the stone slabs had become a stunning but practical pathway to our cabin.

At the base of the hill there were dump truck loads of gravel that glittered with gold flecks. When the rocks were wet they shimmered like they were meant for royalty. Over the course of a couple of weeks, bucket after bucket of beautiful gravel also made its way up the hill. The gravel conveniently filled in the cracks of the walkway and also paved the steep areas where the rocks wouldn't stay in place. By the first of September, the mushy soil around the cabin was finally under wraps. Being able to observe the natural beauty everywhere I looked made me feel content.

If I wasn't picking up flat rocks or shoveling gravel, I was scoping out branches for towel racks or coat hooks. Each subsequent discovery became my new favorite one! Some of the limbs that Tom had trimmed off the cedar trees from around the cabin offered the best configuration for the coat hangers we desperately needed. Others branches made beautiful towel racks and even a rod for our shower curtain. Even though Tom couldn't see their potential during my gathering process, once it was usefully installed inside the cabin, he would eventually acknowledge how valuable a plain old branch can be.

As I examined the area around the cabin in search of functional branches, I became aware of the endless supply of berries along the beach. Huge bushes teeming with wild blueberries and huckleberries kept us in the fruit during our stay. Lucky for me, Tom despises fruit. As a result, Pup and I had the juicy treats all to ourselves. At the peak of the season I picked and then stored the berries in plastic water bottles in the fridge.

Besides berries, wild mushrooms were plentiful as well. Since some of them were varieties that we had eaten before, we knew they were safe and harvested them regularly. One day we found a peculiar mushroom crop which appeared to have come straight from a colorful children's story book. Each of the waxy, bright red domes was evenly decorated with white puffy dots. We assumed that because they were so beautiful, they were most likely poisonous.

As annoying as the ravens were on our first trip to Alaska, the resident seagulls of our summer stay weren't too far behind on the irritation meter. Instead of just two or three pests, though, there were closer to fifty. Unlike the ravens, however, the seagulls wanted nothing to do with our camp. But unfortunately for us, the screeching hyena noises the birds would make day after day more than made up for their lack of interest in our belongings.

For the seagulls, the local attraction was definitely the creek next door. Their ear-piercing communications echoed continuously from the small canyon there. The salmon were spawning; consequently, the creek was packed with fish. After closer examination, however, we discovered it was not the fish the seagulls were after; it was their eggs. We had come to that conclusion after realizing that all the dead fish carcasses littering the beach had provoked not so much as a glance from the seagulls. The creek, on the other hand, was full of freshly deposited eggs. Every morning just before dawn, the squabbling began as all the freshly laid eggs became visible at first light.

The tide's relationship to the creek also initiated quite a ruckus. At high tide, the lowest part of the creek was flooded in deeper water which allowed the fish to easily move further up the creek to spawn. As the tide receded, the water in the creek became very shallow again, exposing many of the fresh eggs which had been deposited during higher water levels. It was at that time when the racket was at its peak as the gulls fought for dibs on the treats. Once the birds had "a place at the table" so-to-speak, then it became important for the seagulls to keep each other at bay. There was often tremendous shrieking about that subject too. I imagined them screaming at each other, "Get Away From Me Already!"

In a way the seagulls became a wilderness alarm for us. Over the course of our stay that summer, we realized that the obnoxious noise would commence for one of three reasons: daylight every morning, outgoing tide, or kindred intruder. If the bears were out, or if we walked into view, simultaneously, the gulls would go speechless, and then as a synchronized team, they would lift off and fly to a gathering place on the rocks where the creek entered the cove.

Once there, they would sit in silence until the coast was clear again. Next year maybe a bear-style scarecrow might be in order, I thought cunningly, as I lay in bed trying to sleep past 4 o'clock each morning!

One of the many mushrooms at the cabin.
This one was bright red with white puffy dots.

33

Fresh Breath of Bear

Since early on during the first trip to Alaska, Tom had been scheming about a more efficient way to manage the boat. After much thought, he felt that he'd devised a plan which would enable us to have the luxury of more flexibility going to and from the property. Instead of constantly waiting for the tide to come and go, the new concept would allow Tom to stand on the shore to retrieve the boat by simply rotating a large loop—as long as the boat was floating, of course. This option would be very helpful in the event that a storm were to roll in because he could easily move the boat closer to shore where he could better monitor the situation.

This pulley system seemed like it would solve a lot of our worries about storing our boat while we were at the cabin. With this set-up, the boat would only be out of service for a brief period twice a day—usually for just a half an hour. The boat needed to be drained every so often anyway; and as a result, Tom would regularly take advantage of the brief time the boat was beached. Every couple of days he would unscrew the steel plug at the stern to empty either accumulating rain water or the excess water which had collected from pulling crab pots.

We had a couple pieces of the proposed loop system already at the cabin, but to implement the plan we needed two pulleys and 750 feet of line which would complete the short list of materials required for the project. The lowest tide of the year was today, so we quickly buzzed into town.

With our supplies collected, back at the cabin, Tom installed a three foot anchor screw out on the beach as far as possible. Using a pipe which he thread-ed through the "eye" of the anchor, he twisted the large screw all the way into the mud until only the eye was visible. Next, he created a 350 foot loop. The saucer-sized pulleys we'd purchased were stationed on each end. The offshore pulley would have a buoy attached to it, so when the tide was in, it would al-low the pulley to float directly above the anchor; the other was tied to a tree on the beach. In no time, the project was completed! Now we had to see if it was going to function as planned. We waited for the tide to return.

At high tide we tested the system, and Tom's plan worked just like we hoped. With the system in place we became accustomed to leaving the boat stationed farther off-shore than we ever had dared before.

In spite of the benefits of our new pulley system, one particular day we encountered quite a problem. The situation was no different than many times in the past; while the tide was out, Tom removed the plug, waited for the hull to empty, and then replaced the plug before the water reached the boat again. After all, it always felt good to be back to square one again with the boat completely drained. On this day, much to our dismay, it was just be-fore dinner time when the wind began to blow. It gave us an uneasy feeling. This sudden turnaround in the weather immediately beckoned our attention! Thinking back on our horrific night when we'd been stranded on the beach a few months back, we knew firsthand how ugly the weather could get with virtually no warning

Even though the weather had been extremely pleasant the entire day, by evening, the troubled skies above were warning us of a vicious storm that was looming. The evil clouds rolling in were clearly indications of a very nasty squall. These unexpected conditions had taken us by surprise because, except for the one early morning thunderstorm, Alaska had given us twelve gorgeous days thus far.

Pup was napping peacefully on the bed as I cleaned up from dinner and did my nightly sweep of the floor. Tom was quietly reading the local paper. In the time since we'd been back this summer, life at the property had been pretty relaxed. With the heater cooking away and the fridge full of food, we hardly felt like we were roughing it in a remote cabin anymore.

By dusk, the intense storm was still building as the water continued to recede. Before long, Tom stepped outside for the first of many random scouting exercises he would be performing on this night. When he returned, he reported disappointedly, "Those waves are huge out there." He explained that our large anchor buoy which was floating just fifty feet behind the boat was barely visible in the rough seas. Tom isn't usually bothered by much, so hearing that news wasn't a good sign. I ventured outside to have a look for myself. It had been just six months since I'd experienced violent water like that, and the battering waves that were rapidly developing outside right now were reminiscent of that dreadful time.

Back inside the cabin, Tom grabbed his reading glasses and the tide book, followed by a glance up at the clock. Disgustedly, he flopped the book down and then the glasses, "We're going to be up half the night tonight—I can see that!" he complained. Because of our ongoing experiences with the tide, we both understood that it was going to be a long wait before we could do much about the current boat dilemma.

"If we get through the storm without damage to our boat it will be worth it to be up all night," I reassured him.

It wasn't the first time that the tide, our boat, and bad weather had all collided. But unfortunately, this time our boat was out as far as it could possibly be in regards to the pulley system. We sensed a stressful night ahead.

"Well, I never should have left the boat out that far," Tom commented regretfully. "And I drained it today, so now it's sitting the wrong way for rough weather," he continued.

This was no fault of his. We both knew that we couldn't predict what the weather would bring on any one day, and leaving the boat out at that specific location generally gave us many more hours of freedom. This was just another go-around of bad luck. We'd have to find a way to endure.

During our previous misadventure when we'd found ourselves stranded for the night, we hadn't had lights to be able to see the big waves; we could only imagine their size as we heard them crashing ashore. Right this minute we could only predict what we'd be up against and it was a helpless feeling to know that our current circumstances were out of our control. From time to time, we gazed out the window toward the water. Our stomachs churned as we waited, and just the sound of the water was bringing back memories of that hellish night. A somber mood hovered over camp since we knew we would encounter serious problems if the weather didn't settle back down pretty soon.

There were two important reasons to be very concerned about our boat; first of all, because of its current position on the brutal rocks. Where it was, there was a very good chance that serious damage might occur as the water slowly surrounded the boat while the tide gradually moved in. It was inevitable. Before our vessel could be safely afloat in deeper water, the brutal waves would cause it to beat against the unforgiving rocks. As a result, the welding seams on the boat's hull would be at risk of being chipped or cracked apart; the resulting damage might leave us no choice but to watch it sink as the water moved up the beach.

The second important reason to be concerned was that the boat was currently aimed in the wrong direction. Due to the fact that Tom had drained it, the stern of the boat was facing downhill toward the water. By then I'd learned that if the bow of a boat is pointed into the waves, it had a much better chance of surviving a storm because the bow kind of divides the waves as they approach. However, the stern is flat, so it gets slapped with waves which continually splash over the stern. In that vulnerable position, eventually more and more water enters the boat. If that were to happen later tonight, by then it would be pitch dark, so even with serious efforts we'd never be able to bail water fast enough, all the while putting ourselves in grave danger. What if the vessel was overcome by the waves and sank? That would be hard to watch, we thought. We knew we couldn't let that happen. Not only did we have plenty of money invested in our vessel, it was our only ride back to civilization. Somehow, we had to get through this! But how?

Periodically, Tom headed outside to make his ongoing assessment. Nothing had changed; the tide had barely moved. Darkness was approaching. There was absolutely nothing we could do to protect the boat from the acre or more of large barnacle covered rocks. We searched our brains for any available options, but we only came up with one solution: as soon as the boat was floating again, it would be urgent for us to spin it around so it was pointing into the weather. Even then, the boat might not make it through the first part of the tide. We'd have to give it our best shot.

Seven o'clock, eight o'clock, nine o'clock came and went. The hours slowly passed. There was no denying that for the remainder of the night we were going to be on high alert. By 10:30 p.m. we had already been playing cribbage for a couple hours in an effort to pass the time. Besides high winds, now a heavy rain had moved in. We discussed our plan of attack all evening long: get the boat turned around as soon as possible!

At last, the time came for us to bundle up and hike out into the storm to see where we were in the battle against the weather. It was pitch dark. The blustering wind and sideways rain was continuously pelting the cabin. It was because of the recent bear activity that we'd decided to go out on the mission together. Tom would take the big spotlight and his shotgun while I packed the bear spray along with a smaller flashlight. We immediately surveyed the situation as we stepped outside. Even though we had yet to see a bear near the cabin, our instincts advised us to be cautious. All was clear, so we stepped off the deck, following the somewhat reflective stone path from the cabin; the lights inside beamed from the three front windows facing the beach.

When we came to the top of the hill overlooking the beach, we stopped for another good spell while we let our eyes and ears adjust to our surroundings. Tom bent down to peer through the trees with a quick flash of his light in order to see what he could before we headed down the makeshift ramp. We saw lots of rain and no bears or wolves, only our lonely boat stranded straight ahead on the rocks. Slowly and carefully we made our way down the treacherous rain-soaked hill. At the edge of the beach just under the trees, we paused to scope out the sights again. Tom panned the spotlight from side to side, looking for glowing eyeballs of any kind. Our search picked up the two yellow marble-like eyeballs in the low creek water.

"That pair of eyes is too close to the water to be a bear," Tom said. We studied them for another few seconds, "unless he is swimming, I guess," Tom decided. But since the tide was out, we calculated that the creek was too low right then for a bear to be swimming.

"It's probably just a seal," Tom concluded.

At that point, we continued to trudge out onto the beach making a beeline for our stranded boat. It was not in trouble yet, but it was on the verge of serious peril from the less-than-friendly water that was approaching. I was leading the way with my small flashlight, which was hardly worth using. In fact, relying on it to observe anything outside a measly ten foot radius was futile; it barely produced a faint circle with a dark, round shadow in the middle. But it was just enough to light our path, ultimately saving the battery life on the bigger flashlight. We paused for a moment at the logical lookout point which was half way out to the boat. Tom scanned left again toward the creek, then straight ahead. I meagerly searched right toward the timber, then around behind us in the direction of the cabin, as I attempted to observe anything of concern within the circle of the dim halo.

Thankfully, the spotlight Tom was carrying radiated clear across the beach like a powerful searchlight on a helicopter. As we stood in the gusting wind, we observed nothing to cause any new concern.

The hair on my neck was already at attention from the darkness and weather alone. Even in broad daylight, during a wind storm I was always relieved to get past the tangled timber at the base of the hill. The treacherous trees we were forced to pass under each time on the way to the beach had grown sideways into each other at angles that defied gravity; one tree propped on the other like an old friend. If the decrepit alder tree at the base of the hill decided to come crashing down at some point, the large cedar tree it had been supporting all these years would have followed like a domino.

All of a sudden I heard Tom's voice quickly utter the word "bear." I was stunned. Even though I thought I was prepared to hear that word, I wasn't! It was different now that I was in the dark.

Instinctively, I asked, "Where?" Even though I should have known where *where* was, because he was obviously pointing straight at the bear with his flashlight.

"Right there," Tom whispered as he held his bright light on the large yet nearly invisible, black, furry silhouette.

"I can't see it, really," I said. My eyes widened while I jutted my head forward to perhaps get a better look.

Looking at a bear in the dark was nothing like I had thought it would be. A big black shadow was all I could make out....but then, the shadow showed us his golden eyes. The bear slowly swung his head toward us, and then away again as if not to be too concerned about our presence.

"He's just a little guy," Tom said in an unthreatening tone. It made me feel better to know that. We quickly assumed he was probably busy feeding on the fish carcasses left in the creek after the tide had receded earlier this evening. That wasn't too bad for a first time bear sighting, I thought, now that it was behind me. But then again, Tom and I couldn't help but wonder how many other bears might be watching us right then.

We walked a little farther out onto the beach only to confirm that we couldn't take care of our mission at the boat; the tide wasn't in far enough yet. With great care, we trailed back through the tide flats, past the feeding bear and back up to the cabin. We'd been gone only fifteen minutes, but as we stepped through the door, Pup reacted as if we'd been gone for two hours. I couldn't discern if it was because he'd never been left home alone, or because he sensed how uneasy I was with the current situation. Either way he was right.

"We didn't get done, so now we have to go out again," I grumbled.

The clock posted a time of 11:00 p.m. as we took off our rain gear and set down the flashlights to take our regular spots at the card table again. We decided that our next patrol would be at midnight. At this rate there was no point in going to bed only to get up an hour later, so we snacked as we played games during the hour-long, nerve-wracking wait.

Just outside the door, the generator noise provided a steady background hum. As the night continued, the wind showed no signs of letting up. We were both grateful that we had not heard any trees crashing nearby. During the day time, it was quite obvious that the forest floor was crawling with exposed roots, which gave the impression that any tree could be uprooted by the slightest breeze. On the other hand, the age old moss hanging from every limb was indicative of each tree's tenure there in the Alaskan wilderness. On many root systems there was plenty of daylight visible clear through to the other side. And even though the structure of the tree appeared questionable in most cases, much of the timber around the cabin had easily been there a hundred years. After some thought, we were pretty certain that we weren't experiencing the worst storm of the century.

At last, the clock finally struck midnight, and we suited up for what we hoped would be our last time out. Like before, Tom would carry the big spotlight, I would pack the little one. He placed his shotgun strap over his shoulder and stood waiting at the door. He explained that the shotgun allowed him to be more prepared for a possible close range bear encounter. Once I was ready, against my better judgment, Tom decided I should pack his rifle for this outing.

Just for the record, I really hate guns! But in the spirit of team work, I agreed to carry the heavy backup weapon over my right shoulder. Next, I pulled the bear spray from my pocket to quickly review the instructions on the canister. Then just for added safety, I grabbed our emergency locator unit. I was simply thinking that in case we got cornered by something ferocious I could possibly send out a signal. Tom was giving me a hard time about my thought process, but he's not exactly the most cautious person I know, so I continued with my preparations as I paid little attention to his insensitive remarks.

Finally, I was ready to step outside again. The weather was worsening. As soon as we closed the cabin door, the wind instantly blew off my hat. We could hear loose metal scraps crashing against the deck. At the same time, the plastic tarp covering our lumber pile down below was flapping furiously like a flag on a pirate ship adrift in blustery seas. The storm's noise was deafening. In spite of the distractions, we scanned for wild animals right away. I instantly gasped, almost jumping out of my skin when my flashlight caught sight of a large black figure just off the edge of the deck. I was understandably nervous following our recent bear sighting. But then, just as quickly, I noticed that the shadow, without question, resembled our canner which was sitting at my feet, casting a large shadow into the woods. I took another deep breath to calm my nerves. I was thankful that due to the wind, Tom couldn't hear my unwarranted outburst.

My heart was racing, but I managed to quickly pull myself together by the time we made our way down the glistening stone path to the top of the hill. Before we descended, Tom squatted down and using his flashlight; he peered through the swaying branches in an attempt to distinguish anything that might be cause for alarm.

Nothing looked out of place. We crept down the steep, water-ravaged trail to where we could stand at the bottom of the hill for a moment. Again, we carefully observed our surroundings before making our way out onto the beach. Just as before, Tom used his flashlight to investigate the vicinity where we had previously seen the bear. There was no black shadow standing there, thank goodness. However, we knew if the bear had been present, at least it would've been accounted for. We took a few more steps in the dark. My head was on a swivel; therefore, I was not paying attention to my own feet as I stumbled here and there on various sized rocks which were scattered across the beach. Tom flashed his light every few steps as well. As I strode forward following him, I did my best to perform active surveillance behind both of us. At one point we each paused for a moment to do a complete security check in opposite directions again.

"There he is!" Tom proclaimed, with his spotlight pointed straight at our boat. "Where?" I whispered loudly, though my voice was barely audible in the gusting winds.

"Right there by the boat!" he said annoyed.

Without a doubt, I could see that this bear was much bigger.

"That's a huge bear. This one is a lot bigger than the one we saw earlier," Tom explained in one quick breath.

Without hesitation I shouted, "Let's go!" In the blink of an eye I'd spun around to make a run for the cabin. Somehow, Tom's quick response time allowed him to barely catch me by the collar before I sped off.

As I regained my balance he ordered me, "Don't Run!" He spoke in slow motion with exaggerated lips as if I was deaf.

"The worst thing you can do is run. Now stand here and hold the light while I fire my gun."

"Okay," I said, panting. "Are you going to shoot the bear?" I whined.

"No," he answered, "I am just going to try to scare it away," he said in a clipped voice. "He's obviously not scared of the boat. He was probably our thief!" Tom assumed.

As we watched for a moment, the bear appeared to be rummaging through the rocks on the beach.

"Okay," he ordered. "Now hold this light and I'll scare him."

I was hopeful that the sound of the shotgun would be able to overcome the noise of the howling winds.

Tom handed me the big spotlight. In my quivering left hand I did my best to hold the bright beam directly on the bear. In my right hand, I clutched my small flashlight while at the same time holding his heavy rifle tight to my side with the strap still slung over my shoulder. He raised the gun up to fire off a shot. As a natural reaction, my eyes squeezed shut as I raised my shoulders to plug my ears.

"Bang!!!" There was instantaneous darkness, and not just because my eyes were closed; I'd let go of the flashlight trigger as well.

The next thing I heard was Tom's irritated voice snapping at me, "Sweetie, you have to keep the light on the bear. Now we don't know where he is. Where'd he go?" he said as he hastily snatched the big spotlight from my limp hand.

Tom should have known by then that any emergency action he might want me to perform would have to be spelled out well in advance of the drama. His vague, on-the-spot instruction was worthless if we hadn't taken time beforehand to entertain all options. Never, as long as I have known him, have I ever functioned well under pressure, and the situation that night was certainly no exception.

He scanned briskly from side to side, panning behind us and then toward the water. Nothing. Thankfully, a few seconds later he finally caught a glimpse of the bear wallowing off into the trees.

Next, we turned our attention to the task at hand. We could see that the boat was not floating, but water was at least gushing under it finally. We walked toward the boat to more closely survey the situation. While flashing our lights to and fro, we attempted to push the boat into deeper water just slightly to be able to swing the stern around toward the cabin. The stern was bobbing some, but somewhere near the bow, it was stuck solid, pivoting on a large rock. Unfortunately, it seemed to have been balancing on the only behemoth stone on our entire beach. The aggressive motion of the waves was violently rocking the boat, but it clearly remained stuck. We shoved and pulled, but while the boat continued to grind away on the barnacles, it refused to budge. We'd been out twenty minutes by then, and we knew our flashlight battery would never last if we waited for the tide to come in far enough. We decided we should head back to the cabin, yet again. We were cold and wet anyway.

Up the beach we went, cautiously flashing side to side and then up ahead into the trees. A quick scan toward the creek revealed nothing. In the midst of the wild weather, the well-lit cabin resembled a sturdy lighthouse. It was a beacon of comfort on the hill, windows glowing in the stormy darkness. Rays of light beamed through the swaying trees and also lit up the flecks of gold which were glistening in the stone walkway. In short order, we hiked up the challenging trail, following the shimmering stone pathway back to the cabin. As we approached, the noise of the generator eventually overcame the sound of the gusting wind. When we finally got back inside the warm shelter, my leg muscles were trembling and my head seemed as if it was spinning. I felt dizzy-drunk from all the adrenaline rushing through my veins. Pup crawled onto the bed to join me where I collapsed for a moment; I realized how thankful I was to be safe and sound. Tom, on the other hand, left on an urgent visit to the outhouse. The frightening bear encounter had taken us both for a ride; we each coped in our own way.

Unfortunately for Tom, our outhouse was a good distance from the cabin, down the trail, across a makeshift bridge and over a small hill. There was no way I would've been able to venture out to it at this point—I would've rather crapped my pants. I knew from then on I'd have a honey bucket inside the cabin for use after dark.

Following that excursion, we knew we'd still have to go out again. After a bit, we regrouped as we chatted about the recent situation.

As convincingly as I knew how, I begged Tom, "If you could just go out by yourself, you might be better off you know. Then you won't have to be disgusted with me."

He barely let me finish my sentence. He was having no part of it. He and I both knew he couldn't safely hold the light, keep an eye out for bears, hold a gun, spin, and then tie off the boat in the rough waves all by himself. He shot a disappointing glance in my direction.

"Alright, I know!" I said as I got bundled back up in my heavy winter coat to go out for what I hoped would be the last time this evening.

We had no other choice than to look after our boat. It was getting thrashed on the rocks. Hindsight kept rearing its ugly head.

"Why couldn't I have just left the boat up higher today?" Tom kept repeating under his breath. "I left it out on the roughest part of the beach in the biggest possible rocks," he complained regretfully over and over.

Because of the calm weather conditions earlier in the day, we both knew that he could not have predicted this scenario. He'd followed the exact same routine before; however, the weather had remained tranquil, and as a result, everything had turned out just fine. Soon enough the time had come again for us to return to the beach.

"Alright, I'm ready," I said nervously, at last, all zipped up with Tom's gun hanging over my shoulder again. "Got your flashlight?" Tom asked.

"Yep!"

"Got your bear spray?"

"Um, wait….no." I said, instantly groping both pockets. After a quick scrounge around the cabin, I couldn't find it anywhere. When I had come in from the last trip I must have been so flustered that I failed to realize that I'd lost my spray.

"Did you drop it on the beach maybe?" Tom quizzed.

"Probably," I answered after a moment in deep thought. "It probably fell out of my pocket when I started to run from the bear. I'll take the other one."

With my ammo in place, I agreed that I was finally ready. We informed Pup, "We'll be right back," as we stepped out on the porch again. We stood for a moment to perform our routine inspection and let our eyes adjust to the darkness again. I took an extra deep breath to prepare myself for the inevitable yet innocent shadow of the canner. All looked well, as usual, so we headed down to the beach. Of course, we automatically checked the locations of the previous bear sightings but saw nothing. Except for our boat, the beach was bare. We observed our small red vessel bobbing up and down like a cork in the water. On our route toward to the boat, we discovered the missing bear spray in the sand. It was exactly where we had been standing when we saw the big bear.

"By morning, the tide would have made sure that was gone for good," Tom pointed out. I swiftly scooped up the bear spray to return it to its position in my pocket before we continued our mission across the dark beach.

Once we were at the boat, we worked together to get it turned around, and then at long last, finally secured it back to the pulley line. For added security, we stretched another line from the boat to the anchor embedded in the sand up the beach. Our thinking was that if for some reason the pulley line were to have failed in the storm, we were hopeful that in the morning the boat would still have been attached to the back-up line. With our tasks finally completed, we heaved a giant sigh of relief as we headed back up the beach to the cabin. The bears were nowhere in sight, and the wind had died down momentarily. As we approached the cabin, we could hear the steady hum of our generator gradually overcoming the sound of the heavy rain.

Our six-hour mission was finally accomplished. Soaked, windblown, and exhausted, we were finally able to get ready for bed. It was 2 a.m. by the time we managed to retire for the evening. The bed seemed extremely cozy that night as the rhythm of the wind and rain chanted steadily outside while we both dozed off to sleep.

34

Coming Full Circle

Even though Tom and I had already been back in Alaska for over a month, I still hadn't retrieved the argument-provoking stainless steel cable we had come across during our previous trip. Since building a pot rack for our kitchen was just ahead on my agenda, I was in need of the main ingredient: my cable. Tom knew I hadn't forgotten about it for a second, and one afternoon he finally agreed to help me get the "trash" hauled back to the cabin.

To save us the long walk in the beating sun, we waited for high tide so we could motor over in the boat. We pulled ashore and after a quick glance around, Tom cheerfully announced, "It's gone!" After my short search in the opposite direction, the cable was right where I remembered abandoning it months ago. In his dreams it was gone, hah! Finally, I was able to close the chapter on the cable.

By early September, the humpies had thinned out and silver salmon season had begun. Even though I still considered myself a novice, fishing had definitely grown on me. Since I had never fished for silvers before, the first time we reeled one in, I was astounded by the shimmering creature that was so big and beautiful.

Fishing for silvers was nothing like fishing for rock fish. Instead of idling over a rock pile and quickly landing a fish, for silvers, we motored along very slowly, dragging our lures while patiently waiting for a bite. Tom attached weights to our line so it would remain fairly deep underwater as we trolled along. If we remembered a bucket, we would drag an empty one behind the boat to slow us down even further than our engine would throttle down.

On any given day, if the weather was even somewhat agreeable, we'd take a few hours to see what we could reel in. During our many excursions I had plenty of fish bite. It was quite a subtle "hello" compared to the aggressive tugs of a rock fish, so even with all the silvers that I'd hooked in Alaska, the ongoing confusion for me was trying to determine whether I actually had one on the line or not.

"I think I've got one," I'd announce.

Following the initial nibble, Tom would constantly quiz me, "Do you have one? Is it on? Is it a big one?"

I was not the person to ask. I could never tell whether I had one, if it was still on, or how big it might be.

My answer was always, without fail, "I don't know!" I would need a lot more practice!

In my mind, the difference between a rock fish and a silver salmon was much like the comparison of a house cat is to a mountain lion. In either situation, they are both in the same family yet very different animals. Although it wasn't quite that extreme, the fishing was as different as night and day. Besides the length of time it took to catch a silver, I couldn't comprehend getting such a large catch into the boat with a relatively small hook, but that was where the landing net came into play. Whenever Tom hooked one, it was my responsibility to capture the squirming fish. The event always provoked plenty of excitement as the fighting fish reached the surface of the water. It would instinctively flail about in attempt to free itself. At first I found the experience extremely nerve wracking! I didn't want to be the one to blame for losing the trophy catch. Tom would always begin by firing off instructions.

"Grab the net, grab the net!" he'd frantically order. "Okay wait, hold it, wait, okay now!" he'd announce.

As time went on, I was surprised at how much I truly enjoyed the whole fishing experience. If I didn't know any better, I might have thought I was becoming addicted to the sport. As I was going to sleep each night, my adrenaline would spike as I relived the events of the day. I couldn't quit thinking about the big one that got away. Next time I vowed; next time! I don't remember dreaming about the act of fishing, necessarily, but when I awoke each morning, I would glance out the window first thing, wondering if and when we could go next. If we had plenty of boat fuel and the weather was cooperating, we always headed for our favorite salmon fishing hotspot just past the dog's leg. The fish always seemed to be jumping there.

Halfway into the month of September, the weather had definitely taken a serious turn for the worse, implying that summer had vanished for good and winter was just around the corner. Our thoughts began to focus on heading home. The fishing season was winding down, and Tom had already pulled the crab pots for the last time. Although we could have easily caught more crabs, at 225 keepers, we had an ample supply in the fridge as well as plenty of full canning jars on the shelf. In addition to all of the crabmeat, we had preserved a large supply of salmon, which we also planned on taking back home to Oregon.

By then, the interior of our cozy Alaskan bungalow was nearly complete—by remote cabin standards, anyway. The walls and ceiling were enclosed. The shower and sinks were working, the heater and fridge had each found a permanent location, and we had built the kitchen cabinets. Due to the fishing ventures that had become quite a priority, the famous pot rack project was not anywhere near finished. Oh well, I thought, there is always next year.

Now that we were preparing to leave for the winter, in addition to the seafood, another Alaskan treasure I wanted to take with us was a stash of cedar boards. In recent weeks, we had been removing sections of a mammoth cedar tree that rested on the beach nearby. There was only one section left and it was my goal to mill the remaining five feet before we left Alaska. As it turned out, just that hunk of cedar alone produced sixty-four beautiful pieces of lumber. I was delighted.

With all of the boards, canned seafood, as well as our personal items we intended to take home, we realized that it was going to require two trips to the car. With the onset of unpredictable weather, we began watching and waiting for an opportunity to get into town.

"This might be the day," was the first thought that came to mind when we awoke one calm morning. The weather seemed agreeable enough. Although it was not a gorgeous day—it was not storming at the moment. The tide was out, and since the boat was much easier to load while it was sitting on the beach, we decided that we'd get started before the tide returned. Unfortunately, where the boat was, it was a bit of a trek to get the goods loaded because Tom had purposely left it out a ways, not only to drain it, but also so we could attempt an early run for town.

A light rain was falling the entire time we were packing; consequently, we wrapped each box of heavy canned goods in its own plastic bag before carefully hauling them one by one on the long jaunt to the boat. We noticed that once it was all in one location, we actually had quite a supply of seafood. What a great feeling! After we'd loaded a sufficient amount of cargo, we patiently waited for the tide to come in. As long as it was only raining, we'd be able to get safely into town. While we took care of a few more details at the cabin, we crossed our fingers in regards to the wind since it was to blame for all the rough water we regularly experienced. Sadly, before long, the wind began to blow. A glance overhead told us that a serious storm was brewing. By the time the water reached the boat, the wind had noticeably picked up. Since Tom was always the one tending to the boat's welfare, he went out to spin it around to face the bow into the rough waves. Just that fast, our plans changed. Frustrated or not, we would be forced to wait out the storm.

Back inside the cabin, we waited. Instinctively, we knew we were not going anywhere for a while. We debated whether to unload the boat. We weren't the least bit thrilled about removing all of our cargo and packing it back up to the cabin. Another hour passed; then without notice, the rough waters settled down. It seemed a bit strange, but we quickly jumped in the boat to make a run for the car. This will be great, we thought, as we sped across the water headed for town. The fantasy of making it to the car on that day abruptly ended as we rounded the dog's leg where a sea of huge white caps greeted us head on. By far, they were the worst I had ever seen in the inlet. It looked like the ocean! It was impassable. It must have been due to a change in the wind's direction. We had absolutely no choice but to turn back. Clearly, we would be unable to deliver our load today.

Once we returned to the beach, we tied up the boat, wondering what to do next. All the hard work we had invested in canning over the last month was held captive in the bobbing boat. Should we pull the boat in and beach it? If we did, we would not have the opportunity to leave until high tide tomorrow. That might be too late in the day to make two trips, we predicted.

Soon, the torrential rain began to pour down. Our situation looked increasingly hopeless. How long were we going to be stuck here? Days? A week? As the hours passed, the intensity of the rain was on the increase; the resulting noise overtook the cabin. Naturally, we were worried about our boat, but at the same time, we felt very privileged to have daylight in which to monitor the effects of the storm. We chose to postpone the unloading project and see what would happen next.

On that day late in September, the ongoing blustery winds were relentless and they were giving the boat an impressive workout. By mid-afternoon, it was high tide, and with the pulley system in place, Tom pulled our boat in close to the cabin. From inside our warm shelter we could see that despite the violent waves, all of the boxes continued to remain exactly where they had been loaded earlier in the day. We watched proudly as the boat took each wave on with such grace and dignity. Amazingly, hour by hour, the trusty vessel managed to hold its own.

We continued to wait with intense anticipation. During Mother Nature's temper tantrum, I had become convinced that I was ready to leave Alaska. And even though Tom was not outwardly disturbed, he had mentioned that he, too, was ready to head for home. Now it would be a matter of when—when would the weather give us a window? We knew from experience that when the opportunity presented itself, we needed to be ready to take it—absolutely no delays! With that in mind, while we kept a constant eye on the boat, we began our final preparations.

Regardless of the foul weather, the first task was to install the shutters, which would help protect the cabin through the winter months. Tom knew that I'd had it with dreary Alaska weather. He offered to stand outside on our rickety ladder as I held the shutters in place from inside while he fastened them over the windows. That afternoon, we also moved our tools inside, stacked the crab pots under the cabin, and covered the outhouse with a tarp.

By early evening, the wind had died down substantially; as a result, we experienced some much-needed relief. Right before bed Tom ventured out to drain the boat in the event we might be able to leave with our first load the following morning. Due to the improvements in the weather, we felt increasingly optimistic. We wondered if maybe we would have the chance to make two trips, because at that point we could leave for good. Man, that would be nice, we agreed, as we drifted off to sleep.

Around 2:00 a.m., we were awakened by another round of strong winds and rain. We knew we had no choice. Half asleep, we geared up and headed out into the storm. Flashlights in hand, we strode down to the beach to check on the only vessel on which we had come to depend. Tom was flashing our spotlight back and forth, checking for bears or other animals at first, and then he highlighted our boat that was bobbing violently due to the rough conditions. We could tell she was riding quite low, probably due to all of the rainwater that she had collected again. At least she wasn't sunk!

Now in the early hours of what was hopefully our final morning, we became very concerned about the boat and her cargo and we were hopeful that the steady downpour of rain wasn't going to do her in. After six weeks of constant worrying about the boat's welfare, I was burned out! I was tired of fighting the ongoing battles with both the weather and the tides. As a result, Tom spent the rest of the night as designated watchman, going back and forth from our bed to the beach, checking to make sure our boat was afloat. Each time he climbed back under the covers, his moist skin was freezing cold next to mine. I sure hope we can leave today, I thought each time he returned.

By daybreak, from inside the cabin we could see that the water was well over the floorboards! We would not be going anywhere this morning, either. The boat would need to spend some time on dry land again in order to drain the massive amounts of water that had accumulated overnight. We would be forced to wait for the next tide to return later in the day.

Once the tide receded and we were up and moving about for the day, Tom and I went down to the boat to perform a wellness check on our cargo. Thankfully, we had twisted the bags closed, so the canning boxes were soggy but still intact. Now if the weather would cooperate, we thought, maybe we can get the heck out of here. We kept the faith although a slight wind was still blowing and the skies were still very gray. All morning long we continued to keep pace with our chores in the event we might be able to make a break for it when the tide returned.

All of a sudden, off in the distance Tom and I heard the faint growl of a floatplane's engine. We both stopped dead in our tracks and looked at each other with great expectations. Was this our signal to escape? Due to the foul weather, we hadn't heard this familiar sound for a few days. Just like in our situation, the wind seemed to be what determined the planes' schedules. It wasn't the wind as much as it was how the wind affected the surface of the water. Perhaps they couldn't safely take off and land their planes in such choppy conditions, we considered.

Even though the water in the inlet was still too risky for travel, it must be clearing up in town, we concluded, or the floatplanes would not be out. This really put a fire under us. It felt like now or never! We each began tending to our final preparations. Having no idea what Mother Nature had on her schedule, we decided to leave the major tasks for later. Tom would drain the cabin's plumbing and the water tank on our final trip, just in case we had to remain there a few days longer.

The energy at the cabin was palpable. Those minutes resembled the urgency during an escape of a building on fire. Even though in anticipation of this very moment I had already taken care of a few tasks, there were just as many items that needed attention at the last minute before we left. The fridge, for instance, was full of food. If I threw the food away and then we had to come back to stay for a day or two because of bad weather, then we would be hungry. However, much of the food in the fridge was still in containers. If I did not empty the dishes and dispose of the food, then I would be leaving dirty dishes that might attract rodents over the winter. It was a gamble. Although my goal was to leave the cabin in a clean condition, under the circumstances it was not a serious concern. Above all, we knew that when it came time for final departure, we would be in a mad dash. I could almost guarantee that there would not be time for dishes. For the time being, I left the food alone.

Twenty minutes later another floatplane's engine hummed in the distant skies. By then, in our camp it was an unsaid rule: one float plane signaled "maybe"....two floatplanes told us "for sure!" Without a word between us, we shifted into overdrive, spending a few intense moments preparing for the first trip to the car. As soon as the boat was floating again we immediately left for town.

The ride was definitely no picnic! This would not be a quick trip; the rough conditions would force us to take our time on the water. During our commute, the turbulent water was barely manageable, but we were determined to get across. Our boat's engine was surging and almost cutting out as the boat lurched into the waves in an attempt to make progress across the choppy seas.

Between the rough current and sideways rain, neither of us could hold a steady gaze ahead. Tom and I gave up trying to dodge the waves that were bursting over the bow with each bounce of the boat; as a result, even in spite of wearing our raingear, we were quickly drenched. As miserable as I was, I was extremely grateful that unlike my first visit to Alaska, I did not feel afraid for my life anymore. Perhaps I was getting used to the rough rides and heavy water assaults, I thought. Honestly, I had never dreamed that such a transition would ever occur. For sure, I had become more confident in the ability of our engine and I had begun to have more faith in our small vessel. I really had come a long way since my first time here.

In the midst of the saltwater showers, we schemed that when we got to the boat launch we would unload the contents of the boat as quickly as possible and then buzz straight back to the cabin to pick up our final load. If the weather was still holding when we loaded up for the second trip, then we would secure the cabin, drain the water tank, and leave for the winter.

Due to the inclement weather, the ride took an extra thirty minutes before we made it safely to the dock. Without a word between us, we efficiently transferred our belongings into the car and jumped aboard our vessel to return to the cabin for our last load. I knew it would be a while before we would see Alaska again. Therefore, even though I was wet and slightly chilled on the return trip, I still made a special point to absorb all of Alaska's incredible sights, which had now become so familiar to me. We most likely wouldn't be back until the following summer. I didn't want to be guilty of taking all of these amazing opportunities for granted.

As we made our way toward the inlet, a sentimental feeling came over me. I noticed that even though it continued to rain, the majestic mountains were still visible from all directions. By the time we had crossed the open water again, the weather had let up and the choppy seas were calming down. Just that fast, the water's surface, which moments ago resembled the perky topping on a lemon meringue pie, was now as smooth as bath water. That improvement allowed the boat's hearty engine to begin a steady hum as we passed one of our favorite fishing holes on the point at one side of the inlet. Then, to our delight, off to our right about twenty yards, a magnificent Humpback whale gracefully surfaced. The noise of an enormous exhale resonated across the water as the powerful burst of mist shot into the air just before the whale disappeared out of sight with the flip of its huge tail. How would I have handled that a year ago, I wondered, but now, lucky for us, the majestic mammal came back into view many times over. The impressive sights continued as the whale paralleled our path until we eventually passed it by as we made our way further up the inlet. It was as if it was saying, "So long," and the emotions I felt caused me to tear up.

Once we reached the dog's leg, everywhere we looked, the silvers were doing belly flops in the water. Perhaps they were happy about the recent weather improvements as well.

"Look at that!" Tom said as if we had been denied the best fishing hole ever.

"Maybe we should stay a couple more days," I said wishfully.

Part of me really did want to stay! I had come to love Alaska, and although I still couldn't imagine living here year round, being here was definitely not as intimidating as I once had thought. My fears were not holding me captive any longer and that was a feeling of great accomplishment.

Even though it was tempting to stay a couple more days, realistically I knew that the current weather change was most likely temporary. Tom and I spoke briefly of fishing but knew that wasn't possible until we returned to Alaska on our next trip. Our fishing poles weren't in the boat anyway; they were already tucked away at the cabin. Jumping silvers are a horrible thing to waste, I thought regretfully, as we passed on by. We were each taking in the sights both on and offshore as we continued on our final journey to the cabin.

When we pulled into our own small cove, we witnessed one lonely black bear fishing peacefully in the nearby creek. He acknowledged that we were closing in but continued to work on his meal. For me, after taking in the recent sights, the trip felt more complete. It truly was our time to go.

As we made our way up the beach to the cabin, I recalled many of the challenging events I'd been exposed to during our recent Alaskan excursions. I thought back to how terrified I'd been when we'd first arrived in Alaska. I'd since learned a variety of new skills and I couldn't believe how much I'd changed. After all, I'd outlasted the brutal elements, learned to cast a hook, and I'd pulled a crab pot or two. I'd gained quite an understanding not only about boats, but also about the pros and cons of living in the tidal zone. I had come to appreciate the solitude, all while watching the beautiful wildlife in their natural habitat. I relished the experience of seeing firsthand how amazing the salmon spawning process really is, while at the same time I was privileged to be able to watch the bears as they scooped those very fish from the nearby creek.

As I reflected on the wide range of experiences, yeah, there were plenty of hard times and bad days, but I had grown so much. What I once considered to be my nightmare had now become a somewhat satisfying lifestyle, if I do say so myself. How could I accurately describe to my family and friends all the attributes of this awesome land and all it holds? Where would I even begin?

We hurriedly spent our last few minutes at the cabin. While Tom drained the water tank and winterized the plumbing, I moved the generator inside before I packed the up the fresh crab we'd be taking with us on our trip back home. With our goods loaded, we locked up the cabin. What about dishes, you ask? Food and all, they were tossed outside for the winter.

We made our final journey to town that morning knowing that our cozy beachfront cabin in the wilderness would be awaiting our return to this unforgettable land of adventure that I affectionately call Alaska!

About the Author

Tammy Jones has always thrived on accomplishing goals far outside her personal comfort zone. These aspirations have landed her in various unrelated jobs and interesting projects. Although she has always enjoyed regaling her family and friends with her own real-life stories, her interest in writing began as a form of therapy after coming to Alaska with her husband, Tom, who has no doubt taken her adventure-prone personality to a new level.

Spring of '05 in her loggin' duds

Shortly after their initial Alaska excursions, they sold their home in Oregon and have since bought a second piece of land up north. Due to their most recent compromise, Tammy now resides with Tom and Pup in their new home on the beautiful banks of Pennock Island. The ever-changing view from their living room window extends across the Tongass Narrows toward Ketchikan and is regularly highlighted by pods of majestic killer whales, robust sea lions, adorable seals, colorful kayakers, and lively shorebirds. It is a place where the whistling of the stately bald eagle is often joined by rusty call of the gangly blue heron. The growl of a floatplane's engine occasionally overtakes the rumble of a tugboat plowing through the channel it shares with barges, crab fishing vessels, skiffs, and ferries as well as the seasonal cruise ships packed with curious, nature-loving visitors from all over the world.

Tom and Tammy still visit their cabin in Carroll Inlet where they continue to experience true isolation from time to time.

For more information and pictures, please visit her website:
www.PennockIslandProductions.com